Corporations and Political Accountability

Mark V. Nadel

D. C. Heath and Company

Lexington, Massachusetts

Toronto

To
BEVERLY AND MATTHEW

ABOUT THE AUTHOR

Mark V. Nadel is a graduate of the University of California at Berkeley and received his Ph.D. in political science from The Johns Hopkins University. He was a Brookings Institution Research Fellow and a National Endowment for the Humanities Fellow. He taught for several years at Cornell University and now lives in Washington, D. C.

Preface

The corporation is a human invention to serve human societal needs. In theory, it is subservient to both the state that creates it and the market in which it competes. If the corporation does not fulfill its social obligations, in theory, the state can amend or even revoke its charter. If it lapses in economic efficiency, its market competitors will force it to improve or force it out.

For most of the almost two million American corporations this theory is also close to a fact. But for a very few giant corporations the theory no longer fits the facts. These few corporations have become much larger in economic size and power than either the states that chartered them or the markets in which they buy and sell. In addition to the absolute size of corporations, the share of wealth held by the largest is also increasing. In the last thirty years, the 200 largest American corporations have increased their share of all manufacturing company assets from under 50 per cent to over 60 per cent. Clearly, the economic, social, and political importance of any business enterprises other than the multibillion-dollar, multinational, multindustry giants is on the wane in relation to these behemoths.

Absolute size is troublesome enough, but that great size has also led to great power. This book is about corporate power and political accountability—a broad and complex subject. But the basic issue may be expressed in that one word—*power*—whether power of an economic, political, or social nature.

It is power to decide what kinds of jobs will be created and what kind will be terminated.

It is power to determine whether new jobs that are made and old jobs that are wiped out will be located in New York, San Francisco, Hong Kong, or Frankfurt.

It is power to influence decisively the decisions of government agencies through overwhelming legal and political muscle.

It is power to influence strongly, if not finally settle, whether Americans will travel about their cities in vehicles that are polluting, expensive, and dangerous or clean, cheap, and safe.

It is power to determine whether small, independent entrepreneurs will or will not have opportunities left open to them to enter, compete, and thrive in particular lines of commerce. It is now many years since small business was forced out of most types of manufacturing, including almost all those of major economic importance. Today giant corporations are making retailing and farming increasingly precarious occupations for entrepreneurs who are not also millionaires.

The issue does not stop at power alone. The more basic problem is that power has been exercised in a way that is unaccountable to those over whom it is wielded. Giant corporate institutions increasingly make decisions *for* people rather than *with* people—depriving citizens of a measure of individuality and control over their own lives. Too many Americans owe their souls to the company store. This book argues that corporate accountability is every bit as essential to a democracy as political accountability. And, in large measure, corporate accountability is part of the larger framework of political accountability.

Recent events—such as payoffs to domestic and foreign politicians—certainly highlight abuses by corporations. At the same time, however, it might be objected that the very uncovering of such abuses demonstrates that corporate excesses are being checked and punished. It might also be argued that corporations are not the only powerful social entities, and one might ask "What about labor unions?" We can offer three responses to these objections.

First, this book is primarily concerned with exercises of corporate power that are either largely legal at the present time or whose legality is not presently settled—problems such as extensive corporate lobbying, excessive economic concentration, and noncompetitive pricing. Furthermore, it should be noted that it took something as extraordinary as the Watergate scandal to trigger the investigations that uncovered a pattern of corporate corruption. Second, it is certainly true that labor unions are powerful institutions and that they are not fully accountable either to the public or even to their own members. In contrast to corporations, however, union power rests fundamentally on the dues and votes of a mass membership of millions. In discussing corporate power, we are dealing with the decisions of only a few thousand corporate executives. Third, and finally, this book makes no claim to analyzing *all* powerful social institutions. Rather, it is about corporations, and we will argue that corporations and the political system each have attributes that make corporations, on balance, exceptionally powerful entities.

At the outset, it should also be emphasized that this book does not present a Marxist or even a particularly radical critique— although some of the reforms urged in Part IV may appear radical to some. To others, they may seem rather conservative. Given the present nature of our economic and political system, corporations have no choice but to try to exercise maximum power. That fact does not make corporate political power any less troublesome, but it does help us understand the problem. This book examines the avenues of corporate political influence, the areas in which the influence is exercised, and the proposals for political accountability.

We do not, however, attempt to deal with the total scope of corporate influence on our lives, and we avoid what can be called the "corporate ethos." Thus, there are some areas that are not dealt with extensively. For example, there is the influence on our value system posed by corporate advertising and the materialist culture it spawns. There are also the underlying effects on the political system inherent in capitalism—such as the assumption by any government in power that it must maintain the "confidence" of business.

We avoid such themes, not because they are unimportant but because we are dealing with the explicit and direct exercise of power in the United States—power that can be analyzed in terms of a specific target of influence and a specific kind of activity to be influenced. If the analysis cannot always be specific about the *effect* of an attempt to exercise influence, it will at least be specific about the attempt itself. It is this kind of specific power that is important in terms of political accountability because it is only explicit actions that can be called into account.

This book is divided into four parts. Following an introductory Part I, Part II—"Corporations in Government"—deals with the major avenues of corporate influence and the targets of that influence in the formal institutions of government. This part is primarily concerned with the effort by large corporations to influence the course of governmental policymaking. In Part III—"Corporations as Governments"—we argue that, in certain situations, corporations not only influence government public policymaking, but that they themselves act as private governments and make public policy that is indistinguishable in effect from the policy made by governments. Finally, in Part IV—"Toward Political Accountability"—we argue that the current discussion of corporate accountability must be reformulated as a discussion of political accountability, and a series of reforms is suggested.

*   *   *

Kenneth Dolbeare and David Vogel provided helpful comments and advice on an earlier draft of this book, and I greatly appreciate their efforts. I gratefully acknowledge the permission of the *Public Administration Review* to use, in Chapter 8, material that originally appeared in an article I wrote for that journal. E. P. Dutton kindly extended its permission to quote (on pp. 190–91) from its publication, *Muscle and Blood* by Rachel Scott (1974).

While I gladly share with my earlier critics the credit for this book, any responsibility for the facts and interpretations presented here is my own.

Mark V. Nadel
Washington, D. C.

Contents

PART ONE
Introduction

1
The Quest for Hegemony

Consider the following events that are seemingly unrelated:

- On February 26, 1972 in West Virginia a mountain of slag and waste below a 14.2-acre lake collapsed and sent down a 30-foot-high mass of sludge into the adjoining valley. The slag heap's collapse left nearly 5,000 residents homeless and 125 dead.

- By 1974 the United States achieved the dubious distinction of joining other countries with double-digit inflation at an annual rate of 12 per cent.

- The average rate of federal taxation on the oil industry in 1972 was 8 per cent.

- In 1973, 54,000 people were killed in automobile accidents.

Although these situations seem unrelated, they have a common root—the economic and political power of giant corporations. Inflation has been linked by many economists to the high level of economic concentration and the subsequent market power of giant corporations. The death toll on the highways would not be so high if the collective corporate power of the highway lobby had not debilitated public transportation in favor of the private automobile. Many oil companies (as well as many other corporations) do not pay their fair share of taxes because they have the political clout to shape the tax laws. Even the first example, Buffalo Creek—which was apparently a natural disaster—actually resulted from corporate action. The slag heap was deposited by a subsidiary of the Pittston Company, the nation's fourth-largest coal producer, in violation of the 1969 Coal Mine Health and Safety Act. Thus, from tax loopholes to "natural" disasters, giant corporations have a profound and far-reaching impact on our lives.

In the wake of Watergate and other scandals that have emerged in the 1970s, we have viewed the spectacle of the largest American corporations engaged in activities we had previously associated only with bookies, crooked contractors, and assorted pushers and racketeers. First it was International Telephone and Telegraph simultaneously trying to undermine the former government of Chile while underwriting the 1972 Republican convention at home. Then corporation after corporation followed the lead of American Airlines and admitted to illegal campaign contributions to the Nixon re-election funds. Gulf Oil, Ashland Oil, Northrop Corporation, Lockheed, and others have admitted payoffs to foreign politicians and assorted fixers. While these revelations amply confirm the dimmest views of American business held by radical critics and even give pause to normal defenders of the American business system, excessive attention to these abuses misses more important points about modern corporations. The question ought not to be whether such abuses are rare or only the tip of the iceberg. The real issue is the power and scope of corporate activities that is manifested in ways that are legal and even widely accepted as legitimate.

This book examines the political role of giant corporations. We will analyze the power of corporations not only in the government but also in society at large. It will be seen that, through the intertwining of corporate and governmental institutions and through the dominance of giant corporations in the economy, there arise profound problems of political accountability—for corporations and governments alike. This chapter discusses the nature and needs of the modern giant corporation and how those factors interact with the political system to create the problems of corporate power and accountability.

The Nature of the Beast

The term *giant corporation* is not merely an attention-getting catch phrase. For most of the companies discussed in this book, the adjective *giant* is, if anything, an understatement. Consider, for example, the revenues of America's largest manufacturing companies as compared to the revenues of the largest state governments. The table below presents such a comparison.

In addition to size, the major American corporations share several organization characteristics that should be briefly noted to provide further clarity of definition. First, they are all "public" in the sense that their stock is publicly traded. Furthermore, they are very widely held; typically, no single stockholder has more than a small percentage of the total. The second characteristic follows from the first: The management of these corporations is separate from the owners. In fact, as Adolf Berle and Gardiner Means pointed out in 1932, the owners have little or no effective control over the management.[1] In a replication of the Berle and Means study, Robert J. Larner found that, of the 200 largest nonfinancial corporations in 1963, 85 per cent were effectively controlled by management rather than by owners—nearly twice as many as Berle and Means found in 1929.[2] Moreover, the management is largely anonymous to the public. Gone are the days when the captains of American industry were widely known (and sometimes vilified) and identified with their corporation)—Carnegie Steel, Rockefeller of Standard Oil, or J. P. Morgan. Only a few families are still identified with and actually have a substantial interest left in their industrial empires, Henry Ford III and the Du Pont family being the leading examples.

A third organizational characteristic is the geographical diversity of the large corporation. While they may be concentrated in a particular geographic region—as in the automobile industry—nearly all large corporations have important plants and offices

Table 1. Sales and Revenues of the Combined 50 Largest States and U.S. Industrial Corporations (in billions).

STATE OR CORPORATION	1973 REVENUES OR SALES
1. General Motors	$35.80
2. Exxon	25.72
3. *New York*	24.58
4. *California*	23.50
5. Ford Motor	23.02
6. Chrysler	11.78
7. General Electric	11.58
8. Texaco	11.41
9. Mobil Oil	11.40
10. IBM	10.99
11. International Tel. & Tel.	10.18
12. *Illinois*	10.12
13. *Pennsylvania*	9.93
14. *Michigan*	9.00
15. Gulf Oil	8.42
16. *Texas*	8.24
17. *Ohio*	7.81
18. Standard Oil of California	7.76
19. Western Electric	7.04
20. U.S. Steel	6.95
21. *New Jersey*	6.62
22. *Massachusetts*	5.87
23. *Florida*	5.77
24. Westinghouse	5.70
25. Standard Oil of Indiana	5.42
26. DuPont	5.28
27. General Tel. & Tel.	5.11
28. Shell Oil	4.88
29. Goodyear Tire & Rubber	4.68
30. *Wisconsin*	4.44
31. RCA	4.25
32. Continental Oil	4.22
33. International Harvester	4.19
34. Ling-Temco-Vought	4.17
35. Bethlehem Steel	4.14
36. Eastman Kodak	4.04
37. Atlantic Richfield	3.98
38. *Maryland*	3.97
39. *Minnesota*	3.97
40. Esmark	3.95
41. Union Carbide	3.94
42. Tenneco	3.91
43. Procter & Gamble	3.91
44. *Indiana*	3.75

STATE OR CORPORATION	1973 REVENUES OR SALES
45. *Georgia*	3.68
46. *Virginia*	3.63
47. *North Carolina*	3.61
48. Kraftco	3.60
49. *Washington*	3.48
50. Greyhound	3.41

SOURCE: U.S. Bureau of the Census, *Statistical Abstract of the United States: 1975* (Washington, U.S. Government Printing Office, 1975); *Fortune*, May 1974.

spread around the country. Furthermore, most of them are multinational in character. While not all large corporations share all the characteristics usually listed as necessary for a true multinational corporation, most do extensive business overseas and have at least some facilities in other countries.

Finally, the large corporations have become increasingly diversified in the products and services they sell. One estimate of diversification concluded that, of the 100 largest nonfinancial firms in 1964, 78 had become more diversified in terms of their economic activities than they had been in 1929.[3] This figure does not even reflect the enormous wave of conglomeration and mergers in the 1960s, which saw previously specialized companies such as International Telephone and Telegraph become, in effect, holding companies for dozens of other previously specialized firms. Moreover, while the diversity of activities within corporations is increasing, the diversity of control over economic activity as a whole is decreasing. For example, from 1947 to 1966 the percentage of value added* accounted for by the 200 largest manufacturing corporations increased from 30 to 42 per cent; the 50 largest increased their share from 17 to 25 per cent.[4]

These characteristics not only define the nature of the modern giant corporation but also point out the social implications of these

---

* The term "value added" is a frequently used economic measure that refers to the increase in the value of a product at each stage of production. For example, if a steel mill buys two million dollars worth of raw materials to produce three million dollars worth of steel, the value added is one million dollars.

firms. Although we will deal with these implications extensively in the chapters to follow, a few of the political implications are worth mentioning now as illustrative of the kinds of problems to be considered in this book. There is, for example, the matter of the separation of ownership from control. While we may feel intuitively that the owner of a small business has a right to control the operation of that business, such control does not actually reside with the stockholder "owners" of the giant corporations. By what right do the managers control firms that they do not own when they are not in fact accountable to or controlled by the legal owners? This becomes a particularly pressing matter when corporate management engages in activities other than trying to earn the greatest possible rate of return for stockholders. The geographical distribution of individual corporations within the United States means that their economic, social, and political influence is likewise spread around, touching scores of communities. The multinational nature of many such corporations also gives their activities profound implications for American foreign policy. Indeed, such firms may be viewed abroad, correctly or incorrectly, as representatives of the American government. Finally, the great merger movement of the 1960s meant that more and more economic power was flowing into fewer and fewer hands.

Behind all these problems, one classic problem of political life looms large—the problem of accountability. Modern economic organization and technology has vested enormous concentrations of resources in relatively few hands. These resources, it will be argued, are readily translatable into political power; and yet that power is hardly accountable even to the nominal owners of those resources, let alone to the larger community. Thus, this book explores two fundamental and related questions: What are the manifestations of corporate political power, and what should be done about these manifestations?

The Needs of the Enterprise

All firms have certain basic economic needs. They need markets, employees, customers, supplies, capital, credit, and so on. But beyond these economic necessities, business enterprises in general and large corporations in particular have three broad needs that intersect with the political system.

1. There is first the need for relative stability in the economic and political environment. This need was dramatically made clear by the plunge of the stock market in 1973–74 as the business community was faced both with a Watergate-related loss of leadership and stability in the White House and runaway inflation with little indication of governmental ability to cope with the economic crisis. Stability, of course, does not mean stagnation, and a static environment is not a prerequisite of stability. Nonetheless, it is essential that most of the basic factors in the social environment of the corporation be stable enough to be predictable into the future— factors such as the value of the dollar, the fiscal and regulatory policies of the government, and the laws under which they do business. This stability is a prerequisite to a second need of corporate enterprise—the ability to plan and affect the future.

2. Both for the development of new products and services and in order to anticipate the market for the corporations' goods, the future cannot be left to chance. The complexity of the tasks required of the corporation, as well as the economic stakes, are too great for a casual approach to the future. Hence, planning is essential. In the view of John Kenneth Galbraith, the need for planning stems from the imperatives of advanced technology and the needs of the managers of that technology—the "technostructure." In a concise summary of his reasoning, Galbraith notes: "From the time and capital that must be committed, the inflexibility of this commitment, the needs of large organizations and the problems of market performance under conditions of advanced technology, comes the necessity of planning. Tasks must be performed so that they are right . . . for that time in the future when, companion and related work having also been done, the whole job is completed."[5]

3. A third organizational need of the large corporation is freedom of action that can be termed *discretionary power*. Galbraith notes that, apart from simple preservation of its own existence, the major protective need of the technostructure is to minimize external interference with its decisionmaking process. The potential sources of such intrusion are owners and creditors, workers, consumers, and the government.[6] Although Galbraith uses the term "technostructure" to indicate managers of large-scale economic enterprise, the need for discretionary power is actually endemic to bureaucratic organizations generally. Bureaucracies are specialized organizations set up to perform certain specified tasks with a structured division of labor. Discretionary power is part of the basic rationale for the existence of bureaucracies, since the specialization of task implies that the specialists have much more to say about the task than nonspecialists, that is, outsiders. There is, however, a tendency in bureaucracies to convert this basic function of specialization into a cult of professionalism. It has become characteristic of the officials of universities, federal agencies, corporations, and other bureaucracies to believe that they can best do their jobs, serve society (and incidentally themselves) if only pesky outsiders would keep their proper distance and let the "real professionals" get on with the business at hand.

The fulfillment of these three organizational needs of corporations hinges in large part upon the formal institutions of government. The policies of the federal government in particular affect the stability of the environment, and planning for the future is frequently dependent on current and anticipated government actions. And, of course, the government is perceived as posing the threat of intervention. The following section traces, in greater detail, the importance of government to the corporation.

The Government: All Things to All Corporations

Although there is a tendency to think of government intervention in the economy as a relatively modern phenomenon, in fact the basic purposes of any government are intimately related to the economy—to the need to provide orderly means of allocating goods and services and to facilitate commerce. Without the security and order that civil government provides, no economic activity can endure; thus order is an inherent part of the basis of government. Seen in this light, the economic aspects of the U.S. Constitution can be readily appreciated. There has been lively debate over the extent to which the framers of the Constitution were concerned with protecting their own commercial interests and status as an economic elite. But this discussion actually involves only the question of the allocation of the economic costs and benefits that result from the political structure laid down in the Constitution. What is *not* debatable is that the Constitution establishes a set of rules providing much greater order and predictability for commerce than had existed previously.

Consider the commercial functions of the new government in the Constitution (Art. 1, Sec. 8): "To regulate Commerce with foreign Nations, and among the several States and with the Indian Tribes; To establish . . . uniform Laws on the subject of Bankruptcies throughout the United States; To coin Money, regulate the Value thereof, and of foreign coin, and fix the Standard of Weights and Measures; To provide for the Punishment of counterfeiting the Securities and current Coin of the United States; To establish Post Offices and post Roads; To promote the Progress of Science and useful Arts, by securing for limited Times to Authors and Inventors the exclusive Right to their respective Writings and Discoveries." Equally important, the Constitution prohibits the states from giving preference "by any Regulation of Commerce or Revenue to the Ports of one State over those of another; nor shall Vessels bound to, or from, one State, be obliged to enter, clear, or pay Duties in another."

These constitutional provisions and the laws subsequently passed had two profoundly important consequences for the continuing relationship between government and business. First, the power of the central government was strengthened in general and made supreme in matters of interstate commerce. Second, a stable and orderly framework was established for the conduct of business on a national basis. The Constitution thus provides the basis for the continued growth of both business and government. It does so through its specific allocations of power and by providing those governmental services essential to the conduct of commerce: a universally accepted currency, a system of law, and a system of security.

The government, however, has not merely provided a neutral framework. It has also intervened more directly, and it is that direct intervention that makes government such an important part of the environment of corporations.

There is, first, the role of the government in setting the limits of permissible behavior and providing sanctions to enforce those limits. Broadly, there are two kinds of police powers exercised by the state against corporations. The most widely agreed-upon type of power is that used to protect the overall system of enterprise from severe dislocations. This protection takes the form of antitrust laws designed to insure that other businesses and consumers will not fall prey to the predatory practices and gross economic inefficiencies of monopolies. As a matter of practical politics, the Clayton and Sherman Antitrust laws resulted from the political pressure of agricultural and other interests that were especially hard hit by monopoly practices. But the theoretical justification for government antitrust activities is that monopolies prevent the realization of an ideally efficient capitalist free market. Under this category, we can also include such government policies as insurance of bank deposits and the regulation of the securities markets—both of which provide the minimum level of investor confidence essential to modern business.

A second police power of the government is less readily accepted but more politically potent. That power stems from the role of the government as the representative of other social groups who need to utilize the government to amplify their claims against particular industries.[7] The National Labor Relations Act of 1935, establishing the guaranteed right of collective bargaining, is a prime example of such a policy. More recently, the claims of consumers have been aggregated in a variety of consumer protection measures in areas such as product safety, advertising, consumer credit, and insurance.

These few examples only scratch the surface of the legislative and administrative constraints surrounding business enterprises. Government agencies now administer both general and specific regulatory schemes. All private corporations, regardless of their product line, face potential scrutiny with regard to particular aspects of their operations, such as antitrust regulation by the Federal Trade Commission and Department of Justice, labor-relations regulation by the National Labor Relations Board, and securities regulation by the Securities and Exchange Commission. Beyond this general policing and enforcement of economy-wide rules, certain industries interact with agencies that regulate the bulk of their operations in areas where rules are vague and agency discretion is considerable. This includes industries whose existence is based on government franchise, such as broadcasting and transportation, as well as those whose products are regulated by the government, such as the pharmaceutical companies and the nuclear-power industry.

The government is also vital to corporations as a major customer and sometimes as their only customer. In 1972, the federal government spent $103.1 billion buying goods and services from the private sector of the economy.[8] Of this sum, $74.3 billion was defense-related, but that figure includes a good deal more than guns and bombs. The Department of Defense is an enormous customer of firms selling clothing, automobiles, food, building supplies, and nearly every other product imaginable. Armaments, however, are extremely important to a few large corporations, such as General Dynamics, for whom the Pentagon is the only important customer.

The government is also a promoter of enterprise. Indeed, the advancement of commerce was one of the earliest activities of government at the state and national level. From the Revolution to the Civil War the individual states were extremely active in the promotion and regulation of commerce. Louis Hartz concluded that, in its efforts to encourage economic development, the state of Pennsylvania's economic objectives "ramified into virtually every phase of business activity, were the constant preoccupations of politicians and entrepreneurs, and they evoked interest struggles of the first magnitude."[9] More recently, the federal government has assumed primacy in this area. Direct and indirect subsidies alone cost the government $5.46 billion in 1972.[10] This sum is composed of investment tax credits, corporate capital-gains tax credit, tax credit for excess bad debt reserves of financial institutions, direct underwriting of research and development expenditures, and the corporate surtax exemption. These aggregate figures do not include occasional large amounts spent to bail out failing corporations such as Penn Central Railroad or Lockheed Aircraft. Indeed, these large-scale bailouts, plus tariff and other forms of relief for industries in trouble, have given us what has been called a "lemon" economy whereby inefficient, mismanaged, and outmoded firms are saved from the negative consequences of the "free enterprise" system. Beyond such direct payments, the federal government undertakes other related policies, such as a generous policy of allowing private companies to patent inventions resulting from government-funded research and development—a policy that does not extend to scientists working directly for the government. In short, the federal government is an active participant in the maintenance and expansion of corporate assets and revenues.

Finally, the government acts not only as a promoter of corporate wealth but also as a creator of that wealth. An increasing amount of wealth exists in the form of rights or status (for example, an exclusive franchise) rather than as tangible real property; and this is precisely the kind of wealth created by the government. Free broadcast licenses are allocated to fortunate recipients by the Federal Communications Commission, awards that may be worth millions of dollars. Licenses and charters granted to bus lines, national park concessionaires, and airlines are of similar value because of the use of government power to limit entry into a particular field of enterprise. On both federal and state levels, other forms of government-created wealth include subsidies, contracts, income and benefits, jobs, occupational licenses, government services, and the use of public resources.[11]

Although it is frequently noted that corporations and businessmen are important constituencies for senators, representatives, and government agencies, the relationship between government and business becomes even more clear when viewed from the perspective of the corporation. The actions of any organization depend greatly on the organization's environment, and government is ubiquitous in the environment of corporations. Government sets the rules of commerce, establishes the framework for the conduct of commerce, and is at once promoter, customer, and creator of wealth.

Just as governmental agencies derive much of their power from their constituencies, corporations also rely on their "con-stituencies"—groups in the environment that can support (or damage) the corporation. There is nothing optional about this relationship. Government itself is the essential constituency for most large corporations in the sense that they depend on the support or acquiescence of that constituency for their survival. Governmental support cannot be left to chance; it must be actively cultivated. In short, the question for large corporations is not *whether* to influence the government, but *how* to do so in order to fulfill the needs of the enterprise for stability, predictability, and discretionary power.[12]

Moreover, corporations do not face a hostile or alien body in the government. Later chapters will discuss various means of corporate influence over government. The remainder of this chapter will emphasize a crucial point underlying corporate influence: that the structure and process of the American political system greatly facilitates the advancement of corporate economic interests.

Corporations and the Political System

Although the deservedly cynical college generation of the late 1970s may assume, in the wake of Watergate and the Nixon presi-dency, that great economic wealth carries with it great political power, that assumption is by no means axiomatic. It is intellectually hazardous to assume that power automatically flows from wealth as an inherent characteristic of that wealth. For example, if the politi-cal party with the most money always won, the Republicans would have been victorious in every recent election. Economic power is important, but it is not the only factor in determining political power. However, the economic system does interact with the politi-cal system, and it is necessary to identify those characteristics of the political system that facilitate the use of wealth as a resource of political power.

These characteristics can be subsumed under what political scientist Theodore Lowi has called "interest-group liberalism." This new public philosophy makes three assumptions: first that organized interests are homogenous and easily represented by any duly elected spokesman; second, that organized interests adequately represent most sectors of the political culture; and third, that government ensures access, particularly to the best-organized groups, and ratifies the adjustments worked out among competing interests.[13] Interest-group liberalism is important in both theory and practice. It is both a statement of how the government should work and how it actually does work. As a theory it effectively undermines the concept of authority based on majority rule. As Lowi notes, "it transforms log-rolling from necessary evil to greater good." In practice, interest-group liberalism means the primacy of organized groups in formulating public policy (thereby co-opting governmental authority), and it means that the interest of organized groups is represented in policy outcomes to the extent of the power and efficiency of their organization.

Even from this brief discursion into interest-group liberalism, the superior political position of corporations can readily be appreciated. In a political system that rewards organization, corporations are highly organized hierarchical organizations able to define and pursue their goals with considerable efficiency. While they may not always act with such sure and precise knowledge of their own interests, they are able to do so more often than other participants in the political system.[14] Furthermore, their financial resources enable them to buy the kinds of legal talent and other services (to be elaborated on in the following chapters) that make for successful political action.

Nonetheless, for our purposes the immediate importance of Lowi's analysis is the fact that interest-group liberalism has become virtually the new public philosophy. That is, we have come to accept as normal, proper, and even desirable the heavy participation of corporate interests in governmental policymaking. The advancement of corporate interests by those in Congress with close ties to them is no longer considered a conflict of interest but simply the representation of constituents. Thus, besides the advantages corporations gain by wealth and organization, they have acquired the crucial advantage of legitimacy.

Even beyond the advantages normally accruing to them in a pluralist system, corporations benefit from an institutional base within government from which organized economic interests are able to amplify their power. The phenomenon of the "captured" regulatory agency has become part of the common parlance of political science. Grant McConnell has attributed this situation to the "legacy of Progressivism."[15] The Progressives of the early twentieth century were alarmed by the power exhibited by great concentrations of corporate wealth and the ensuing corruption of the political process. Their remedy was to disperse power and to take the maximum number of decisions out of "politics." Hence, the primary election and the long ballot. Furthermore, in the eyes of Progressives, politics was bad and administration was good—thus the city-manager movement and the establishment of independent regulatory agencies.

The Progressives proceeded from a narrow and naive view of politics and administration and only succeeded in further insulating centers of political decisionmaking against the mechanisms of majority rule and other vehicles of political accountability. The Interstate Commerce Commission was insulated against what was perceived as the evils of political parties, but it was not insulated against the influence of railroads. As McConnell noted: "simple insistence upon the virtue of administrators as wardens of the public interest led deviously but certainly to ties with the special interests, opposition to which had been the point of Progressive beginnings."[16]

If, as McConnell argues, the legacy of Progressivism was to create the institutional setting in which private power could flourish, another legacy was the political drive of private groups that seized the opportunity handed them by Progressive policies. This drive was not new, but it accelerated from the beginning of the twentieth century onward. Business interests have increasingly seen the advantages of utilizing governmental power to further their own economic interests. For example, as Gabriel Kolko points out, the early legislation on meat inspection came at the instigation of the large meat packers, who needed enforced standards of purity in order to take advantage of a growing export market. Agencies such as the Interstate Commerce Commission and the Federal Trade Commission were either created for or utilized by corporate interests. Rather than being a restraint by government, these agencies have often provided a more accessible framework for the exercise of corporate power.

The Quest for Hegemony

As the preceding sections have shown, there are three major factors that shape the political role of business in our political and economic system:

1. The large corporation seeks to control its environment.

2. The government is an ever-present part of that environment.

3. The political system facilitates the exercise of political power by corporations.

Taken together these factors result in a corporate quest for hegemony—preponderant influence over their economic environment—and exercise by corporations of great political power in the formal institutions of government and in society as a whole.

The concept of hegemony is a useful one in analyzing corporate political power. Just as powerful nations seek hegemony over their area of the world (the Soviet Union over Eastern Europe, the United States over Latin America), so too do great corporations seek to maintain a non-hostile environment around their "borders." Hegemony is a useful concept also because it connotes the limitations of power. The biggest and most powerful nations or corporations do not always succeed in getting their way. Corporations do not "run" the government. Hegemony does not mean absolute power over all aspects of all situations. It does connote, however, a high degree of domination relative to other groups and an ability to maintain structures that benefit the source of power. Corporations, like other organizations, seek a stable environment and the minimization of risk from the environment. Unlike most other organizations, however, they have the ability to seek hegemony over that environment. Although this may be to *their* advantage, it is not always so for those outside the corporate structure.

Different facets of the corporate quest for hegemony and the consequent problems of political accountability are examined in the remainder of this book, which is divided into three parts. Part Two ("Corporations in Government") deals with the corporate attempt to establish and maintain hegemony over the formal institutions of government—the Congress, the Executive Branch, and especially the regulatory agencies—that is, to influence the course of public policymaking.

In Part Three ("Corporations as Governments") the broader effects of the corporate quest for hegemony are examined. It will be argued that giant corporations not only influence governmental policymaking but also make public policy in their own right. Their actions necessarily have major and even binding effects on all citizens in that corporate attempts to establish hegemony over the environment leads them to act as private governments that make public policy. Such policy is as important to citizens as that of federal, state, or local governments.

Political accountability means that citizens have some control, some method of holding accountable those who exercise political power. Yet, corporations exercise such power, and there is no widely accepted theory of corporate political accountability. In Part Four ("Toward Political Accountability") various reform proposals are analyzed; and it will be argued that the discussion of corporate accountability must be reformulated as a discussion of political accountability.

Notes

1. Adolf Berle and Gardiner Means, *The Modern Corporation and Private Property* (New York: Commerce Clearing House, 1932; rev. ed., Harcourt Brace Jovanovich, 1968, available in paperback).
2. Robert J. Larner, "Ownership and Control in the 200 Largest Nonfinancial Corporations, 1929 and 1963," *American Economic Review* 56 (September 1966), p. 777.
3. U.S. Congress, Senate, Committee on the Judiciary, *Economic Concen-*

tration, hearings before the Subcommittee on Antitrust and Monopoly, 89th Congress, 1st sess. (1965), pt. 2, statement of Dr. Joel Dirlam, p. 973.

4. U.S. Bureau of the Census, Department of Commerce, *Concentration Ratio in Manufacturing*, 1967, 1970, pt. 1. Cited in John M. Blair, *Economic Concentration: Structure, Behavior and Public Policy* (New York: Harcourt Brace Jovanovich, 1972), p. 69.

5. John Kenneth Galbraith, *The New Industrial State* (Boston: Houghton Mifflin, 1967), p. 16.

6. John Kenneth Galbraith, *Economics and the Public Purpose* (Boston: Houghton Mifflin, 1973), p. 93.

7. It should be noted that the distinction between these two types of policies is not universally accepted. Thus, Gabriel Kolko argues that much of the regulatory legislation seemingly hostile to business interests was actually instigated and supported by those interests for their own benefit. Nonetheless, I would argue that a government policy may be opposed by corporate interests and, once implemented, work to the benefit of those interests. This was the case with automobile safety legislation. The policy in the first instance is indeed an aggregation of claims against business. Cf. Gabriel Kolko, *The Triumph of Conservatism: A Reinterpretation of American History, 1900–1916* (New York: Free Press, 1963).

8. U.S. Bureau of the Census, *Statistical Abstract of the United States: 1973* (Washington, D.C., 1973), p. 390.

9. Louis Hartz, *Economic Policy and Democratic Thought: Pennsylvania 1776–1860* (Cambridge: Harvard University Press, 1948), p. 289. See also Oscar and Mary Handlin, *Commonwealth: A Study of the Role of Government in the American Economy: Massachusetts, 1774–1861* (New York: New York University Press, 1947).

10. Figures from *Statistical Abstract: 1973*.

11. Charles A. Reich, "The New Property," *Yale Law Journal* 73 (April 1964), pp. 733–87.

12. There is a substantial sociological literature on the relationships between organizations and their environments. See, for example, Roland Warren, "The Inter-Organizational Field as a Focus for Investigation," *Administrative Science Quarterly* 12 (December 1967), pp. 396–419.

13. Theodore Lowi, *The End of Liberalism: Ideology, Policy, and the Crisis of Public Authority* (New York: Norton, 1969), especially pp. 55–97.

14. Raymond Bauer, Ithiel de Sola Pool, and Lewis Anthony Dexter, *American Business and Public Policy* ('New York: Atherton, 1973), pp. 127–53.

15. Grant McConnell, *Private Power and American Democracy* (New York: Knopf, 1967), pp. 30–50.

16. Ibid., p. 30.

PART TWO
Corporations in Government

2
Corporations and Elections

Although the chapters in this section deal with the influence of corporations on the government, it is first necessary to go outside the formal boundaries of government in order to examine the starting point of that influence. Corporate power in government begins with corporate influence in determining who gets into government, particularly who gets elected to high office. For corporations, the primary means of electoral influence are campaign contributions. This chapter looks at campaign contributions by giant corporations as a system of attempting to control as much as possible the uncertainties of the political environment by determining beforehand who occupies that environment.

Corporate Campaign Finance

As former California politico Jesse Unruh put it, "Money is the mother's milk of politics," and therein lies the key to corporate influence in electoral politics. That influence stems from two intersecting factors. First, as was discussed in Chapter 1, is the corporate need to exert hegemony over its social environment, in which government is the dominant factor. The second factor consists of the needs of politicians seeking office, of which the need for money is paramount. Running for major office costs an increasingly large amount of money, and few politicians have been able to do it cheaply. In eleven out of the thirty-five senatorial races in 1970, one or more of the contenders reported expenditures of more than $150,000.[1] In general, reported expenditures greatly understate the actual costs, which, for all national offices in 1972, were estimated at $400 million.[2] Even though the Federal Election Campaign Act Amendments of 1974 placed limits on spending—a campaign chest of $120,000 is the federal limit for most states—a senatorial campaign still puts a premium on the ability to raise money.

Who underwrites this massive expense? Although a variety of loopholes in the law (especially prior to 1974) and various subterfuges make a precise answer impossible, in the past the funding of most campaigns was dominated by large contributors. For example, in 1968, 47 per cent of the contributions to the Republican presidential campaign came in amounts of $500 or more—the minimum amount for what are generally considered "fat cat" contributions. At least half of Hubert Humphrey's 1968 general-election revenues were accounted for by contributions and loans from about fifty individuals.[3] According to a recent study, newly wealthy, self-made men are more likely to be large contributors than people from long-established financial dynasties. The typical big contributor is the near-absolute controller of his own business empire who has a great deal of easily disposable wealth. Such contributors tend to be in the newer industries such as electronics, pharmaceuticals, and conglomerates.[4]

These newer, individually dominated corporations are not, of course, alone in contributing to political campaigns; they are probably just the most dramatic and visible evidence of the overall role of large corporations. Because of the variety of devices used to filter and conceal contributions, it is impossible to prove conclusively how important corporations are in campaign financing. Nevertheless, one known indication of the importance of that role can be seen in corporate America's financing of the national conventions of both parties. Since 1936, political parties have sold advertisements in their convention program books in order to defray convention costs. In 1972, full-page advertisements in either the Democratic or Republican program cost a minimum of $10,000 each and netted the Democrats $750,000 and the Republicans about $1,000,000. Thus corporations, through this form of tax-deductible spending pay at least half of the costs of this phase of the presidential campaign.[5]

Post-Watergate Legislation

In the wake of the Watergate scandal, in which campaign contributions played an important part, Congress passed the Federal Election Campaign Act Amendments of 1974. This legislation has the laudable goal of reducing the importance of large campaign contributions by limiting the amount that can be given and the amount that can be spent, as well as providing for public financing of presidential campaigns. Although the legislation received a great deal of fanfare as a reform that would end the domination of the fat cats, corporate donors should still be able to slip by this law as they have past legislation. A careful review of past experience shows that the 1974 reforms may mitigate corporate funding somewhat but not by much.

The 1974 legislation, like the Corrupt Practices Act of 1925 and its replacement, the Federal Election Campaign Act of 1971, prohibits corporations and labor unions from making *direct* contributions to a political campaign. The law, however, has served as more of an inconvenience than a barrier to corporate financing of campaigns. A good deal of funding slips through a provision that allows corporations to establish and solicit voluntary contributions for a separate fund to be used for political purposes. Currently, such committees are limited to contributing $5,000 to a particular candidate, but they are not limited in the number of candidates or total amount they may contribute. Indeed, a representative of the Business-Industry Political Action Committee stated that "the law has had a liberating effect on corporate activity instead of an inhibiting effect." By allowing the formation of corporate-based political action committees and repealing the old prohibition against political activity by government contractors, the corporate mobilization of campaign funds has increased.[6]

An increasing number of corporations are utilizing such funds. A typical example is the Merrill Lynch Effective Government Association, which accepts contributions from all employees and determines where those funds will go. Another of the growing number of banks using such funds is the Chemical Bank of New York, whose Fund for Good Government solicits contributions from vice-presidents and above but allows contributors to designate where the money will be spent.[7] While giving at the office is a noble and widely accepted method of raising money for charity, the extent to which such political contributions are truly voluntary is highly questionable. As Kent Cooper of the National Information Center on Political Finance noted: "Is it voluntary if your boss comes to you and asks for a contribution? How are you going to refuse him?"[8] Some companies even make specific recommendations concerning the amount to be contributed.

It has, in fact, long been suspected that many such allegedly voluntary employees' funds were merely covers for campaign contributions that actually come from the corporations themselves. Occasionally, evidence emerges that lends weight to that suspicion. According to a former executive's affadavit filed in the Federal District Court in New York, the International Telephone and Telegraph Corporation had a systematic plan of extracting campaign contributions from company executives and then reimbursing them for those contributions. According to his affidavit, John T. Naylor, a former executive, was instructed to give $1,200 to Lyndon Johnson's vice-presidential campaign in 1960. Naylor quoted a company senior vice-president as saying, "You are down for $1,200. This can be financed for you by the company if necessary. Jim Lillis (comptroller) will handle it. You will be expected to recover the amount by covering it up in your traveling expense account. The board of directors wants us all to cooperate." Naylor was later told, "Of course, if there ever were an investigation, you would have to testify that this was all voluntary and simply a personal payment made from your home."[9] Although the FBI did investigate, this information only came to light because of a civil suit and the increased attention to the political activities of ITT. This particular dodge is probably widely utilized. According to Naylor's affidavit, ITT president Harold Geneen asserted, "Everybody does it. . . . It is paying off big in Washington."

Fraudulent Bookkeeping

A variety of other ways around the law are practiced and masked by fraudulent bookkeeping. Payments are made, supposedly for legitimate business expenses, that are merely covers for campaign contributions. For example, a company may agree to pay on phony invoices to a candidate's advertising or public relations firm for services supposedly done for the firm but actually done for a candidate. Companies also funnel money through law firms or phony trade or educational associations. Corporations are often able to provide direct services to candidates or pay for a variety of campaign expenses by lending credit cards, providing company airplanes for travel, and providing hotel accommodations for candidates.[10] Additionally, corporations that are creditors of campaign committees (airlines, telephone companies, and the like) may partially or completely write off those debts.

These activities, it should be emphasized, are not mere utilizations of legal loopholes; they are manifestly illegal. Under Section 205 of the Federal Election Campaign Act of 1971, the phrase *contribution or expenditure* (which corporations and labor unions are prohibited from giving) includes "any direct or indirect payment, distribution, loan, advance, deposit, or gift of money, or any services, or anything of value."[11] Despite this flat prohibition, corporate violations of the campaign financing laws reached an alarming level during the 1972 election campaign, and in the wake of the Watergate scandal we have available more information than ever before on such illegal activity.

The first Watergate case of this type to develop involved American Airlines; the case offers a specific example of the kinds of activities outlined previously. George A. Spater, former board chairman of the airline, admitted that the company had contributed $55,000 out of corporate funds to the Finance Committee to Re-Elect the President in response to a solicitation from President Nixon's lawyer, Herbert Kalmbach. The funds were generated by issuing a false invoice for payment of a commission to a Lebanese firm, Amarco, for the sale of used aircraft. Amarco had in fact performed services for American airlines in the past. But for purposes of the contribution, $100,000 was "laundered" through an Amarco bank account in Switzerland and transmitted to the Chase Manhattan Bank in New York. A Lebanese agent of Amarco withdrew the money in cash and transmitted it to officials of American Airlines. Payments totalling of $55,000 of these funds were made to the Nixon re-election committee; the remaining $45,000 was eventually turned back to the airline.[12]

By 1976, more than a dozen corporations had pleaded guilty to illegal contributions to the Committee to Re-Elect the President. These included $100,000 from Phillips Petroleum, $30,000 from Minnesota Mining and Manufacturing, $100,000 from Gulf Oil, $40,000 from Goodyear Tire and Rubber, $100,000 from Ashland Oil, and $40,000 from Braniff Airways.

Illegal contributions, of course, did not start with the Nixon campaign and have not been confined to Republicans. The Associated Milk Producers Inc. has been convicted for a variety of illegal contributions, including contributions to the 1968 presidential campaign of Hubert Humphrey. Indeed, the scope and size of corporate political contributions became even more clear in early 1976 when investigations by the Securities and Exchange Commission uncovered giant political slush funds that had been maintained over a long period by some major corporations. Gulf Oil, for example, used a Bahamas subsidiary to "launder" $12.3 million used for political purposes, while the 3M Company established a Swiss bank account for the same purpose. Nor was the political activity confined to domestic politics. Congressional investigations uncovered mammoth payoffs to foreign officials by McDonnell-Douglas, Northrop, United Brands, and, most of all, Lockheed Aircraft Corporation. While the foreign payments were generally not campaign contributions, they nonetheless demonstrate the use of hidden reserves of cash to obtain desired policies.

An indirect but legal funnel of corporate money into campaigns is through autonomous political organizations or committees. The most prominent of these is the Business-Industry Political Action Committee (BIPAC), which was established by the National Association of Manufacturers in 1963 as a business counterpart to organized labor's Committee on Political Education (COPE). (The latter highly successful and well-funded organization provides substantial funding for candidates favored by labor.) BIPAC has individual businessmen rather than corporations as members, but, as we have seen, this is often a distinction without a difference. In the interests of anonymity, the dues system is structured to encourage contributions under $100. (Contributions over $100 must be reported.) BIPAC contributes money received from contributions to business-oriented candidates for Congress with a reasonable shot at victory. Although it claims to be bipartisan, in 1968 BIPAC contributed to the campaigns of twenty Republican candidates for Congress and no Democrats; in House races, BIPAC gave to 117 Republicans and 9 Democrats. Although it does no lobbying, BIPAC has a separate educational fund, which it uses to send newsletters and other information to Congressmen and its own members.[13]

He Who Pays the Piper

Corporations (technically, businessmen as individuals) become involved in electoral campaigns for a variety of reasons. There is, first, the high-minded belief in the importance of the two-party system. This reason is usually cited by large contributors who give to candidates of both parties and even to candidates opposing each other. More commonly, and more realistically, corporate interests seek to aid in the election of politicians who will be generally sympathetic to the business perspective over a wide variety of issues. For example, in announcing the support of the National Association of Manufacturers for BIPAC, NAM president Werner P. Gullander stated that NAM support was forthcoming "not because we want business to dominate politics, but because we don't want the nation's politics and policies to be dominated by those who apparently do not understand the needs of our free economy."[14] The needs of our "free economy" presumably coincide with the needs of big business. Overall, the desire for a sympathetic ear has led corporate interests to back Republican candidates far more often than Democrats.[15]

Large contributors may expect not only a sympathetic attitude toward business in general, but also a quick and direct hearing of their particular problems. Gaining direct access to members of Congress, and high executive officials is a major reason for large campaign contributions. While most givers and recipients of large contributions do not expect a specific *quid pro quo*, they do expect (but rarely state explicitly) that the contributor's problems will not be answered with a mere form letter or a polite runaround. The contributor may not get his way, but he can be confident of getting at least an attentive hearing. Orin Atkins, chairman of Ashland Oil, told the Watergate Committee (Senate Select Committee on Presidential Campaign Activities):

. . . I think all we were attempting to do was to assure ourselves of a forum to be heard. Were we a large factor in our respective industries, we could expect to have access to administrative officials in the Executive branch of Government with ease, but being a relatively unknown corporation, despite our size, we felt we needed something that would be sort of a calling card, something that would get us in the door and make our point heard.[16]

Contributions with an eye to access can be viewed as a form of insurance. There may be no specific problems at the moment, but in the age of big government and big business there will always be areas of interaction. The wise company knows it is helpful to have the ear of attentive government officials when the need does arise. This is particularly true in regulated industries such as those in transportation and communications.

Contribution or Bribe?

The system of private campaign contributions has been castigated in terms such as *deferred bribery*, using *the politician as an investment,* and *who owns Congress?* It is impossible to know how heavily unsavory motives weigh in corporate campaign contributions. Clearly the desire for a substantial return on a contribution is not an uncommon feature of corporate campaign activities. Thus, contributions usually go to representatives and senators on committees handling legislation of direct interest to the corporation or business group. In an unsubtle directive to its executives announcing the collection of "voluntary" employee contributions, Sterling Drug, Inc. said the political fund was "to be allocated to those legislators . . . whose re-election or election is *important* to our industry and to *Sterling Drug, Inc.*" [emphasis in original].[17]

The line between campaign contribution and bribe is especially thin or even nonexistent in cases in which corporations have important matters pending before government agencies or are the subject of legislation pending in Congress. For example, what are we to make of a $100,000 contribution to President Nixon's 1972 re-election campaign by Gulf Resources and Chemical Corporation, a company whose major subsidiary, an Idaho mining operation, was under pressure by the Environmental Protection Agency to correct extensive air and water pollution problems? Since that time, the pressure has diminished.[18]

Sometimes favor seeking is formalized and handled in a particularly blatant way. When he was Secretary of Commerce, Maurice Stans established two advisory committees of businessmen on pollution and consumer issues. A *Washington Post* survey found that at least a dozen corporations whose officials were on the committees were solicited for contributions by Stans or other officials of the Finance Committee to Re-Elect the President. An executive of U.S. Steel Corporation said that Stans gave his company a quota to be contributed by its executives and that, in his solicitation, Stans reminded the company he had spoken up for the business viewpoint on pollution issues when others in the administration sought to impose strict controls. In another pointed reminder, Stans allegedly discussed a contribution with officials of the Greyhound Corporation in the context of the corporation's interest in legislation to allow wider buses on federal highways.[19]

Finally, corporate contributions may arise not from a desire that the government do something, but from a desire to let sleeping dogs lie—to either keep the government out of an area of concern to an industry or to maintain the favorable position already acquired by the industry. One of the major impediments to regulatory reform is opposition to change by regulated industries that have grown comfortable in a noncompetitive environment in which they cooperate with regulators. For example, a major goal of the airline industry is to preserve the virtual monopoly that, due to regulatory policies, they now share. The same is true for the trucking industry, which is regulated by the Interstate Commerce Commission.

There is another desire for government restraint or inaction that arises from more insidious circumstances. According to American Airlines chairman George A. Spater, much of the corporate money contributed to campaigns is given in fear of possible retaliation from winning candidates. At the time of the airline's illegal contribution, Spater noted that it had been solicited by Herbert Kalmbach, then President Nixon's lawyer. Spater's assessment of his own motives is revealing. He stated, "I knew Mr. Kalmbach to be both the President's personal counsel and counsel for our major competitor. I concluded that a substantial response was called for."[20] In less genteel circles, this pattern of behavior is known as extortion. Nonetheless, adding insult to injury, the Civil Aeronautics Board later rejected American's merger proposal. Not unlike the victim who hands over his wallet and is hit over the head by the mugger anyway, American Airlines was taken. But this obviously is not the norm or campaign coffers would not be so well-laden with corporate money. What, then, is the usual return on this corporate investment?

The Return on Access

If access is the most common and pervasive reason for contributions, it is also the most common response to contributions. On one level, access is largely symbolic and ego-gratifying. This is particularly true in presidential politics. Guest lists for large White House dinners and other such functions have traditionally been made out with an eye to who gave how much. Presidents Kennedy and

Johnson had a President's Club composed of $1,000 contributors, and President Nixon's large contributors were referred to as RN Associates or the Lincoln Club. Club members normally received invitations to White House functions, briefings on government policy, and personal but usually symbolic meetings with the President himself.

Contributions to the Nixon re-election effort apparently were keyed to higher levels of access in proportion to contributions. Currier Holman, an executive of Iowa Beef Processors, Inc., said that a Nixon campaign aide told him, "If you gave $25,000, if you had a problem, you could talk to someone in the White House, a Cabinet officer or someone like that. For $50,000 you get to talk to the President." The campaign aide, Clayton Yeutter, later an Assistant Secretary of Agriculture, admitted that rewards were geared to contributions but claimed it was purely ceremonial: "I probably said something about the large contributors getting invited to a White House function, and maybe medium contributors having lunch with Stans or Cabinet officers. It was definitely not that you could come and talk to the President about your problems."[21] Even in these days of rising food prices, the average citizen might wonder whether lunch with Maurice Stans was worth $25,000.

If buying access to decisionmakers is helpful to corporations, buying a position as a decisionmaker is even better. On the level of personal ego-gratification, the buying of ambassadorships is a long-established folk custom of the very rich. A more pernicious and economically harmful practice is the placement of large business donors on regulatory commissions and other agencies. For example, by conservative estimate $800,000 was contributed to political campaigns by petroleum company executives in 1968. Of that amount, 93 per cent went to Republicans. Judging from President Nixon's appointments to the Federal Power Commission, the regulatory agency most relevant to the oil industry, the oilmen had invested their money wisely. Nixon appointed as chairman John Nassikas, formerly general counsel of a gas utility in New Hampshire. According to Senator Frank Moss, chairman of the Senate Commerce Committee's consumer subcommittee, Nassikas' views "consistently paralleled the position of industry on major policy matters." As commissioners, the President appointed Pinckney Walter, a former dean of the University of Missouri business school who had frequently consulted for natural gas companies, and Rush Moody, Jr., a lawyer who was sponsored by the president of Pennzoil United Corporation—a man who later supplied $700,000 to the Nixon re-election committee.[22]

The direct buying of government policy is probably less pervasive than buying access or appointments, but it has the advantage for the donor of being less indirect and of bringing quicker results. Although the matter concerns agribusiness rather than industrial corporations, the case of the tainted milk subsidies affords us a rare glimpse of the potential payoff on a political investment. The facts and documents in the case were first developed by separate lawsuits brought by the United Farm Organization and Ralph Nader and were later the subject of investigation by the Senate Watergate Committee and a federal bribery prosecution.[23]

The Great Milk Caper

We can begin the chronology of the great milk caper on March 13, 1971, when then-Secretary of Agriculture Clifford Hardin announced that the Department of Agriculture would maintain the price support for milk at $4.66 per hundredweight and would not raise it for the new marketing year beginning April 1. The following week legislation was introduced by 29 senators and 116 congressmen to raise the price support of milk. Nearly half of those legislative sponsors had received a total of $187,000 in campaign contributions from dairy groups in the previous three years.

The plot thickens on March 22, 1971, when the Trust for Agricultural Political Education (TAPE), the political arm of the Associated Milk Producers, gave $10,000 to various Republican campaign committees. The next day, a dozen dairy industry representatives met with President Nixon and Secretary Hardin to discuss the milk subsidy level. On March 24 another dairy political organization, the Trust for Special Political Agricultural Community Education (SPACE), delivered $25,000 to four national Republican campaign funds. Yet a third dairy group, the Agricultural and

Dairy Educational and Political Trust (ADEPT), pledged $50,000 to the Republicans. The next day, March 25, Secretary Hardin announced that the Department of Agriculture had revised its original decision and would, after all, raise milk price supports from $4.66 to $4.93 per hundredweight. As the *Washington Post* cryptically commented, "We don't know, of course, what the nation's cows did between March 12 and March 25 that might have caused such a dramatic reconsideration by the administration."[24] The cows didn't do much, but the dairymen did. Confirming the obvious, Gary Hanman, chairman of ADEPT, the political arm of Mid-America Dairymen, Inc., wrote to a Mid-America member that contributions "played a major part" in changing the decision.[25]

The changed decision removed the need for the dairymen to further pressure Congress and subsequently, according to data collected for Ralph Nader's suit, dairymen's contributions to congressmen declined to a fraction of the former rate. Contributions to national Republican campaign funds, however, increased tremendously. After the White House meeting and consequent policy change, TAPE, SPACE, and ADEPT contributed another $287,000 to the Nixon re-election drive through scores of dummy committees. Much of the money was solicited and channeled by veteran Nixon political hatchetman Murray Chotiner. When asked about the additional contributions subsequent to the policy change, ADEPT chairman Gary Hanman said: "It's not unusual to bleed you more later."[26]

One of the clearest statements of the realities of corporate campaign contributions and their relation to public policy was supplied (perhaps unwittingly) by William A. Power, president of Mid-America Dairymen, Inc. In a letter to a member, he wrote:

> The facts of life are that the economic welfare of dairymen does depend a great deal on political action. If dairymen are to receive their fair share of the governmental financial pie that we all pay for, we must have friends in government. I have become increasingly aware that the sincere and soft voice of the dairy farmer is no match for the jingle of hard currencies put in the campaign funds of the politicians by the vegetable fat interests, labor, oil, steel, airlines, and others.
>
> We dairymen as a body can be [a] dominant group. On March 23, 1971, along with nine other dairy farmers, I sat in the Cabinet room of the

White House, across the table from the President of the United States, and heard him compliment the dairymen on their marvelous work in [the] consolidating and unifying of our industry and our involvement in politics. He said, "You people are my friends and I appreciate it."

Two days later an order came from the U.S. Department of Agriculture increasing the support price of milk to 85 percent of parity, which added from 500 to 700 million dollars to dairy farmers' milk checks. We dairymen cannot afford to overlook this kind of economic benefit. Whether we like it or not, this is the way the system works.[27]

It later turned out that the blatant attempt by the milk producers to buy influence not only went beyond the bounds of discretion but also beyond the bounds of the law. In August 1974, the Associated Milk Producers, Inc., pleaded guilty in federal court to rampant violations of federal election laws and was fined $35,000. The 1971 donations exceeded the bounds of the law in other ways as well. As part of the same case, allegations of outright bribery emerged. Harold S. Nelson, former general manager of the Associated Milk Producers, and Jake Jacobson, a Texas lawyer, both pleaded guilty to bribing former U.S. Treasury Secretary John Connally to obtain his help in securing the 1971 rise in milk subsidies. Connally was indicted and tried in the case, but he was found not guilty.

In reviewing the uses of campaign contributions to influence governmental decisions, it is difficult to draw generalizations from the few cases about which there is adequate documentation. Are these the worst cases, or are these typical cases that just happened to be discovered? On a superficial level, the milk subsidy case tends toward the former view since it involved bribery. On the other hand, the case richly illustrates the ambiguities of the relationship between campaign finance and political influence. The original facts and allegations in the case (as developed by Ralph Nader and others) were developed before the bribery was uncovered as part of the much wider Watergate prosecutions. It was only the close timing of the contributions and the reward of higher subsidies and the explicit statements of dairy-industry officials that led to the discovery of an undeniable *quid pro quo* relationship—improper but not criminal. The admission of outright bribery did not come until much later. Thus, it is bribery (in a legal sense) when a high government official receives money for his personal use in exchange for favors; but it is not bribery when he received it as a campaign contribution *implicitly* given for the same favors.

This may well be a distinction without a difference. This ambiguity is further seen in the investigation by the Watergate prosecutors, prior to President Nixon's resignation, of charges that the President was influenced by the $2 million campaign pledge by the milk producers in his decision to raise price supports. These allegations may never be conclusively resolved, but the entire situation illustrates that the difference between an outright bribe, improper influence, and a legitimate campaign contribution is largely a matter of degree. Thus, as a practical matter, the dairy case may be untypical only in the explicit *quid pro quo* nature of the transaction and in the fact that it became entangled in the sordid Watergate scandal.

The Campaign Finance Merry-Go-Round

Given the high incidence of secrecy (and the premium placed on secrecy) and the various subterfuges devised by lawyers, the complete story of campaign contributions can never be known. But even from what is known, a rather dismal picture emerges. The current system of financing requires candidates to raise huge sums of money, which generally come from large donations. This system breeds the dependence of many politicians on corporate interests and leads to the dominance of corporations in the campaign finance system. This, in turn, leads to increased access to government and sometimes to buying favors or government inaction in regulatory or antitrust cases.

The amendments to the Federal Election Campaign Act passed by Congress in 1974 were supposed to reduce the dominance of large contributions and the subsequent dependence of many politicians on corporate interests. While the legislation is a step forward, particularly in its more comprehensive disclosure requirements, it still falls far short of effectively curbing large-scale corporate financing of political campaigns. Presidential contenders in primary-election campaigns are still required to raise substantial sums from private contributors; the legislation does not provide public funding for congressional candidates, nor does it require financial disclosure by members of Congress. In addition to the loopholes and subterfuges already discussed, donors can still give up to $25,000 a year to the national committee of their political party—and donors in that range are quite closely identified with their corporate interests.

In 1975, the United States Supreme Court ruled on a challenge to the campaign-finance amendments. The Court upheld most features of the amendments but did declare that, except for presidential candidates who accept federal funds, limitations on campaign spending are unconstitutional. The Court also ruled that individuals could not be limited in the amount they spend to support a candidacy by means other than direct campaign contributions. Thus, the net effect of the Federal Election Campaign Act Amendments and the Supreme Court ruling is probably to increase the power of big money in politics. Since corporations, directly or indirectly, are the prime suppliers of big money, they come out as the big winners.

It is difficult to determine how much influence is purchased through campaign contributions. It might be argued that the buying of influence so widespread in the Nixon administration was unusual. It is more probable that the Nixon people were unusual only in the blatant manner with which they sold favors and extorted contributions. The system of preferred positions for large donors has long been a feature of the presidency and Congress; and it will continue as long as large, identifiable contributions are needed and permitted.

As the Watergate scandal demonstrated, it is not only and completely corporations that are to blame for the excesses of the campaign-finance system. Just as there is a fine line between contribution-induced political influence and bribery, there also is a fine line between bribery and extortion. The giant corporations would not have been buying if former President Nixon had not been selling. Moreover, there is a fundamental institutional problem as well. The political system as a whole makes it essential for corporations to exert whatever influence they can. Within it, the system of campaign finance requires the donation of private funds

—funds that are readily supplied by corporations. Nor has the public done much to reduce the need for large donors. Provided with the opportunity to check off $1.00 on their income tax returns to be allocated for campaign financing, fewer than half of the taxpayers did so. If the majority of citizens will not take even so simple a step to provide for campaign expenses, we must expect corporations to seize the opportunity to fill the void. For them it is a good opportunity to pursue the essential goal of hegemony in the political environment.

How Much Does It Matter?

This still leaves open the question of how much it matters—of how much influence is exerted due to contributions. The cases cited in this chapter show that, at times, the influence is substantial indeed. Looking at the political system as a whole, the answer is harder to come by. Perhaps the most reasonable answer is to rely on the corporations' own assessment of that influence. As Galbraith has reminded us, modern corporations must engage in extensive planning of the wisest investment of their resources. There is some disagreement about the extent to which giant corporations are able to control their environment, but there is little doubt that they try to reduce uncertainty and influence their environment to the maximum extent possible. Before making substantial investments in physical facilities, new products, or acquiring other companies, large corporations must calculate whether a suitable return on investment will be forthcoming. This being so, we must conclude that corporations calculate that they are also getting something in return for the many millions of dollars spent as campaign contributions. In fact, their contributions can be viewed as investments with the expectation of a return—like investments in research, machinery, and property. As with other investments, the payoff is not certain; but on the whole a good return is usually expected.

In short, we can conceive of campaign contributions by large corporations as a large-scale system of attempting to control as much as possible the uncertainties of the political environment by rewarding friends for past favors and by insuring future access.

Corporate money does not always or automatically buy public policy, but it buys a lot more than the individual votes and small contributions of average citizens.

Notes

1. Congressional Quarterly, *Dollar Politics* (Washington, 1972), pp. 62–63.
2. *New York Times*, November 19, 1972, p. 1.
3. Herbert E. Alexander, *Financing the 1968 Election* (Lexington, Mass.: D. C. Heath, 1971), pp. 147–52.
4. George Thayer, *Who Shakes the Money Tree?* (New York: Simon and Shuster, 1973), pp. 133–35.
5. *Congressional Quarterly Weekly Report* 30 (July 8, 1972), pp. 1656–60.
6. Michael Malbin, "New Campaign Finance Law Faces Legal, Political Tests," *National Journal Reports* 28 (July 12, 1975), p. 1016.
7. Martin Tolchin, *New York Times*, September 17, 1974, p. 37.
8. Ibid.
9. *New York Times*, July 7, 1973, p. 1.
10. Jerry Landauer, "Delinquent Donors," *Wall Street Journal*, November 21, 1969, p. 1.
11. U.S. Code, Title 18, Sec. 610.
12. U.S. Congress, Senate, *Watergate and Related Activities, Phase III, Campaign Financing*, hearings before the Senate Select Committee on Presidential Campaign Activities, 93rd Congress, 1st sess. (1973), Vol. 13, pp. 5494–5501.
13. Jonathan Cottin, "Washington Pressures/BIPAC Seeks to Elect Business Members to Congress," *National Journal* 2 (July 18, 1970), pp. 1525–31.
14. Cottin, "BIPAC," p. 1525.
15. *Congressional Quarterly Weekly Report* 30 (October 21, 1972), pp. 2720–27.
16. Senate Select Committee on Presidential Campaign Activities *Watergate and Related Activities*, Vol. 13, p. 5442.
17. *Washington Post*, October 8, 1970, p. 1.
18. Bob Woodward and Carl Bernstein, "$100,000 Gift to Nixon Campaign Is Traced to Texas Corporation," *Washington Post*, Oct. 6, 1972. The money was part of the infamous "laundered"-in-Mexico scheme.
19. Nick Kotz and Morton Mintz, "Business Executives were GOP's Big Pre-April Donors," *Washington Post*, October 22, 1972, A1.
20. *New York Times*, July 7, 1972, p. 19.
21. Mary Breasted, "G.O.P. Fund Plea Tied Rewards to Size of Gift," *New York Times*, July 19, 1973, p. 18.

22. Morton Mintz, "Moss Charges Payoffs," *Washington Post,* September 30, 1972, p. A19.
23. For a fuller explication of this case with supporting documents, see Senate Select Committee on Presidential Campaign Activities, *Final Report,* pp. 579–767.
24. *Washington Post,* August 31, 1972, p. A22.
25. Letter published in Senate Select Committee on Presidential Campaign Activities, *Final Report,* p. 671.
26. *Washington Post,* August 25, 1972, p. A9.
27. Letter published in Senate Select Committee on Presidential Campaign Activities, *Final Report,* p. 671.

3

The Corporation as Lobbyist

*The host of contractors, speculators, stock-jobbers and lobby members which haunt
the halls of Congress all desirous . . . on any and every pretext to get their arms into
the public treasury are sufficient to alarm every friend of his country. Their progress
must be arrested.*

James Buchanan in a letter to Franklin Pierce, 1852.

Lobbying is probably the most pervasive form of political activity,
and it has been with us for a long time. The term originally
referred to those seeking special favors from the government by
huddling with legislators in the lobbies of Congress and state legislatures; it was in general use by the 1830s. The goals of lobbyists
have not changed much since James Madison addressed himself to
the problem in the Federalist Papers. What we now refer to as
pressure groups, Madison called factions as he observed in *The
Federalist No. 10:*

. . . the most common and durable source of factions has been the various and unequal distribution of property. A landed interest, a manufacturing interest, a mercantile interest, a moneyed interest, with many lesser
interests, grow up of necessity in civilized nations, and divide them into
different classes, actuated by different sentiments and views. The regulation of these various and interfering interests forms the principal task of

43

modern legislation and involves the spirit of party and faction in the necessary and ordinary operations of government.

The process of advancing those "various and interfering interests" is the very core of democratic politics, and lobbying is a major element of that process. We will be using a broad concept of the term *lobbying* to refer to the attempt to shape public policy by directly and indirectly influencing government officials. We will first examine the more formal and direct types of lobbying and then proceed to its broader scope.

The Nature of Lobbying

Although the popular image of a lobbyist is that of a cigar-smoking purveyor of pressure stuffing hundred dollar bills into the pockets of legislators, the day-to-day work of lobbyists is considerably less exciting and less unsavory. In fact, the lobbyists work as much with the groups that employ them as with the government, for half of their job is to keep clients appraised of government actions or policies that may affect them. The other side of that job is to inform government agencies and Congress of the position of their employer on pending legislative or administrative proposals. In what is euphemistically referred to as an educational function, lobbyists present to government officials their industry's version of the economic and technological limits of legislation. Finally, when push comes to shove, lobbyists engage in the hard business of persuading members of Congress to take their side in legislative battles. This process of persuasion is more likely to take the form of working out strategies and providing information to legislators who are already friendly and trying to persuade neutrals than trying to convert opponents. Working closely with representatives, senators, and congressional committees and staffers, lobbyists are active participants in every phase of the legislative process.

While Congress is the most visible target of lobbyists, it is certainly not the only target; nor is it always the most important target. Many lobby groups concentrate extensively on the agencies of the Executive Branch since the process of formulating public policy does not end in Congress. Nearly all government programs leave considerable discretion in the hands of the executive agencies that administer and implement those programs. Administrative agencies set *specific* policies in vital areas such as occupational safety, food and drug purity, and antitrust regulations. Before government became so big and so complex, Woodrow Wilson, while still a professor of government, wrote that there was a necessary distinction between politics and administration. The job of the administrator, Wilson asserted, was to be politically neutral and to implement the policies decided on by Congress. If that distinction was neat and clear in Wilson's day, it certainly is not so easily discernible today. Because of the great amount of discretion vested in administrators—born of the scope and complexity of government activities—they are an inherent part of the political process. For all parties interested in political issues, including lobbyists, the policymaking process merely changes arenas when a law goes from Congress to the Executive Branch. Thus, lobbyists engage in much the same process of communication and persuasion as they attempt to influence public policy as they do when they are working to affect the lawmaking process.

Although we are primarily concerned here with business lobbying, it should be noted that there are many other important types of lobby groups. One of the most formidable groups of lobbyists comes from within the government itself in the form of representatives of the executive departments and agencies. Every sizable agency has a congressional relations office to cultivate members of Congress and to push the agency's own legislative proposals.[1] The labor unions, particularly those that constitute the AFL-CIO, have an extensive, sophisticated, and particularly powerful army of lobbyists to advance the interests of organized labor. Other traditionally powerful lobby groups include the American Medical Association, the American Farm Bureau Federation, and the American Legion. Far down the list in terms of money and power are groups representing more widespread and dispersed public interests such as the Consumers Federation of America.

Lobbying and Political Power

Although lobbying has long been the subject of sober analysis and sensational exposés, there is little agreement among observers about the power and effect of lobbyists. Instead, there have been two dominant modes of writing about lobbyists. There is, first, the muckraking mode, in which lobbying is described in terms such as *the Washington payoff*, replete with images of legislators being pressured and bought off by special interests. A number of recent books on corporate power have chronicled many instances in which corporate pressure on Congress and the Executive Branch has led to policy highly favorable to corporate interests.[2] Among the notable examples is the case of the oil industry, whose immense political power has been channeled into obtaining major tax and other commercial advantages in the states and federal government.[3]

Although lobbyists deny unethical or illegal activities, they rate their own effectiveness very highly. Indeed, a major part of their work rests in assuring their clients of their own importance in the councils of government. Studies by political scientists, however, have found a more limited impact. Lester Milbrath concluded that "there is relatively little influence or power in lobbying per se. There are many forces in addition to lobbying which influence public policy; in most cases these other forces clearly outweigh the impact of lobbying."[4] Similarly, the authors of a major study of business political activity directed toward tariff legislation conclude that their findings "tend to cast doubt on the stereotype of pressure politics, of special interests effectively expressing themselves and forcing politicians either to bow to their dictates or to fight back vigorously."[5]

There is clearly an important conflict among the prevailing views of lobbying power. A major problem of analyzing the impact of lobbying stems from the larger problem of studying political influence generally. The concepts of power and influence are among the most elusive in political science. Scholars who are commonly called pluralists contend that attributions of power must be extremely specific: Citizen X has power over citizen Y on a particular specified issue, and it must be proven that Y's action was a result of X's influence.[6] Critics of the pluralist school maintain that this is a too-restrictive view of influence since influence extends beyond specific decisions considered separately. For example, a major criticism is that the ability to prevent a given question from even being considered may be a stronger evidence of political power than prevailing on a particular decision. In that case, the holder of power controls the political agenda.[7] One of the major issues at the root of this conceptual controversy is the problem of causation. In the study of power, as in the use of statistics, correlation does not prove causation. Simply because a business group lobbies for a piece of legislation which is then enacted does not prove that the enactment was caused by lobbying. On the other hand, it requires a giant and naive methodological leap of faith to believe that the maintenance of the oil-depletion allowance is independent of the enormous political efforts put forth by the oil industry.

Another problem in assessing the impact of lobbying is that it is not always clear exactly what constitutes a victory or a loss for an interest group. Although the passage of Medicare in 1965 was commonly regarded as a defeat for the powerful American Medical Association, the legislation came only after thirty years of effort, and it fell considerably short of the original goals of the reformers. Even if we could compile a scorecard of wins and losses for corporate interests, we would not know how important or permanent such successes or failures are.

But even with these cautionary notes and with due respect for the complexities of the political process, it cannot be concluded that corporate lobbying is without significant influence. To say that there is a large number of participants in any policy controversy and that larger forces are at work does not mean that the participants and forces are independent of each other. Nor does it mean that corporations and other interest groups are but one minor factor out of dozens of minor factors. In assessing lobbying, two points can be made that help to clarify the impact of corporate power.

First, the American political system is highly favorable to the exercise of power by organized groups. The structure of policymaking in America is such that organized aggregations of interests are permitted and even expected to formulate public policy by funneling their preferences through governmental channels that reflect their power and facilitate their needs. We have gone from the Madisonian conception of faction as a necessary evil to be regulated to a conception of interest-group government as a positive expression of the facilitative role of government.[8] Furthermore, the making of regulatory policy is a process of high-interest-group activity relative to other policy areas; and it is in this regulatory area that we find the most frequent expression of corporate political activity.[9] Thus, the political system facilitates the activities of organized groups in general; and in the area of the most interest to corporations such group activity is most prevalent.

The second point to be made is that this chapter focuses on lobbying as one avenue of corporate influence, and no claim is made that lobbying alone caused a particular result or that corporate lobbying is all-powerful. Instead, we examine the ability of corporations to utilize that avenue of influence as one part of their overall political impact.

In an environment that requires the participation of organized interests, corporations as lobby groups are well-prepared to exert influence since they have, in greater measure than other social entities, two kinds of resources that are richly rewarded in the political system: superior "presence" and a relatively high degree of control over communications and information. While corporate interests are not omnipotent, they are very nearly omnipresent in the political environment; that is, business representatives are able to spend a lot of time in professional and social contacts with legislators. The influence of superior access is compounded by a relative corporate dominance of the channels of political information. It has long been observed that control of information is a major source of political power. While corporations rarely have complete control over relevant information, they are able to distribute more information sympathetic to their own ends than other interest groups. Thus, the following discussion of corporate lobbying proceeds in the context of the power of access and information.

Corporate Lobbyists: Being Seen and Being Heard

Major corporate interests enjoy superior formal access to policymakers. As we have noted previously, campaign contributions buy a good deal of access. The representative of a corporation that has been responsible for delivering a few thousand dollars to a senator's campaign fund rarely has to wait long for an audience. In the case of administrative agencies, access is sometimes institutionalized. For example, the Grocery Manufacturers of America (GMA), one of the most important and powerful trade associations, has regularly scheduled meetings with top officials of the Food and Drug Administration. At the meetings they discuss topics such as regulations pertaining to food labeling, food additives, and standards. Nor is the GMA unique, for other industry associations also hold regular meetings with FDA officials. At a lower level, GMA lobbyists try to maintain continuing contact with staff members of the FDA. One FDA official told a reporter that the GMA is "constantly calling . . . trying to ascertain where we are and to get information."[10]

The Grocery Manufacturers also deal regularly with the Federal Trade Commission. The association naturally has an interest in the FTC's jurisdiction over advertising, packaging and labeling, and antitrust. About twice a year, the FTC commissioners meet with GMA board members. The FTC also has meetings with other industry groups, and in 1970 they started meeting with consumer groups as well. Although pending legal cases are off-limits at these meetings, the GMA and other industry groups do work with FTC staff in discussing proposed regulations such as those covering marketing and advertising practices.

Corporate interests can be even more successful in shaping new legislation or administrative regulations by working directly with industry-oriented departments such as the Department of Commerce or Agriculture. For example, the GMA worked closely with officials of the Department of Commerce in its effort to delay legislation requiring unit-pricing in supermarkets. Utilizing a strategy of delay, the GMA argued that more study was needed— then offered to sponsor such studies. In 1970, grocery industry representatives held several meetings with Commerce Department officials, ostensibly to review information on unit-pricing. In fact, the implicitly understood purpose of the review was to determine whether sufficient studies were available to justify a Commerce Department position opposing unit-pricing proposals. They were unable to come up with the requisite studies in time, and so the Commerce Department refrained from taking a position.[11] Although it fell short of its original goal, the grocery lobby nonetheless succeeded in shifting its role from outside lobbyist to inside participant. The power of the Grocery Manufacturers can readily be appreciated by noting that the Commerce Department shares responsibility for implementing the Fair Packaging and Labeling Act—a piece of legislation the GMA had bitterly opposed in the first place. The shrewd lobbyist knows that what is lost in Congress can be regained in the bureaucracy.

Lobbyist Watering Holes

Utilizing the advantages conferred by their wealth and social position, corporate representatives constantly attempt to cultivate continuing friendly relations with government officials. Lobbyists know they are more effective in dealing with officials with whom they have long and continuing contacts rather than trying to approach people sporadically and in relation to specific issues. To this end, Washington abounds in plush watering holes where lobbyists can entertain members of Congress, congressional staffers, and administrative agency officials. While the officials are not always buying, the lobbyists are always selling—however subtly.

A more questionable practice in maintaining friendly relations is the industry-sponsored excursion for public officials. Many members of Congress are paid large fees to speak at industry functions, often in plush places the rest of us would pay handsomely to attend. Picking its speakers carefully, for example, the National League of Insured Savings Associations paid Senate Banking Committee chairman John Sparkman $1,000 for addressing one of its meetings. Another Banking Committee member, former Senator Wallace Bennett of Utah, received $1,200 for addressing the National Mortgage Banking Association. On many other occasions, industry groups simply invite representatives and senators to join them in all-expense-paid junkets; or they pick up the tab at semiofficial functions. For example, a group of giant corporations paid a third of the cost of the 1975 National Governors

Conference—a practice that has become customary. Provided for the nation's governors and their parties was breakfast sponsored by Dow Chemical, Coca-Cola, and J.C. Penney; evening cocktail parties were held courtesy of Xerox, Martin Marietta, and the Federation of American Hospitals; and a lavishly appointed riverboat ride for gubernatorial staffs and reporters was sponsored by the Mid Continent Oil and Gas Association.[12]

Probably most lawmakers who are on the receiving end of such gratuities believe, or convince themselves, that there is no relation between what they receive and their legislative activities. Thus, in explaining why he flew to Bimini in 1973 on a private flight sponsored by defense contractor Rockwell International, Senator Herman Talmadge said, "Al Rockwell, Jr. has an operation in Albany, Georgia. He has been a friend of mine for quite a number of years. . . . He invited me to join him on a fishing trip, and I went."[13] Yet, whether in committee or on the floor, legislators are continually making judgments of great financial interest to defense and other industries. However the legislators perceive the situation, corporate lobbyists no doubt prefer to have such decisions made by their fishing and poker companions who have frequently been their guests. The object on such occasions is never to seek a vote or commitment on a particular piece of legislation, but rather to create a sympathetic mood. As one of the lobbyist hosts at the National Governors Convention put it, the aim of the lavish hospitality was "getting ourselves known in the hope that we can follow up later on specific issues." It would take, after all, an ungrateful and hard-nosed legislator to believe that Ford Motor Company or General Motors is less than sincere in its environmental concerns if he is personally and pleasantly acquainted with officials of those corporations.

While it is almost inevitable that legislators of all ideological persuasions will be friendly with America's economic and industrial elite, propriety at least demands that such relationships be limited to simple mutual friendship rather than corporate sponsorship of a lawmaker's leisure time. The situation is further compounded by the dominant buying power of industry. Environmental, consumer, and other public-interest groups are in no position to compete in favor giving. While Nader's Raiders humbly talk to congressional staffers in the House or Senate cafeterias, other officials are ceremoniously wined and dined in more commodious and expensive surroundings. Taking a leisurely trip in a company airplane is more conducive to the process of influencing a legislator than hearing the earnest entreaties of Ralph Nader in a congressional office.

The Military-Industrial Complex

Although the preceding discussion considered senators and representatives as *recipients* of lobbying influence, it should also be noted that they themselves often act as internal lobbyists for important economic interests in their districts. In concert with corporations and unions, they participate in formidable lobbying coalitions. The biggest, most important, and most expensive coalition is the military-industrial complex. Although the largest fruits of its labor go to defense contractors, the corporate interests are only one component of the military-industrial complex. Other elements include the armed services themselves, local government officials in areas with heavy defense spending, some labor unions, military alumni associations, the reserves and National Guard, and, most significantly, members of Congress from defense-oriented districts. No one has to lobby such legislators to support major new weapons systems. It is already their inclination, and perhaps their responsibility, to get as much financial advantage from defense spending for their district as possible. Conversely, every member of Congress is in favor of closing down obsolete and wasteful installations—unless they are in the home district, at which point they become vital components of the national security system.

The important point to be made about the military-industrial complex is that it is the epitome of the nearly unstoppable lobby coalition. It is not unique, however, only bigger and more successful than other such attempts. At the heart of the matter is the fact that corporations and trade associations—such as the Aerospace Industries Association and the National Security Industrial Association—are joined in their efforts by agencies of the Executive Branch, sometimes by the White House, and by many members of Congress. Each element of the coalition pursues the coalition's common goals in order to fulfill their diverse interests. For the industrialists the goal is almost unabashedly financial gain. In the case of industrial giants such as General Dynamics and Lockheed Aircraft, upward of two-thirds of their revenues come from defense orders. For them the goal is survival.

The military, like any other bureaucracy, seeks to expand its budgets, programs, and power. Legislators enlist because of their sincere belief in the virtues of a strong defense establishment and their equally strong instinct for electoral survival—a survival that may hinge on their ability to bring home the federal "pork" for their districts. This phenomenon can most clearly be seen in the career of Representative Mendel Rivers, the late chairman of the House Armed Services Committee. His district—which consisted of Charleston, South Carolina, and the surrounding area—had a naval station and shipyard, an air base, an Army base, a missile plant, and a mine warfare center. It was suggested that, with one more installation, Charleston would sink to the bottom of the sea.

The lesson of the military-industrial complex for the student of corporate interests is that it is most successful in achieving its legislative goals when it can tie those goals into the self-interest of other powerful political forces and the widest possible range of localities. It is a lesson that has not gone unheeded. For example, in planning for NASA's space shuttle, an explicit goal of the space agency and the contractors who were bidding for the contract was to allocate the project in such a way that subcontracts would be spread as far and as evenly around the country as possible. While this was a laudable display of fairness, it also created economic interest in the shuttle in a greater number of congressional districts and hence put more pressure on Congress to vote for the shuttle.

The Washington Connection

The political influence inherent in the superior presence and information capability of corporate interests is clearly seen in the complex network of professional and personal relationships that can be called *the Washington connection*. An important but little-known element of the connection is the system of advisory committees to various government agencies. The utilization of outside committees to provide advice to the government is a long-standing practice. It gained momentum during the New Deal and particularly during World War II, as hundreds of businessmen worked with government agencies on matters of war production. These committees—some formal, some informal—are supposed to provide expertise to aid government policymaking. To call the advisory system network "little-known" is not to fault the public. Until recently no one knew fully the scope and impact of advisory committees, including even their total number. Fortunately, this situation has recently changed.

In 1970 and 1971, hearings were held on advisory committees, and in 1972 the Federal Advisory Committee Act (PL 92-463) was enacted. The First Annual Report of the President to Congress on Federal Advisory Committees revealed that, as of the beginning of 1973, there were 1,439 advisory committees. The largest number were in the Department of Health, Education, and Welfare—367. Most of the advisory committees are not business-oriented nor even composed predominantly of corporate representatives. Nonetheless, our concern is with those that are composed of corporate interests and with the potential for influence inherent in the advisory system.

It is beyond the scope of this book to analyze comprehensively the entire advisory network. Indeed, the President's Report on Advisory Committees requires more than 5,700 pages to just list and briefly describe federal advisory committees. So we must content ourselves with just a brief look at some committees and the problems they present.

The avowed purpose of business advisory committees can be seen in the statement of mission of the National Business Council for Consumer Affairs, an advisory committee in the Department of Commerce established in 1971:

. . . The National Business Council for Consumer Affairs is established as a primary focus for action by American industry on consumer issues and as a basic source of industry information for the Federal Government in this area. The Council will encourage and assist in the establishment of voluntary programs for industry action to anticipate and resolve consumer problems, and when appropriate, make recommendations concerning legislation or executive action.[14]

In his statement announcing the formation of the council, President Nixon stated:

. . . The Council will allow businessmen to communicate regularly with the President, the Office of Consumer Affairs, the Federal Trade Commission, the Justice Department, other government agencies as appropriate and private organization which are directly concerned with consumer affairs. This dialogue in a forum involving all consumer product and service industries will provide greater awareness and sensitivity for both consumer concerns and responsive corporate action.[15]

Since there was already a Consumer Advisory Committee attached to the Executive Office of the President, it might be wondered why business representatives were simply not added to that group to provide "greater awareness and sensitivity for both consumer concerns and responsive corporate action." The basic reason is that the purpose of such advisory groups is not to provide an enlightening "dialogue" but to press a particular point of view. This advocacy role can be seen in the organization statement made to the initial meeting of the National Business Council for Consumer Affairs by its chairman Robert E. Brooker, chairman of Marcor, Inc. (Montgomery Ward):

. . . Some of you might be surprised at the high level of consumer distrust of big business. But when one considers the large and varied group of consumer advocates and the amount of media coverage given to these groups, it is not surprising that these attitudes have won wide acceptance. Since all of us in this audience can also be categorized as strong consumer advocates, I believe we must combine our resources and data and present our briefs to the public and governmental representatives.[16]

In effect, the advisory committee system is a formalized lobbying process, as Ralph Nader asserted, "giving a Government imprimatur, giving exclusive access to Government councils and civil servants and, in effect, severely imbalancing the right of unorganized citizens and citizen groups to have relatively equivalent access."[17] Although the 1972 advisory committee law requires "balanced" representation on the committees, Nader's charge remains well founded. For example, in the Department of the Interior's National Petroleum Council nearly all the members are industry representatives; and all the new members appointed by the Secretary of the Interior in 1974 had close ties to the industry. The rather lame explanation for this bending of the law was that the law "does not tell us whether it means balance within the industry or balance in society."[18]

The Fox in the Chicken Coop

While no one doubts industry's right to press forth its point of view, we can wonder why it is necessary to provide this kind of legitimized super access—a situation that further bolsters big business's already considerable political advantages. Moreover, some advisory committees are composed not only of representatives of corporations with an interest in certain problems, but also of corporations that are themselves the problem. For example, one-third of the companies represented on the Business Council for Consumer Affairs are the subject of some form of complaint from the Federal Trade Commission. Being a polluter seems to be a prerequisite for membership in another Commerce Department advisory committee, the National Industrial Pollution Control Council. The council is composed of board chairmen or presidents of major oil, automobile, electric utility, mining, timber, coal, airline, and manufacturing companies—most of them major contributors to pollution. Capping off the Pollution Control Council, President Nixon named as its chairman Bert Cross, board chairman of Minnesota Mining and Manufacturing—a company that, at the time, had ignored a 1966 state order in Wisconsin to stop discharging sulfurous waste into municipal sewers.

Beyond the fox-guarding-the-chicken-coop problem, an additional peril of the advisory groups to the public interest is their penchant for secrecy. Although this danger has been alleviated by the 1972 reform legislation, it is still worth mentioning, inasmuch as it illustrates the natural proclivities of the advisory network. Until 1972, meetings of both the Business Council for Consumer

Affairs and the National Industrial Pollution Control Council, among others, were closed to the public. At best, only summary minutes of the proceedings were provided. The total description of the business discussed at the first meeting of the Subcouncil on Warranties and Guarantees was "a brief discussion on warranty and guarantee problems in various industries and segments of industry." The secrecy of the meetings was no accident; it was avidly sought, and the participants went to great lengths to maintain secrecy. After a confrontation with representatives of ten environmental groups in October 1970, subsequent meetings of the Pollution Control Council were held at the State Department building—a restricted-access building where only those with prior appointments are admitted. Similarly, the initial meetings of the various subcouncils of the Business Council on Consumer Affairs were held either at the State Department or the White House.

In testifying against proposals to open up advisory committee meetings, William D. Lee, executive director of the Business Council for Consumer Affairs, stated that open meetings "would have the ultimate effect of vitiating the informal atmosphere that I believe a necessary adjunct to receipt by the government of knowledge and advice concerning matters of significant importance in the public interest otherwise difficult, if not impossible to obtain."[19]

It is precisely because the matters discussed are of "significant importance in the public interest" that Congress ordered such meetings to be open. The reasons advanced for secrecy were generally couched in terms of the necessity for "informal" deliberations and "candid" discussions. What it all boiled down to was that the corporate representatives were advancing positions they feared could not stand the light of day. What else is the big secret? Indeed, when we look at the accomplishments of some advisory committees, we can more readily understand the penchant for secrecy.

Consider first the Business Council on Federal Reports (originally the Advisory Council on Federal Reports). The Council on Federal Reports advises the Office of Management and Budget on questionnaires that federal agencies want to send out to businesses. Under a 1942 law, all agencies that desire to send a questionnaire to ten or more businesses or persons must be cleared by the Office of Management and Budget. The purpose of the law was to prevent needless duplication and overburdening of small businesses with questionnaires; the council was set up by the first Budget Bureau director to administer the law. While efforts to streamline federal data-collection should be welcomed by all businesses and taxpayers, the Business Council on Federal Reports goes a good deal further than merely providing neutral advice.

In 1963 the Federal Trade Commission proposed a survey to study ownership and interlocking directorates of the 1,000 largest corporations. At the OMB (then organized as the Bureau of the Budget), business representatives reportedly objected vigorously to the *purpose* of the study. Nonetheless, the study was approved. Having the benefit of an advance tipoff, the corporate representatives took their fight to Congress, where they succeeded in scuttling the project. Congress refused to appropriate money for the survey and even forbade it for the next three years.[20] Similarly, an FTC attempt to collect more detailed information on the various divisions of conglomerate corporations was thwarted at an OMB advisory committee meeting in 1971.

Since 1963, successive attempts by the Public Health Service and the Federal Water Pollution Control Agency to survey industrial water waste disposal have been pigeonholed in the wake of objections by OMB advisory committees. An inventory of air contaminants sent out by the National Air Pollution Control Administration was not cleared by the Budget Bureau until it had been severely watered down—after negotiations with representatives of large polluting industries.[21] Thus, secret meetings were being used to protect further corporate secrecy. With results like these, the change in name from Advisory Council on Federal Reports to Business Council on Federal Reports was extremely apt.

As a result of these abuses, legislation was enacted in 1973 to permit regulatory agencies to seek information from corporations without obtaining permission from the Office of Management and Budget. This reform and the Federal Advisory Committee Act have at least insured that the public's business will be conducted in the open, mitigating the conspiratorial aspects of business advisory committees. Nonetheless, the past excesses of the system demonstrate the uses to which some corporate leaders wanted to put the committees. Furthermore, corporate lobbyists are still attempting to undermine or repeal the 1973 legislation. The advisory committees must still be counted as potent instruments of corporate influence in the heart of government. Indeed, as noted by Senator Lee Metcalf, "the industry councils enjoy a favored position over the non-industry special interests and even public-interest groups. This, of course, is just one small step short of the manner of operation of the 'corporate state'—where dominant political power is *officially* and *legally* vested in massive industrial and financial conglomerates."[22]

Musical Chairs

If advisory committees allow corporations to exercise influence by entering government, a frequently more profitable but more circuitous route to corporate influence lies in the two-way traffic of personnel between business and government—a high-stakes game of musical chairs. Information stemming from a study for the House Interstate and Foreign Commerce Committee shows that in 1975 at least 350 officials on the nation's regulatory agencies once worked for the industries they now regulate. While this practice may be justified in the name of obtaining necessary expertise and first-hand experience, the possibility that these officials may be partial to their former employers or be swayed by the prospect of returning to industry is also present. Particularly troublesome is the fact that the Food and Drug Administration leads the list in the number of former industry people now working for it. More than one hundred FDA officials, who decide on the safety of drugs and food additives, once worked for drug or chemical companies. Other agencies with large numbers of former industry personnel are the Federal Trade Commission, with 66; the Securities and Exchange Commission, with 36; the Environmental Protection Agency, with 51; and the Federal Power Commission, with 30.[23]

The traffic, of course, moves the other way as well. Because of their experience and access to old colleagues still in government, high-level policymaking officials command a high price from corporations seeking the good graces of the federal government—a category that excludes few corporations. Some recent examples are illustrative. James Needham was a largely unknown New York accountant until he became a commissioner on the Securities and Exchange Commission in 1969. After leaving that post he ascended to the chairmanship of the New York Stock Exchange. The former administrator of the Environmental Protection Agency, William Ruckelshaus, returned to private law practice and represented the plastics industry in a case before the EPA. And former FCC commissioner Robert Wells returned to a high position in a Kansas broadcasting corporation—the employer whom he had left for a brief two-year stint in the FCC.

Government Alumni as Lobbyists

The movement between government and business is not confined to administrative officials. In high demand as lobbyists are former members of the House and Senate. They have the dual advantages of knowing intimately the ways of Congress and having close personal ties to sitting members of Congress. Furthermore, they have the lifetime privilege of entering the floor of Congress. Lobbying is not limited, moreover, to past members of Congress; several present members are partners in law firms that are registered as lobbyists. From the passage of the Federal Regulation of Lobbying Act in 1946 until 1968, 113 present or former members of Congress or their law firms were registered as lobbyists. Seventy-six of them represented one or more corporations or business trade associations.

The movement of high government officials to related activities in private enterprise is a natural development. After all, they have to do something after government service if they are not to retire, and their expertise is a valuable commodity on the labor market. But it is clear that they are hired as much or more for their influence as for their expertise. The capitalization of government experience is widely accepted and easily defended as legitimate in a capital accustomed to influence peddling as a way of government. The laws of the United States provide a safeguard against the more flagrant conflicts of interest. For example, it is against the law for a former official to act as an agent for anyone in a governmental proceeding relating to a matter in which he participated "personally and substantially" while in the government. Furthermore, one year must elapse before a former official can personally appear before a government agency in relation to a subject that was "under his official responsibility" during his last year of government employment. While these regulations appear strict, they only apply to formal and personal appearances and do not affect the giving of advice to new employers or deal with subjects that were not the specific responsibility of the ex-official. This leaves a lot of leeway for influence peddling from a privileged position, as can be seen in the activities of a couple of former officials.

Bryce Harlow was a close personal aide to Presidents Eisenhower and Nixon, and served Nixon for a time as chief White House lobbyist. He took his skills, experience, and influence with him when he left the White House to become chief lobbyist for Procter & Gamble. When a controversy over the environmental safety of phosphates in detergents surfaced, Procter & Gamble, together with the other members of the Soap and Detergent Manufacturers, led by Harlow, persuaded the government to reverse its previous position and recommend the continued use of phosphates.[24] Important lobbying victories such as this make the value of ex-government officials readily apparent.

Harlow's former position and current successes make him something of a superstar among Washington influence peddlers. More typical is Carl Bagge, who became the head of the National Coal Association after leaving his post as a commissioner of the Federal Power Commission—the agency that regulates major coal customers and competitors. In 1972, Bagge filed to his former agency two pleas on behalf of the coal group in opposition to a regulation that was also being fought by the electric utilities. Privileged position does not always mean success, however, and Bagge's plea was turned down by the FPC. In defense of the practice of regulatory officials taking jobs in the industries they regulated, Bagge told a reporter: "You couldn't get people except elitists on regulatory bodies if they couldn't utilize the knowledge and insights they've acquired about how a system operates. If that's a deferred bribe, then so be it."[25]

Some officials are more circumspect about their private dealings after they leave the government. There is, for example, former Attorney General Nicholas Katzenbach, now of IBM—a company being sued by the government in a major antitrust case. Although three years elapsed between the time he left Justice and the time he came to IBM in 1969, Katzenbach took the precaution of obtaining from the Justice Department antitrust division a memorandum certifying that there was no indication that Katzenbach had "any direct decision-making involvement" in the IBM investigation.

Unfortunately, other corporate ambassadors have been less scrupulous and appear to have been working for their future corporate employers while still serving in the government. Among the many suspicious circumstances surrounding the Soviet grain deal in 1972 was the role of former Assistant Secretary of Agriculture Clarence Palmby. While with the Agriculture Department, Palmby led a trade delegation to Moscow in April 1972 to discuss the big grain purchase by the Soviet Union. In June he left the Agriculture Department to assume a vice-presidency in the giant Continental Grain Company. Shortly thereafter the Soviet buying team (some of whose members he had escorted on a tour of Washington) bought five million tons of grain from Continental. The close timing between his government activities and his private employment prompted some critical inquiries; and Palmby at first denied that his Continental job was settled at the time of his participation for the government in the Soviet grain deal. It was later learned, however, that a few days before his trip to the USSR, he had signed a purchase agreement for a New York apartment and listed four Continental Grain officials as credit references. For Continental Grain, the Washington connection (which included contacts other than Palmby) proved very profitable.

The Interchange Program

Some aspects of the interchange between business and government have even become formalized. In 1969, President Lyndon Johnson launched the President's Commission on Personal Interchange, which was to come up with a plan for young executives in government and industry to occupy temporary positions in the other sector. The exchange program finally got under way in the Nixon administration in 1970: forty business executives occupied positions in government for twelve to eighteen months, and an equal number of government executives worked in industry. The purpose of the program is to "improve individual understanding for more effective working relationships between government and business," and to "encourage a continuing interchange of management practices." While these are seemingly laudable objectives, the program cannot help but increase the influence of giant business in government by furthering the clubby atmosphere that so much enhances that influence. Every company involved in the program is, of course, a giant corporation. Furthermore, one must be suspicious of a plan whose avowed purpose is to improve executive performance in the same administration that sought systematically to decimate and politicize the senior career civil service.

Occasionally the utilization of corporate representatives on temporary assignment in Washington yields even more direct and profitable returns for their companies. During the height of the energy crisis in late 1973, many oil company executives went to work in the new Federal Energy Administration and in other energy-related capacities. The ample opportunities for the enrichment of industry through this scheme did not go unexploited. The most prominent example of the remunerative use of government position by oil executives came to light during a congressional hearing in late 1974. It was disclosed that a Phillips Petroleum executive, John Bowen, who was temporarily with the FEO, was primarily responsible for initiating a regulation in January 1974 that permitted the major oil companies to gain windfall profits estimated as high as $300 million. This provision permitted the companies that shared crude oil under the mandatory allocation program to recover their costs twice. It also turned out that, far from being an innocent mistake or coincidence, this "double-dip" provision was initially opposed by FEO lawyers, who correctly foresaw that it would lead to excessive compensation for the oil corporations. Nonetheless, the provision was vigorously pushed by Bowen and his immediate superior William A. Johnson, and it was approved by William Simon who was then head of the FEO. In June 1974, after a year with the government, Bowen returned to Phillips Petroleum, which had netted $52 million in double-dip profits as a result of the regulation he had sponsored.[26]

The problem of corporate-government personnel interchange is exemplified by an incident that points out the real perceptions and expectations of the people involved in the system. In 1971, Richard Spears, then in the process of becoming the general manager of the National Transportation Safety Board, recommended outgoing White House patronage chief Harry Fleming for a part-time job at Continental Airlines. The recommendation is interesting for two reasons. First, four-fifths of the board's work involves airplane accidents, but Spears blissfully asserted that he saw no conflict of interest in his recommending Fleming. Secondly, the qualifications cited in the letter of recommendation are instructive. Spears wrote to Continental president Robert F. Six, advising him that Fleming would be valuable to Continental because he had strong access at the Justice and State Departments and a good relationship with Peter Flanigan, then the White House liaison man with big business.[27] So here we had the spectacle of a political appointee in a regulatory agency recommending to a regulated company the employment of a man whose chief qualification would be that he had political clout in Washington. The corruption of this arrangement lacked even the subtlety usually characteristic of such influence peddling. The Spears-Fleming case only illustrates the worst tendencies of the Washington connection. To the extent that the interchange system flourishes—formally or informally—we tend to have a government of men, not laws.

A Lobbyist—Who, Me?

Although we have been discussing lobbying as though lobbying and lobbyists were generally agreed-upon terms, the matter is not so simple. In fact, much, if not most of the lobbying that occurs in Washington is, according to its practitioners, not lobbying but something else—education, public relations, or legal representation. And therein lies another substantial advantage for corporate lobbyists. Although the 1946 Regulation of Lobbying Act requires that lobbyists register with the Clerk of the House and the Secretary of the Senate, the law itself and subsequent court interpretations have left gaping loopholes that allow many lobbyists to avoid registration and, more importantly, reporting on lobbying expenses. One major loophole required registration only from those whose "principal purpose" was influencing legislation through direct contacts with legislators. Thus, politically powerful organizations such as the National Association of Manufacturers, the International Telephone and Telegraph Corporation, and the National Rifle Association could blithely claim not to be lobbyists.

A further weakness in the law allows lobby groups themselves to determine what portion of their overall expenses are allocated to lobbying. Naturally enough, associations with huge Washington offices have reported only miniscule amounts for lobbying, claiming that the bulk of their activity was "public relations," "education," or some other beneficent activity. The resultant figures serve only to mislead the public. For example, the American Association of Railroads initiated a $1 million public-relations campaign in 1972 in support of the Surface Transportation Act; it reported lobbying expenditures of less than $5,000. Similarly, the politically potent El Paso Natural Gas Company reported no lobbying expenses in 1971, although it actually spent $439,862 "for purposes of influencing public opinion."[28] Such thinly disguised fraud in reporting is a form of corporate secrecy that denies the public the right to know how much money is going into corporate efforts to influence legislation.

The Hidden Persuader: Grass-Roots Lobbying

The most important unregulated aspect of corporate lobbying is in the area of advertising and public-relations campaigns—so-called grass-roots lobbying. Here the purpose is to influence Congress indirectly by trying to sway public opinion. Usually the aim is not to attack a specific legislative proposal but rather to portray the corporation as the greatest of contributors to solutions in broad policy areas such as the environment or agriculture. The line between building customer goodwill and indirect lobbying is admittedly a fine one, but one that is usually interpreted as mere advertising by the corporation.

Recently, the greatest area of corporate political advertising has been in the realm of environment. A Council on Economic Priorities survey of environmental advertising in 1970 found that nearly $6 million was spent on such advertising in *Newsweek, Time,* and *Business Week.* Ironically, the five industries that had the most ads were those that also had the greatest amount of pollution clean-up to do in their own backyards. These were electric utilities and iron and steel, petroleum, paper, and chemical firms.[29] Typically, the advertisements present the corporations as passionate ecologists whose industrial practices either do not pollute or who promptly curb pollution and restore the landscape to a new height of loveliness and ecological balance.

Capitalizing on the environmental-advertising bandwagon, *Reader's Digest* published an advertising supplement in its September 1971 issue in which eight companies and trade associations participated. The general tenor of the supplement was that pollution is everyone's problem. The ads stressed the individual's responsibility not to litter and carefully downplayed the environmental damage caused by the companies doing the advertising. Thus, the advertising by the Glass Container Manufacturers Institute and the Can People (the can trade association) stressed: (1) that only a small percentage of U.S. solid waste and litter is made up of bottles and cans; (2) that they had campaigned against littering and had provided reclamation centers; and (3) that they supported basic research on solid-waste disposal.

Of course, corporations have the right to tell the public of their good works and about the "realities" of the environmental problem. The difficulty here is that these ads are frequently distortions, and outright falsehoods are not uncommon. Often what is most revealing is left out. For example, the glass and can ads neglected to mention that, in 1969, an estimated 43 billion cans and bottles were disposed and that the figure was heading toward 100 billion by 1980. In tonnage and cost of disposal, this is a staggering amount. In spite of its claims, the industry has done precious little in the field of recycling beyond providing disposal barrels that companies can place on their premises. None of the container companies has been known to establish centers in convenient urban locations.

Nor is this ad a rare example of misleading advertising. Environmental ads are like statistics and bikinis—what they show is revealing, but what they conceal is crucial. A two-page U.S. Steel ad in national magazines posed the question "What is U.S. Steel doing to help restore our environment?" and proudly answered by asserting that they reforested land after mining operations. What U.S. Steel neglected to mention was that it vigorously opposes the federal industrial-waste-discharge permit program, and it was only under threat of legislation in 1971 that U.S. Steel agreed to certify that the information on its applications for discharge permits was true.[30]

Going beyond mere misleading advertisements, some corporations perpetrate outright hoaxes. An ad for Bethlehem Steel featuring a picture of seemingly pristine Fishpond Lake, Kentucky, with a boy and his grandfather fishing stated: "Where mining shovels once pulled coal from the earth's surface, Sonny and his grandfather—retired miner George Mullings—now pull bluegills and large-mouth bass from this 45-acre man-made lake." The lake and 900 acres of surrounding park were built on property that had been surface mined more than a decade ago. Actually, however, the lake is so polluted from mine acids and other pollutants that it has never been open to the public for swimming, and the Kentucky Fish and Wildlife Department states that Fishpond Lake is not considered a fishing lake because the fish with which it was once stocked have not prospered in the polluted waters. Although the ad states that the land around the lake is "in the near-perfect spot for good reclamation," more than twenty years after it was mined and "reclaimed" "it remains ugly and unnaturally barren," according to *Environmental Action* magazine.[31] Moreover, the state of Kentucky, *not* Bethelehem Steel, did most of the work. The company donated the land—for which it received a tax writeoff—but it retained the original mineral rights. Bethlehem Steel certainly could have written the book about adding insult to injury.

The environmental ads are clearly aimed at improving industry's image in the wake of public concern about the environment. But the ads have a deeper purpose than getting the public to love their neighborhood conglomerate or even creating customer goodwill. The average consumer, after all, does not buy several tons of steel from Bethlehem. If corporations succeed in persuading the public that they are already preventing pollution and restoring the environment, there will be less public pressure and support for government action. It is in this sense that such advertising campaigns are properly conceived of as lobbying—more subtle and indirect, but lobbying all the same.

An important lobbying technique through advertising is to frame the discussion of political issues in a narrow and misleading way that is completely advantageous to the advertising company. The various members of the highway lobby are adept at this technique. Their ads are aimed at building public support for continued highway building at the expense of mass transit. An advertisement by Caterpillar Tractor touted the fact that the accident rate on the new Interstate Highway System was half that of the old highways. In an obvious dig at public officials, the ads state: "we still have 12,000 miles left to finish. We could be saving 2,000 more lives each year. That alone is reason enough to push the Interstate Highway System to completion without delay. Let's get it finished. Before more lives are." Caterpillar might have added that they would sell a lot more heavy machinery. More importantly, however, the ad misleads the public regarding the relative safety of various modes of travel. Interstate highways are undoubtedly safer than old highways, but automobile travel on any highway is far more hazardous than its alternatives. Compared to a death rate per million passenger miles of 1.2 for Interstates, domestic airlines have a rate of .23, and on railroads the rate is only .09.[32] In fact, by its constant pressure to prevent widespread mass transit—thus requiring Americans to rely primarily on private passenger automobile travel—the highway lobby has doomed thousands of Americans to a tragic highway death. This is particularly true in urban areas, where alternative modes of safer and less polluting transport could be readily implemented if funds were available from the Highway Trust Fund.

If the news media were found to have so seriously distorted the discussion of major political issues, they would be justifiably subject to harsh criticism. If a politician had tried to perpetrate the same sort of fraud, he would be called to account by his opposition. But who holds corporations to account for their fradulent political advertising?

Softest of the Soft Sells

Lest anyone object that no one believes advertising anyway, it should be noted that the corporate-image advertisements are the softest of soft sells. When such ads are in the guise of public-service messages, the normal skepticism of consumers toward ads for toothpaste, deodorants, or soap seems not to be present. And these ads do indeed fool some rather sophisticated people. Take, for example, a campaign by St. Regis Paper Company. For several years, the company ran advertisements giving information on trees and forests. The ads were graphically attractive and correct as far as they went. The overall theme of the ad campaign was that "nature will cooperate with man if man learns to cooperate with nature." The ads created an impression of a company earnestly concerned with its effect on the environment. Reprints of the ads have been used in schools, and the company has received awards for the ads, including one from *Saturday Review* in 1965 for distinguished public-interest advertising. Unfortunately, however, St. Regis' own record in the environment is a far cry from the image portrayed in the ads. As noted by the Council on Economic Priorities, St. Regis has a "dismal pollution control record." The CEP found that

. . . six years ago St. Regis had not shouldered any responsibility for preserving these resources, and today [1971] it is only beginning to do so. The company has inadequate air and water pollution controls at all but one of its pulp mills; it discharges 175 million gallons of untreated waste water daily from these mills; and it is cleaning up this pollution only in response to pressure from state agencies.[33]

Nonetheless, the ads have fooled intelligent audiences such as readers of *Saturday Review* and *Advertising Age*, whose columnist Jim O'Gara wrote: "Its [St. Regis'] notions of conservation long preceded today's acute awareness of the need to protect what's good in the environment. . . ."[34]

In some cases, such as the Bethlehem Steel ad, the FTC has investigated and demanded evidence of the advertisement's claims. But the usual "punishment" is simply an agreement that the advertisement will no longer be run—by which time the damage has already been done. A more effective remedy is the requirement that the offending corporation run corrective advertising to rectify false impressions created by earlier advertising. This device is rarely used, however, and is more suitable for regulating advertising of specific consumer products. Public-interest and environmental groups have challenged many of the offending ads through the Federal Trade Commission; but they do not even come close to having the immense resources to counter the barrage of false information disseminated to the public. In short, "public-interest" advertising represents a potent and unchecked form of corporate grass-roots lobbying.

Such covert lobbying techniques point out another significant advantage of corporate lobbying—it is indirectly subsidized by the government through income-tax deductions as business expenses. Direct lobbying expenses and other overt political activity are not tax deductible by corporations or any other organizations. Nonprofit, tax-free organizations such as foundations are prohibited from engaging in such activity as a condition of their preferred tax status. However, as we have seen, the line between what is and what is not "lobbying" is very blurred; the result is that, like regular product advertising and other marketing expenses, "public-interest" or political-issue-oriented advertising by corporations is generally considered tax deductible. Even organized campaigns to influence a particular piece of legislation may sometimes be tax deductible. For example, in 1956 the oil and gas industry tried to prevent government regulation of natural gas prices. The industry set up the Natural Gas and Oil Reserves Committee whose purpose was "to present to the American public at the grass roots a better understanding of the natural gas industry." Nearly $2 million was spent on this effort. Although the industry lost the battle, the companies involved were able to treat the expense as a tax-deductible business writeoff.[35] Thus, the government ultimately helped finance the effort by giving up tax revenues it otherwise would have gained. Ultimately, of course, it is the average taxpayer who bears the burden of this and other such lobbying campaigns. In general, the tax treatment of grass roots lobbying is a gray area full of inconsistencies, and the law is ambiguous.[36]

However, the law can be applied selectively to the detriment of public-interest groups. If a nonprofit group actively lobbies, the donations made by its members are no longer tax deductible. Thus, the Sierra Club lost its exempt status in 1968 when it lobbied against the proposed plans to construct dams on the Colorado River in the Grand Canyon. Yet, by masking their environmental propaganda as a marketing expense, corporations are free to pursue their own aims. This aspect of lobbying is doubly unfair. In the first place, the immense wealth of giant corporations enables them to make their views heard far more extensively and effectively than any countervailing interest. Secondly, corporations can make consumers pay for the propaganda twice—through higher prices that reflect overall business expenses and through the tax deductibility of such expenses.

Conclusion

In pointing out some of the problems of corporate lobbying, it should not be thought that such political activity is entirely devoid of utility, legitimacy, and even some degree of necessity. First, corporations and their officers have as much right to petition the government and try to sway public opinion as any other citizen or groups. Second, as is generally acknowledged, lobbying of all types serves an important communications and informational function. In drafting legislation pertaining to a particular industry, it is both fair and essential for legislators to learn the position of that industry. Finally, as we have noted above, corporate lobbying is sometimes only one element of a broader lobbying coalition; corporate interests may coincide with other broad and important interests in society—interests that, as a practical and ethical matter, should be taken into account in legislative and regulatory policy.

Nonetheless, a listing of the positive features of corporate lobbying does not demonstrate that it is one of the more democratic features of our political system. The key factor must be balance. While corporations should pursue their interests in the political system, other societal interests should not be neglected nor given short shrift, as they often are. Superior access to policymakers for corporate leaders plainly means inferior access for others. It cannot be otherwise in a world of limited time and information. Without attempting to enter the complex debate over the character of "public interest," it suffices to say that corporate lobbying frequently triumphs over broader and more numerous societal interests. It is not enough to assert, as apologists for large corporations do, that corporations do not always win their legislative fights.[37] Of course, they do not. But in key areas such as consumer protection, the issues in which the economic and political stakes for corporations have been highest—consumer class-action, for instance—have usually been resolved in favor of the corporate interests.[38]

Notes

1. See, for example, Abraham Holtzman, *Legislative Liaison* (Chicago: Rand McNally, 1970).
2. For example, see Morton Mintz and Jerry Cohen, *America, Inc.: Who Owns and Operates the United States?* (New York: Dial Press, 1971) and Mark J. Green, James M. Fallows, and David R. Zwick, *Who Runs Congress?* (New York: Bantam Books, 1972).
3. Robert Engler, *The Politics of Oil* (Chicago: University of Chicago Press, 1961).
4. Milbrath, *The Washington Lobbyists* Chicago: Rand McNally, 1963), p. 354.
5. Raymond Bauer, Ithiel De Sola Pool, and Lewis A. Dexter, *American Business and Public Policy* (New York: Atherton, 1963), p. 484.
6. See especially Robert A. Dahl, "The Concept of Power," *Behavioral Science* 2 (July 1957), pp. 201–15.
7. Peter Bachrach and Morton Baratz, "Two Faces of Power," *American Political Science Review* 56 (December 1962), pp. 947–52.

8. Theodore Lowi, "The Public Philosophy: Interest Group Liberalism," *The American Political Science Review* 61 (March 1967), pp. 5–24.
9. Theodore Lowi, "Four Systems of Policy, Politics and Choice," *Public Administration Review* 32 (1972), pp. 298–310.
10. Andrea F. Schoenfeld, "Sophisticated GMA Lobby Represents Grocery Item Industry in Era of Consumerism," *National Journal*, March 13, 1971, p. 570.
11. Ibid., pp. 572–74.
12. *Washington Post*, June 12, 1975, p. A7.
13. *New York Times*, August 2, 1973, p. 21.
14. U.S. Congress, Senate, Committee on Government Operations, *Advisory Committees*, Hearings before the Subcommittee on Intergovernmental Relations, 92nd Congress, 1st sess. (1971), pt. 3, p. 917.
15. Statement of the President, August 8, 1971.
16. *Advisory Committees*, p. 901.
17. *Advisory Committees*, p. 984.
18. *Washington Post*, September 10, 1974, p. A4.
19. *Advisory Committees*, p. 914.
20. Jan Nugent, "Unheralded Committees Molding Statistics," *Journal of Commerce*, November 26, 1968, p. 3.
21. Vic Reinemer, "Budget Bureau: Do Advisory Panels have an Industry Bias?" *Science* 169 (July 3, 1970), pp. 36–39.
22. U.S. Congress, House, *Advisory Committees*, hearings before a Subcommittee of the Committee on Government Operations, 92nd Congress, 1st sess. (1971), statement of Senator Lee Metcalf, p. 16.
23. *Washington Post*, September 7, 1975, p. A2.
24. "Why the Corporate Lobbyist is Necessary," *Business Week*, March 18, 1972, pp. 62–65.
25. Michael Jensen, "Musical Chairs in Business and Government," *New York Times*, November 12, 1972, Sec. 3, pp. 1–2.
26. Bob Kuttner, *Washington Post*, September 26, 1974, p. A2.
27. Jack Egan, "Ex-White House Aide Got Airline Job Through Transportation Safety Chief," *Washington Post*, May 24, 1973, p. A3 (based on Senate Commerce Committee hearings).
28. Alan B. Morrison, "How Not to Regulate Lobbying," *Washington Post*, September 7, 1975, p. B2.
29. "Corporate Advertising and the Environment," *Economic Priorities Report*, September–October 1971.
30. *Air and Water News*, October 4, 1971; *Economic Priorities Report*, p. 35.
31. May 15, 1971.
32. *Environmental Action*, July 24, 1971.
33. *Economic Priorities Report*, p. 30.
34. Ibid.

35. George Cooper, "The Tax Treatment of Business Grassroots Lobbying: Defining and Attaining the Public Objectives," *Columbia Law Review* 68 (May 1968), pp. 801–59.
36. Ibid.
37. Neil H. Jacoby, *Corporate Power and Social Responsibility* (New York: Macmillan, 1973).
38. Mark Nadel, *The Politics of Consumer Protection* (Indianapolis: Bobbs-Merrill, 1971), pp. 219–32.

4

Corporations and
Regulatory Agencies

The preceding two chapters have dealt with the major processes by which business corporations attempt to exert their influence on the government. The funding of political activities, congressional lobbying, and mass public-relations campaigns are all methods directed at leaving the corporate imprint on government policy in general—in Congress, in the Executive Branch, and in the state governments. As noted in Chapter 1, these activities are all part of the corporation's quest for hegemony over its environment. The present chapter is more narrowly focused and examines the relationship between corporations and a particular kind of government organization—the independent regulatory agencies and the regulatory agencies within the Executive departments. As will be detailed below, these agencies pose a major *potential* threat to the stability and freedom of the corporation; and for many corporations they are the most visible and important part of the corporation's political environment.

Starting with the Interstate Commerce Commission in 1887, these regulatory agencies have been created by Congress in order to provide the day-to-day implementation of broadly drawn laws passed by Congress to regulate an increasing amount of the nation's commercial life. With wide discretion and rule-making authority, the regulatory agencies have emerged as important, and independent, public policymakers in their own right. The major independent agencies are the Civil Aeronautics Board, the Consumer Product Safety Commission, the Environmental Protection Agency, the Federal Energy Administration, the Federal Trade Commission, the Federal Communications Commission, the Interstate Commerce Commission, the National Labor Relations Board, and the Securities and Exchange Commission. Two major agencies in the Executive Branch are the Food and Drug Administration in the Department of Health, Education, and Welfare and the Occupational Safety and Health Administration in the Department of Labor.

It is useful to single out regulatory agencies for special attention for at least two reasons. First, regulatory agencies are the prime targets of corporate influence in government. This is to be expected because the regulatory agencies are at the front lines of government policymaking in regard to business. The economic health and power of most industries are intimately bound up with the regulations and other decisions continually promulgated by the agencies. Thus, the rates of all freight carried by rail and interstate trucks and the routes by which they move must be approved by the Interstate Commerce Commission. The Civil Aeronautics Board does the same for the airlines. All drugs marketed by the nation's pharmaceutical companies must be cleared by the Food and Drug Administration. Radio and television stations can only broadcast under a license and regulations granted by the Federal Communications Commission. Even industries that are not so specifically regulated come under the jurisdiction of the general-purpose regulatory agencies. All securities offerings by public corporations must be cleared by the Securities and Exchange Commission. The Federal Trade Commission has antitrust and deceptive-practices jurisdiction over all companies engaged in interstate commerce— virtually all companies of any significance in the national economy.

A second reason for special concern with the regulatory agencies is that the subject is particularly timely. In the late 1970s, government regulation of business has once again become the focus of attention in and out of government. President Gerald Ford mounted his own attack on regulatory agencies early in his administration. Simultaneously, several congressional committees have undertaken major investigations of the agencies. Critics as diverse as Ralph Nader and the United States Chamber of Commerce have taken their own potshots at the agencies—for entirely different reasons. In Chapter 7 we will sort out some of the major proposals involving the agencies. For the present, suffice it to say that there is no lack of suggestions in this regard and that the regulatory agencies are the subject of extensive political interest. Our concern here is with the methods and effects of corporate influence on the agencies and some of the underlying factors behind the relationship between corporations and agencies.

The Avenues of Influence

Although President Ford has portrayed American business as being hobbled and helpless before the federal regulators, such an image does not do justice to the efficacy and ingenuity of American corporations. Given the importance of regulatory decisions, large corporations do not leave such decisions to chance. Nor do they limit their efforts to the mere pleadings of legal briefs. They have many opportunities to influence the agencies, and they pursue those opportunities vigorously and successfully. At the outset it should be emphasized that we are not discussing a simple notion of great conspiracies or of industries "capturing" agencies and remaining dominant over agencies. The influence of business is less than and more subtle than that. Nonetheless, over the long haul, business in general and large corporations in particular have the predominant influence over the regulatory agencies that are supposed to regulate them in the "public interest."

Influence at the Creation

The influence of business on the regulatory agencies goes all the way back to their formation. Despite the common view that the agencies were born in a burst of reform furor in an effort to control the worst excesses of the robber barons, many elements of the business community were in fact not displeased with the creation of such agencies as the Federal Trade Commission. As historian Gabriel Kolko has shown, many large corporations viewed regulatory legislation and agencies as a way of protecting and controlling their markets and profits.[1] Thus, early pressure for national meat-inspection regulations came from the large packers who needed government certification of meat quality in order to maintain their European markets.

Similarly, the formation of the Federal Trade Commission was welcomed by many large business interests, and the FTC quickly became involved in the policing of false advertising with primary emphasis on protecting competitors rather than consumers. Even when industry originally opposed legislation, some business leaders were shrewd enough to foresee the benefits of federal regulatory legislation. The classic example of this attitude can be seen in the case of the Interstate Commerce Commission. In 1892, Richard S. Olney, a railroad attorney who was about to become President Cleveland's attorney-general, wrote a letter to reassure the president of the Burlington Railroad that the new Interstate Commerce Commission "is or can be made of great use to the railroads. It satisfies popular clamor for a government supervision of railroads, at the same time that supervision is almost entirely nominal. . . . The part of wisdom is not to destroy the Commission, but to utilize it."[2]

After awhile, big business saw the wisdom of Olney's counsel, and the tendency for business to utilize the agencies for their own benefit began. Of course, some agencies were more cooperative than others, and business influence was then channeled into jurisdictional battles to restrict the control of unfriendly agencies. For example, during the fight to pass the Food, Drug, and Cosmetic Act of 1938, one of the major issues concerned advertising. The original legislative proposal called for regulation of food and drug advertising to be housed with the then-vigorous Food and Drug Administration. The food and drug industries fought this provision tooth and nail, and for several years the legislation was blocked. The Food and Drug law was passed only after a separate bill—the Wheeler-Lea Amendment to the Federal Trade Act—

placed authority over advertising in the industry-favored Federal Trade Commission.

Agencies that started out as vigorous champions of the consumer and the public interest have tended to slow down and stagnate over time. One leading scholar of regulatory commissions refers to this process as the "life cycle" of regulatory commissions. Toward the onset of the agencies' old age—a period of debility and decline—they become highly responsive to the interests of the industries they are supposed to regulate, with a consequent exclusion of other, wider interests.[3] Finally, in their old age, these patterns are firmly set, and the agencies become incapable of innovation and adaptation to changing political and economic conditions. It is, however, doubtful that regulatory agencies completely lose the capacity for change. The new aggressiveness of the Federal Trade Commission after 1969 shows the dramatic results of new leadership. Nonetheless, a wealth of evidence confirms that such agencies tend increasingly to view regulation from the perspective of the major regulated industries.

The process was well analyzed some years ago by Samuel Huntington in a study of the Interstate Commerce Commission. After a period of vigorous regulation of the railroads in the early years of this century, the ICC began to change around 1920. After the worst abuses of the railroads had been corrected, there was less reason for interest on the part of the reformers who initially brought about the creation of the commission and who were keenly interested in its early activities. Also, the period of the 1920s heralded a return to "normalcy" under President Harding. Regulatory fervor declined, and the ICC, which like other bureaucracies needed outside political support, turned to the railroads for that support. In the term used by political analysts, the ICC was *captured* by the very industry it had been charged with regulating. Whereas prior to the 1920s the railroads had opposed the commission at every turn, they now praised it, defended its independence, and supported expansions of the agency's power. This support was not brought about by a change in heart on the part of the railroad men. Rather, it resulted from ICC policies that proved highly beneficial to the railroads—such as rate increases, expanded exemption from antitrust laws, and, for awhile, competitive advantages over other forms of overland shipping.[4] This pattern has been the general trend of regulatory-agency response to industry demands and political pressure.

The Exercise of Political Influence

The simplest and probably most pervasive form of industry influence on agencies is through direct communication and pressure. Representatives of regulated industries are present at all stages of regulatory decisionmaking and pursue the regulators with all the persistence, thoroughness, and tenacity their great corporate resources can muster. When former Food and Drug Commissioner Herbert Ley resigned after being criticized by the drug companies for not acting fast enough on drug applications (while consumer advocates charged the agency with acting too fast), he complained that he had been under "constant, tremendous, and sometimes unmerciful pressure" from the drug industry.[5]

Nor is this pressure confined to the man at the top. In 1962, Americans were shocked to learn that this nation had been narrowly spared a massive drug tragedy that had afflicted Europe. A new sedative, thalidomide, had been widely prescribed in Europe; its users included thousands of pregnant women. It was learned, tragically late, that use of the drug by women in the early stage of pregnancy caused terrible birth defects. In 1961, the giant pharmaceutical company Richardson-Merrill had filed a new drug application with the Food and Drug Administration for thalidomide under its trade name Kevadon. When the case exploded in the press (in the *Washington Post*, of later Watergate fame), Americans learned they had been spared the epidemic of birth defects only because of the medical expertise and stubborn courage of a new FDA doctor, Frances Kelsey. Although Richardson-Merrill had already sent the drug out to more than 1,000 physicians in the United States and had assured company salesmen that it was safe, Dr. Kelsey was not so sure and proceeded cautiously to evaluate thalidomide.

When it became apparent that the drug was not going to be approved rapidly, Richardson-Merrill began to exert great pressure on Dr. Kelsey. She was continually pestered by more than fifty "contacts" from Merrill; her complaint that the company had been something less than candid about its knowledge of side-effects elicited a response from Merrill that seemed to threaten her with legal action. Although executives from Merrill went over her head to gain clearance, Kelsey stood firm until, finally, word came back from Europe that the birth defect epidemic had been traced to the use of thalidomide by pregnant women. There is a bitter irony in the fact that Dr. Kelsey subsequently received the Distinguished Federal Civilian Service award for preventing the marketing of thalidomide in the United States. The award was an implicit recognition not simply of a scientific accomplishment but of great courage in not knuckling under to the enormous pressure brought by a pharmaceutical corporation.

It would be comforting to report that the thalidomide situation was an isolated case of industry pressure. Unfortunately, congressional hearings conducted by Senator Edward Kennedy in 1974 revealed that industry pressure has become rampant, and successful, in some parts of the Food and Drug Administration. Eleven FDA medical doctors and pharmacologists testified that there was always pressure to approve new drugs, and that there was never trouble when they did so. However, when medical officers came up with negative findings, they were harassed, transferred to other assignments, or even overruled. The researchers were never overruled when they approved a drug, but all of them had been overruled when they recommended against a drug. For example, Dr. Carol Kennedy, a psychiatrist, found that evidence presented in support of Abbott Laboratories' drug for hyperactive children, called Cylert, was inadequate. Two advisory committees were called in to review her findings, but these committees supported her conclusions. Finally, she was transferred to an FDA office studying soft contact lenses. She also was asked to sign reports from which her comments and data were deleted. The researchers revealed to the Senate committee that agency supervisors often went behind the backs of the drug evaluators by consulting with the drug companies and reporting to them on the deliberations in progress. In short, contrary to the image often projected, the top levels of the FDA are not overcautious and obstructive to the drug companies. On the contrary, medical officers who disapprove drug applications may find their FDA careers taking a "downhill course," in the words of one doctor.[6]

Doctors and the FDA

The Food and Drug Administration is also the recipient of another particularly questionable technique of exerting pressure on agencies. This technique involves the use of practicing physicians by drug companies to amplify the companies' claims to the FDA. A recent example of this method was demonstrated in the wake of the FDA's action on antibiotics. As a result of the enactment of the Kefauver-Harris Act of 1962, the National Academy of Sciences, under contract with the FDA, undertook a study of the efficacy of drugs put on the market between 1938 and 1962.[7] One of the principal subjects of consideration was combination drugs—single fixed dosages that contain two or more specific drugs. The NAS study was highly critical of fixed combinations, particularly antibiotics. Both the Food and Drug Administration and the NAS agreed that "the use of two active ingredients in the treatment of the patient who can be cured by one . . . is irrational, illogical, unscientific, and is a disservice to the patient." Hence, in 1969 the Food and Drug Administration announced that it proposed to remove certain fixed-combination antibiotics from the market and, as required by law, invited comments before that proposal became final. In response, the affected drug companies mounted a blitz campaign in opposition to the proposed regulation.

The Food and Drug Administration received 3,500 letters opposing its proposals and only ten in favor. While at first glance it would appear that the weight of opinion was against the FDA, the matter was not so simple, as disclosed by evidence submitted to the monopoly subcommittee of the Senate Select Committee on Small Business. Most of the letters were from practicing physicians, and from their form and content it was obvious they were prompted by the efforts of the Squibb and Upjohn companies, makers of Mysteclin-F and Panalba (two of the fixed-combination antibiotics) respectively. Upjohn sent out a "Dear Doctor" letter to physicians encouraging them to protest; Squibb sent similar letters and instructed its detail men (salesmen) to encourage doctors to write. And write they did. A typical letter came from a doctor in Fort Wayne, Indiana. He wrote: "Mysteclin-F has had a definite useful place among the antibiotics prescribed in my practice, particularly for those types of patients prone to candidal infections. . . . I have used Mysteclin-F for several years and feel the FDA order to withdraw Mysteclin-F from availability for prescription use would create an unnecessary and inconvenient restriction on my prescribing freedom to the detriment of my patients." A Philadelphia doctor provided a typical scientific touch: "The NAS-NRC panel's report on Mysteclin-F indicates that they are not aware of evidence of proved efficacy in the prevention of disease due to monilial organisms, although suppression of growth of moilia may be accomplished."

These statements were not merely typical, but in fact they appeared word for word in scores of physicians' letters around the country. A coincidence? Hardly. The same lines and several others appeared in a Squibb pamphlet, "Guidelines Which Physicians May Want to Include in Letters to the FDA." There was also a variety of identical letters from a given locality that were the result of a form letter prepared by a detail man. One doctor, apparently inadvertently, enclosed with his testimonial letter a note from his Squibb detail man saying: "Dear Dr. Dawson: Hope the enclosed letter is satisfactory for your signature." The Senate Select Committee on Small Business received other evidence of letters wholly prepared by Squibb (even mailed in Squibb envelopes), which were to be passed off as the independent appraisal of physicians. The Maine Medical Association circularized its membership with a paraphrased list of Squibb's "Guidelines," which, in turn, were sent in to the FDA. Given the testimonial nature of letters purporting to represent physicians' professional judgment, the ethics of Squibb and the physicians are, at the very least, questionable.

Furthermore, contrary to the impressionistic evidence testified to by the protesting doctors, the drugs were being withdrawn precisely because the best impartial scientific evidence was that their benefits were outweighed by their risks—evidence that went back at least twelve years before the FDA order. Nonetheless, the drug companies attempted to use their economic and political muscle to overcome the results of scientific examination in a matter of public health and welfare. The power of the drug companies in this regard can be seen in their ability to con so many doctors into making unsubstantiated claims to influence the FDA—claims that flew in the face of the National Academy of Science's findings as reported in the prestigious *New England Journal of Medicine*, among other places. Fortunately, this self-serving, crude attempt at pressure failed; the FDA concluded that "no useful data could be obtained from this mass of correspondence."[8]

Corporate Shaping of Regulatory Power

Corporate influence is present not only in the day-to-day decisions made by agencies, but also when basic changes in the authority of an agency are proposed. As noted before, there was intense corporate involvement during the early part of this century, when the form and jurisdiction of regulatory agencies were first being legislated. Current legislative proposals affecting agency rules and jurisdiction evoke no less active participation. A good example is the Federal Trade Commission's recent assertion of its rulemaking power. In the 1970s the FTC, as a result of vigorous new leadership, began asserting its authority to issue trade regulation rules— rules that would apply to an entire industry with the force of law and that could declare a specified trade practice unfair and hence illegal. Previously, the FTC had proceeded on a case-by-case basis. In Congress, proponents of wider FTC authority attached an amendment to a federal consumer product warranty bill. The amendment would have clarified any doubts about the FTC's authority in this regard by giving the agency explicit statutory authority to issue industrywide trade regulations. The amendment was the target of intensive pressure from many sides. Another provision would have extended the scope of FTC authority to banking, transportation, and communications—fields that are now exempted. Not surprisingly, the amendment was given a chilly reception by the affected businesses. Testifying to the power of business, the Senate dropped the rulemaking amendment so as not to lose the warranty bill.

Another example concerns Congress's responsibility for the organizational form of the agencies. In 1950, President Truman presented to Congress a reorganization plan for the regulatory agencies. Its main feature was to allow the President to designate the chairman of each regulatory commission and to pinpoint the responsibility of the chairman for hiring top-level agency officials. Previously, chairmanships had rotated, and staffing responsibility had been spread among the commissioners. Congress agreed to the plan for all the agencies except one—the Interstate Commerce Commission. The railroads were dead set against having as the powerful chairman of their regulatory agency anyone chosen by Harry Truman, and they were able to exert enough political muscle in Congress to prevent extension of the reorganization plan to the ICC. They were also able to prevent the incorporation of the ICC into the Department of Transportation when that cabinet-level department was formed by merging other transportation agencies during the Johnson Administration.

Corporations and the Judicial System

Another important avenue of corporate power vis-à-vis the regulatory agencies is the judicial system. The courts are often used in an attempt to reverse important adverse rulings by regulatory agencies. For example, companies that were targets of the Federal Trade Commission's industrywide trade rules quickly went to court to challenge the FTC's authority to issue such rules. Although the FTC lost the first round in a federal district court, it won on appeal in June 1973 in the U.S. Circuit Court of Appeals.

Like other social groups and individuals, corporations have a right to advance their legitimate interests through the judicial process. The problems of power and accountability enter, however, in the case of giant corporations that are able not only to participate in the legal process but also to dominate it by sheer weight. For example, the Justice Department's antitrust case against IBM has dragged on since January 1969 and only went to trial in May 1976. In 1974 the giant computer manufacturer settled a civil antitrust suit with its competitor Memorex; as a result, IBM destroyed a computerized index that Memorex had constructed in order to utilize the voluminous number of documents in the case. Although the Justice Department has access to the documents, the lack of a computer-access system has slowed down the case even more.

In some areas, particularly regulation of advertising, corporate legal muscle can thwart government legal action *regardless* of the final judicial disposition of the case. For example, the Federal Trade Commission's deceptive advertising case against J. B. Williams Company, for its misleading advertising of Geritol, dragged through the commission and the courts for nearly ten years. During that time, Geritol continued to be advertised as a cureall for listlessness and went through several different advertising campaigns—all with the same underlying deceptive theme. The net result of the final disposition of the case was that Geritol advertising now admits that only a small fraction of listlessness is due to iron deficiency; instead, the nostrum is touted as a way of preserving beauty and sexual energy in middle-aged women. Typically, a healthy-looking couple is portrayed on television with the husband testifying to his wife's many attributes. Should the government wish to pursue this questionable claim, we can anticipate that Geritol will have gone to another campaign and another malady by the time a final disposition is reached.

Corporations and the Executive Branch

Another conduit of corporate influence is the top levels of the Executive Branch. The lines of influence from a large corporation to the Executive Branch may be stronger than those directly to agency officials. Executive intervention in the regulatory process gives regulated corporations a double opportunity to exert their influence: first, in the agencies directly, and second, through recourse to executive intervention. Such a process was evident in the government's action against the artificial sweetener cyclamate. In 1959, the Food and Drug Administration included cyclamates in the Generally Recognized as Safe (GRAS) list, which meant that cyclamates could be added to foods at the discretion of the manufacturer without further proof of safety. The endorsement was given and continued despite a series of warnings about cyclamates dating back to a 1954 report by the National Academy of Sciences/National Research Council. The warning against the uncontrolled distribution of cyclamates was repeated, with no effect, in 1955, 1962, and 1968. By 1968, the FDA had received more than a dozen warning signals, linking the artificial sweetener with damaging effects on the liver, the intestinal tract, on blood anticoagulants, and, ominously, with possible genetic damage. The evidence came from as far away as Japan and as close as one of the FDA's own biochemists, Dr. Helen Verrett. In 1968, however, another report by a committee of the National Academy of Sciences appeared, minimizing the dangers of cyclamates. This report was criticized severely by the FDA's own scientists; nonetheless, based on its findings, FDA Commissioner Herbert Ley decided to keep cyclamates on the GRAS list.

Finally, one year later, in October 1969, Robert Finch, then Secretary of Health, Education, and Labor, announced a ban on the use of cyclamates. The ban, however, was based on the flimsiest evidence of cyclamate danger—that the additive was carcinogenic (cancer-producing) in test animals and thus subject to total prohibition under the 1958 Delaney Food Additives Amendment to the Food and Drug laws. In his press conference, Secretary Finch conveyed the impression that he was somewhat reluctantly banning cyclamates and that this rather weak evidence of their carcinogenic danger was the only possible reason for banning the additive. Other studies were not mentioned. In fact, there were better studies done later that showed that even in low doses cyclamates could be carcinogenic. However, even without such studies, Finch could and should have relied clearly on a specific requirement of the Delaney Amendment that only additives *proven safe* could be introduced into the food supply. The clear intent of the law was that burden of proof

of safety of potentially unsafe substances should rest with the manufacturer.[9] Given the many adverse findings on cyclamates, Finch
could have removed them on this basis alone, and more importantly,
he could have advised the American people of the wider range of
potential dangers. But, instead of thus exercizing his legally
sanctioned administrative discretion, Finch waited until he was
forced to act by the Delaney Amendment, which mandates that
carcinogenic substances be withdrawn; and, in the process of announcing its implementation, he criticized the amendment.

   The ban had serious economic consequences for a number of
American corporations—especially manufacturers of cyclamates
and of "dietetic" soft drinks. They had always insisted that cyclamates were safe, and they started an intensive rearguard political
effort to salvage what they could from the situation.

   Whether or not there was a specific political link, the comments of
Secretary Finch on the issues at stake in the cyclamate controversy
are impressive evidence of the power of corporations to shape the
terms of public dialogue. Secretary Finch, in grudgingly announcing the ban, said: "But who's to say that using Fresca or some other
diet drink . . . isn't better for you than the problems of overweight
or diabetes?" He thus both bought and broadcast the advertising of
cyclamate makers and corporate users that use of "diet foods" with
artificial sweeteners is an effective means of weight control. In fact,
as the FDA reported in 1969, "none of the few controlled studies
reported to date have established a useful role for non-nutritive
sweeteners as weight-reducing aids except under the most carefully
controlled conditions."[10] Thus, high-level political leadership undermined the regulatory mandate of the Food and Drug Administration by presenting to the public the industry version of the risks
and benefits of cyclamates rather than the facts adduced by independent scientific studies.

   The ban did not last long. One month later, Secretary Finch
rescinded the total ban and allowed distribution of cyclamates
when labeled as such in dietary foods and in tablet and liquid form
as a sweetener. Although labeled as drugs, the new ruling permitted the uncontrolled promulgation of cyclamates to anyone willing
to ignore the warning on the label. It was later learned that this

action was bitterly opposed by scientists within the FDA and had come about through the intervention of Finch and Roger Egeberg, the Assistant Secretary for Health and Scientific Affairs, and Surgeon General Jesse Steinfeld. Administratively, the episode finally ended in August 1970, when the FDA returned to a complete ban on cyclamates after releasing a report showing cyclamates to be of little or no value in controlling diabetes or obesity. These conclusions were supported by evidence that had been around for years but which had been obscured by political leadership more sympathetic to the plight of affected corporations than affected consumers.

More recently, after nearly a decade of warnings, the Food and Drug Administration finally banned Red Dye No. 2, a potential carcinogen that was widely used as a food color. Against the great risk, the dye provided only the benefit of prettier chocolate, soda, toothpaste, and other products.

Occasionally, Executive Branch intervention can be traced to considerations of partisan political advantage. While it is not known how typical such intervention is, even in the Nixon administration, one example suffices to show the possibilities. In 1972, the Federal Trade Commission's Bureau of Competition recommended that the FTC challenge the acquisition of a major California wine producers cooperative, United Vintners, Inc. by Heublein, Inc., a large liquor and wine distributor. Before the full commission voted whether to issue the antitrust challenge, Secretary of Agriculture Earl Butz met with FTC chairman Miles Kirkpatrick to argue against any FTC attempt to block the merger. During the forty-five-minute meeting, Butz reportedly made an economic argument for the merger and, in closing, pointed out to Kirkpatrick the political implications of the case. According to Kirkpatrick, Butz's partisan claim was "kind of an off-hand remark at the end. He said maybe we should bear in mind that California was a critical state and that the case could have an effect on the upcoming election."[11] Although Kirkpatrick did not consider the remark improper, an aide understood Butz to have asked directly that the FTC challenge be delayed until after the election.[12] In any case, Butz's intervention was to no avail since the FTC went on to approve the challenge. Nonetheless, the case illustrates yet one more technique of attempting to dampen the ardor of regulatory enforcement.

Corporations and the Commissioners

Finally, corporate influence is directed toward the people who head up the commissions. While the law requires that regulatory commissioners appointed by the President be confirmed by the Senate, informal politics requires prior confirmation by regulated industry. A recent study of independent regulatory commissioner appointments from 1953 to 1974 found that politics and patronage rather than competence generally were the primary criteria employed by presidents in appointing commissioners. In particular, it was found that consumer and public-interest groups have been excluded from consultations, leaving regulated industries as the dominant voice in the selection process. The White House frequently solicits the reaction of regulated industries to proposed appointments, and prenomination meetings between proposed commissioners and industry representatives have been commonplace.[13]

While it is difficult to predict how most individuals will act as regulatory commissioners, the regulated industries go all out to ensure that commissioners they perceive as having acted detrimentally to their interests are not reappointed. One classic case of this phenomenon concerned Leland Olds, a Federal Power Commission member whose position in favor of greater regulation earned him the fervent enmity of the oil industry. Olds was nominated for a third term to the commission by President Truman in 1949. He had previously testified in Congress against a bill that would have prevented FPC regulation of natural gas producers. This was the height of heresy to the oil industry, and an all-out effort was mounted in the Senate to deny him confirmation—an effort led by then-Senator Lyndon Johnson of the prime oil state of Texas. In an unmistakable tribute to the power of oil in politics, Olds was denied confirmation by a 53–15 vote.

The Washington Connection Continued

There are also a variety of informal avenues of corporate influence on the regulatory process that are of considerable importance. One such avenue is the "Washington connection" discussed earlier. It is a common practice for regulatory commissioners to join the ranks of regulated industries when they leave the commissions. Similarly, many young lawyers for the agencies join firms specializing in regulatory matters after developing expertise in those areas. The problem in this situation is usually not one of ethics but of political influence. There are strict provisions against divulging confidential material or representing clients in cases on which a former official had been active. Nonetheless, this type of career movement gives regulated corporations a valuable source of expertise and general, if not specific, inside information that greatly bolsters their ability to pursue their interests.

A second avenue of influence consists of a variety of informal contacts between the regulators and the regulated. It is a common practice for regulatory commissioners to give speeches and meet informally with representatives of regulated industries at conventions and other professional gatherings. Many agencies allow regulated companies to pay expenses and honorariums to commissioners for excursions to major cities and resort areas around the country. While the Federal Power Commission and the Federal Communications Commission prohibit acceptance of fees or reimbursements from regulated industries, other agencies are not so circumspect. Although precise figures are unavailable, it appears that Interstate Commerce Commission members are the most frequent guests of those they are charged with regulating; but the ICC commissioners may accept only reimbursement for actual expenses.[14] In addition to speeches and meetings, these excursions may include private railway tours for ICC members or participation in gala inaugural airline flights for members of the Civil Aeronautics Board.

Except in rare cases, these meetings and trips do not constitute unethical conduct on the part of the commissioners. It would be stretching even a polemical point to think of such activities as bribery or other *unethical* influence. The problem is at once more subtle and deeper than that. While junketing with industry representatives may not be a manifestation of unethical influence, it is a manifestation of industry influence. Trade association representatives usually refer to these informal social meetings as an opportunity for regulatory officials to have a "clearer understanding of the issues." What is left unsaid is that this is clearer only as industry understands the issues. In fact, most commissioners probably do avoid speaking of specific cases before them. But in the long term actual discussion is probably less important than the subtle adoption of the perspective of the regulated industry.

In general, the involvement of regulatory officials in the social circuit of regulated industries is part of an industry effort to soften the regulatory process, to create closer and cozier relationships with those in a position to make decisions substantially affecting profits. In the attempt to exert political influence by cultivating personal relationships, this lobbying technique is similar to that employed with members of Congress and other governmental officials. As it applies to regulatory agencies, however, the situation is particularly detrimental to the public interest for two additional reasons.

First, most regulatory commissions are quasijudicial agencies. Commissioners hear evidence and make rulings in accordance with federal administrative law. We do not tolerate judges ruling on cases in which they have close personal ties with plaintiffs or defendants. Why should we be less stringent with regard to quasijudicial officials?

Second, these contacts might not be so troublesome if they were counterbalanced with similar contacts with consumer groups, but they are not. Consumer groups do not have the resources, the organization, or the opportunities to engage in the frequent socialization with regulatory commissioners. The "clear understanding of the issues" thus tends to become very narrow. Ralph Nader summed up the situation well when he asserted that such industry-agency contacts create a one-sided state of affairs with commissioners rarely, if ever, going to speak to consumer groups. . . . The socialization, the fraternization, the comradeship, the first name familiarity between commissioners and the industry people . . . is one of the most important underminers of the public interest.[15]

Although most regulators are loath to admit it, regulation is inherently an adversary process. Most regulatory legislation was enacted because there was some conflict between the public interest and activities that would result if an industry were free from government restraint. While it is no doubt more comfortable for regulators to mute this inherent conflict, close cooperation does not always serve the public interest. In fact, one good indicator of the extent to which an agency is derelict in its duties is the extent to which it is praised by the regulated industry. This can be seen in the case of the Food and Drug Administration. By this standard, the FDA was a disaster area for the public interest during the late 1950s and early 1960s—the period of George Larrick's tenure as commissioner.[16]

The rewards for casual regulation can be great, and laxness in law enforcement can be seen in industry's response. Thus, the general tenor and lack of vigor of Larrick's term as commissioner were highlighted by the fact that in 1958 he received an award from the Pharmaceutical Manufacturers Association for "devoted service to the public welfare" and for his "understanding of mutual problems." Commissioner Larrick reciprocated with a constant faith in industry. In a 1963 interview he stated that "by and large people in industry are just about as honest as people in government." Since this statement came a year after it was revealed that the chief of the FDA's antibiotic division had received more than $250,000 from the drug industry during the preceding eight years, Larrick was hardly reassuring on either count. Further indicating an excessively cozy relationship between the FDA and the drug industry, an FDA Citizens Advisory Committee (whose members were chosen by Larrick) issued a report in 1962 urging that self-inspection and self-regulation should eventually supersede formal regulation and enforcement by the agency. Although the report was prepared during the period in which the cause of the thalidomide tragedy was emerging, no mention was made of new drug-testing problems. This was perhaps due to the fact that the chairman of the drugs subcommittee of the advisory committee was James B. Mintener, a former Assistant Secretary of Health, Education, and Welfare who was then engaged in private law practice specializing in food and drug regulation and whose clients included Richardson-Merrill, the American manufacturer of thalidomide. Not surprisingly, the report was praised by the Pharmaceutical Manufacturers Association.[17]

Corporate Power and the Problems of Regulation

Although the influence wielded by corporations over the regulatory agencies is considerable, it should not be concluded that the problems of the regulatory process are due only to the political power of regulated industries or to weak or corrupt regulators. These factors do not exist in a vacuum, and there are inherent structural features of the regulatory system that accentuate the political and economic power of regulated corporations. As with other areas of corporate influence over government, corporations are responding to a need to affect and even control their political environment. Because of the shortcomings of the regulatory process, the major corporations in regulated industries actually are able to accentuate their economic and political power. The point to be emphasized is that it is not only the actions of the corporation but of the regulatory system as a whole that give some corporations unwarranted power over society.

Some of these problems are traceable to the very origins of regulation—to the drafting of regulatory legislation by Congress. Regulatory legislation invests the agencies with sweeping discretionary power. For example, the typical regulatory mandate is that policy be made (licenses granted, rates approved, new services approved, and so on) in "the public interest, convenience, and necessity." And what does this vague triad of a phrase require? Congress has provided little specific guidance, and one administrative-law expert observed that "it means about as little as any phrase that the drafters of the act could have used and still comply with the [Constitution]."[18] The commissions, therefore, have little in the way of specific criteria to guide their decisions, and their enormous discretionary power paves the way for industry domination.

Beyond the statutory problems there are three other related problems of the regulatory process: secrecy and informality, the inadequacy of government resources for the current purposes of regulation, and, finally, the very purposes of regulation themselves.

Regulation as a Closed Policy System

Although most of the federal regulatory agencies have an impressive array of formal legal powers and sanctions in their dealings with regulated industries, the agencies prefer to rely on a more informal system of policymaking—bargaining and reliance on self-regulation by industry. Probably the prime example of this method of operating is the Securities and Exchange Commission, in which an informal, secret, and highly discretionary regulatory pattern defines the agency's relationship with the securities industry—particularly the New York Stock Exchange.

The SEC maintains a two-level regulatory pattern. The agency directly regulates various aspects of the securities markets. It also oversees, and may override, the rules that the securities exchanges impose on their members. It has been this second level, self-regulation—that has been the mode traditionally preferred by the government, even though the SEC is vested with a comprehensive set of formal powers. The SEC must approve the organization and rules of the exchanges; and the commission can "alter or supplement" these rules if, after an appropriate request, the exchange does not make needed changes on its own. This authority applies to most areas of exchange operations, including rates, trading hours, and members' financial responsibilities. The SEC also has direct authority to prescribe rules covering various aspects of securities trading in the exchanges. This direct rulemaking power supersedes exchange self-regulation.

In practice, however, there is minimal use of the SEC's direct rulemaking power. The SEC, like other regulatory agencies, traditionally has preferred a regulatory pattern stressing self-regulation. As former SEC chairman and Supreme Court Justice William Douglas put it: "Government would keep the shotgun, so to speak, behind the door, loaded, well-oiled, cleaned, ready for use but with the hope that it would never have to be used."[19] There is nothing inherently wrong with relying primarily on a voluntary regulatory process backed up with agency authority. Problems of excessive influence can and do arise, however, when interests other than those of the securities industry are shut out of the process.

Under the more formal direct rulemaking authority of the SEC, federal law requires advance notice of proposed rules, with an opportunity for participation by all interested parties. However, the SEC is not formally required to provide opportunities for this participation when it merely ratifies proposed self-regulations by the securities exchanges. Elementary fairness ought to require at least the opportunity for other interested parties to be involved in decisionmaking, even when an exchange complies with SEC requests voluntarily. In spite of the requirements of law and propriety, the regulatory framework of the SEC has placed itself in a very close and even cozy relationship with the securities industry, particularly the New York Stock Exchange. This regulatory pattern consists of *private* meetings at the agency's headquarters and at industry conventions, daily telephone calls, and contacts at social affairs. The implications of this arrangement can be seen in some of the cases in which the agency was involved in the 1960s.

Throughout the 1950s there had been little intervention in the New York Stock Exchange by the SEC. This situation changed in the 1960s, however, because of scandals in the American Stock Exchange and the threat of antitrust action against the New York Exchange. The impetus for more vigilant SEC activity thus came largely from interested parties other than the agency—worried investors, Congress, the Justice Department, and brokers who were not members of the New York Stock Exchange. The SEC proceeded to work out more stringent rules; but in its bargaining with the New York Stock Exchange, other interested parties were denied access to the decisionmaking process—even though it was these forces that had prodded the SEC in the first instance. For example, in 1964 the SEC promulgated rules for "floor traders" with minimal input from outside parties. Floor traders have an advantage over other traders due to their on-the-spot contact with trading; and this advantage can cause manipulated stock-market fluctuations. Yet it was not until 1964 that floor traders were the subject of direct regulations by the SEC.

Beginning in the summer of 1963, the SEC and Exchange officials held private negotiations on floor-trading rules. Not until the agency broke off meetings in March of 1964 were the public and other members of the investment community informed of the issue. At that time, a public hearing and the consequent involvement of other interested parties appeared imminent. Nonetheless, before this could happen the New York Exchange and the SEC reached a compromise that allowed some floor trading to continue. Only *after* the announcement of this compromise was public comment solicited. Two months later, without any discussion of the comments received from outside parties, the new SEC and Exchange rules were adopted.[20] Thus, in a matter of great political and financial interest to members of the investing public, that public was shut out. This pattern has been repeated in many other instances as well. This situation is not presented in order to single out the SEC as a villain among regulatory agencies. Indeed, this case is particularly significant precisely because the SEC usually has been considered one of the best of the regulatory agencies.

The Imbalance of Resources

A major problem of corporate influence over regulatory agencies is the tremendous imbalance of resources in some regulatory situations. The prime example is the almost ludicrous imbalance between the American Telegraph and Telephone Company (1973 revenues of $23.5 billion) and the agency that regulates its interstate services and rates, the Federal Communications Commission (1973 fiscal year budget of $34.2 million for all regulatory functions). The imbalance in overall financial resources is notable because it highlights the more relevant advantage of AT&T in terms of legal resources and expertise. The FCC would probably have to rely on AT&T's version of information needed for regulation, even if the agency were otherwise disposed. Even more fortuitous for AT&T is the fact that the regulatory agency is more than willing to "understand our mutual problems" and cooperate to insure a high and stable rate of return to the giant corporation. This can be seen in the events surrounding the 1969 approval of a higher rate of return for the Bell system.

On November 5, 1969, the FCC announced: "Reductions in rates for interstate long distance telephone calls will be submitted shortly by the Bell System telephone company to the FCC. It is estimated that the reduced rates will save users of telephone service about $150 million, representing an offset to increases in revenues resulting from higher rates recently filed for program transmission, Telpak and teletypewriter exchange (TXW) services when the latter increases become effective. *The Commission anticipates that the new rates will permit the companies to achieve earning in a range needed to attract capital under today's conditions.*" (Italics added.) Previously, in 1967, the commission had ruled that a fair and reasonable rate of return for AT&T was 7 to 7.5 per cent. With this new release, the commission held that an earnings level that exceeds 7.5 per cent was "not unreasonable" and that "it is anticipated that the rate adjustments announced today will not, in themselves, prevent the company from achieving earnings" in the range of 8 to 8.5 per cent. AT&T itself was more direct about what had transpired. John D. deButts, then vice chairman of AT&T, welcomed the "recognition by the FCC of our need for a higher interstate rate of return." He noted that the company had claimed a requirement for profits in the range of 8.5 to 9 per cent and that this had been "taken into account by the commission." Thus, the corporation was allowed a substantially higher rate of return—in the upper 8 per cent range. The question is how this came about.

In 1967, the ruling establishing the 7 to 7.5 per cent rate of return was arrived at after formal hearings and the compilation of an extensive record. The decision of November 5, 1969, however, was reached after only an informal review was conducted, according to the agency, "as part of the continuing surveillance of the Bell System's interstate operations and participated in by representatives of the Commission's staff, Bell System officials and several outside consultants." The only published record of this multimillion-dollar decision is the FCC's three-page press release and a dissent filed by Commissioner Nicholas Johnson.[21] Apparently, AT&T overwhelmed a not-unwilling commission with a massive lobbying effort. As one FCC employee put it: "Bell believes it can push this agency around—and with good reason. They lobbied everybody in sight except for Nick Johnson and his staff. There was no leavening from outside consumer representatives . . . even though the New York City Consumer Affairs Department requested (and was denied) the opportunity to appear."[22] Johnson further accused the commission of "contempt" for consumers. Johnson, however, was a maverick commissioner—one whose avowed goal was to "add a little salt and pepper of competition to the rather tasteless stew of regulatory protection that this Commission and Bell have cooked up."

The case of the Bell profit increase is one more demonstration of the effect of industry lobbying, industry control of information, and a largely acquiescent regulatory commission. While one can easily peg the problems of this case to the enormous size and power of AT&T, the commission has similarly sacrificed consumer interests in other areas. Thus, the FCC has been singularly inactive in opposing the concentration of media ownership in the form of newspaper-owned broadcasting companies.[23]

Simpler examples of regulatory acquiescence abound in the contexts of other agencies and other commissions. We are not suggesting, however, that agencies are always acquiescent, that they are "captives" of regulated industries, or that corporations always win. Rather, the point is that large corporations have learned how to live (and live well) with their regulatory agencies. They have substantial resources that they utilize to good effect in cultivating a regulatory environment generally more favorable to them than to consumers. Through a variety of means, regulatory agencies are usually induced to define the "public interest" as containing large components of corporate interest.

Protecting Privileged Position

Much of the political clout of regulated industries is directed toward the most useful service provided to industry by certain regulatory agencies—the protection of a monopoly or legally fixed share of the market and the protection of cartels. This regulatory process primarily involves the Interstate Commerce Commission, the Civil Aeronautics Board, and the Federal Maritime Commission. Regulatory protection is a key component in any consideration of corporate economic power in that it frees industry from even the semblance of competition and forces consumers to accept prices and services that are administratively (which is to say *politically*) set. Thus, the specific regulatory subsystems, with industry as a dominant partner, determine unilaterally what the rest of us have to pay for essential services. This regulatory protection is manifested basically in two ways—price regulation and the granting of franchises.

Price regulation stemmed from a need to protect consumers from price gouging by monopolistic industries—a problem initially responded to by the creation of the Interstate Commerce Commission in 1887 with the power to set *maximum* rates. Ironically, through a later grant of authority to set minimum fixed rates for railroads and trucks, the commission has been the chief instrument for charging far higher shipping costs than would prevail under competitive conditions. The object of the ICC is not to provide the cheapest, most efficient shipping service for the nation, but to assure that each mode of transportation (e.g., railroads, trucks) has preserved for it some of the market for each type of shipping service. The most common application of this policy is to prevent railroads from lowering their charges for long-distance shipping and thereby capturing a large share of that business from long-distance trucking.[24] So, instead of each mode charging prices based on the actual costs of providing the service, the ICC often sets prices according to what could be charged by the transportation mode with the highest costs.

Furthermore, much of the actual rate setting is done by industry cartels and only ratified by the ICC. Under the Reed-Bulwinkle Act passed in 1948, transportation-industry rate conferences or rate bureaus set rates for particular segments of the industry. While the law allows common carriers to submit their own rates individually to the ICC, the incentive is clearly for them to join the price-setting cartel, and most of them do so. The rate-conference prices are then considered and ratified by the ICC.

The second aspect of regulatory protection is the granting of government licenses and franchises in an industry, thus limiting the number of competitors in that industry. In some instances, the government must award a franchise due to technological considerations or where a "natural monopoly" exists. Thus, the FCC has to apportion the limited number of broadcast frequencies. Other government franchise awards, however, serve only to limit competition and enhance protected monopoly positions in an industry. (This protection is defended as preventing "wasteful" competition; read "wasteful" here to mean threatening.) This is particularly true when, as with the ICC, franchise awards are coupled with price regulation. Indeed, the ICC proudly admits its anticompetitive role: "From the beginning of federal motor carrier regulation, restrictions generally have been imposed to protect already authorized carriers from unintended and unwarranted competition."[25] All ICC-regulated common carriers must get their routes of service approved, and this includes even the specific highways and regions through which they travel. The result is a constant battle by carriers to keep competition out of their service area. Indeed, this type of regulatory activity comprises 70 per cent of the ICC caseload.[26]

The excess costs of this regulatory system are substantial. A 1969 Brookings Institution study estimated that the direct costs to society of ICC regulation of freight transportation came to $500 million annually.[27] Indeed, the waste and cost to consumers of the present system is one aspect of economic regulation that has been criticized by economists and other observers as diverse as the President's Council of Economic Advisors, conservative economist Milton Friedman, and Ralph Nader.[28] Furthermore, it should be emphasized that large corporations do not present a united front on this issue. Few, if any, industrial shippers benefit from this arrangement, and even some common carriers might do better under competition. However, as anyone who has moved household goods can testify, regulation-protected profits are more comfortable for the common carrier, allowing them to be sloppy, inefficient, and not work particularly hard for commercial or public business. Together they have managed enough political power to impose these costs on the public at large.

Conclusion

Regulatory agencies are of great concern to all large corporations; and for certain closely regulated industries, such as pharmaceuticals and common carriers, they largely determine the economic health of the industry. Thus, the stakes are high. We should not be surprised that regulated corporations present their cases vigorously to the agencies, and indeed it is their right to do so. Problems, however, arise when the political impact of corporations on regulatory commissions ranges from vigorous to overwhelming and agencies lose sight of their original mandate to promote the public interest. When this occurs, regulatory agencies present only the illusion of protecting the public interest. The ultimate degeneration of the system is seen in the case of surface transportation; in this case an agency, the ICC, protects a noncompetitive system that is inefficient, costly, and opposed to almost any version of the public interest.

As with other manifestations of corporate influence, the problem is not that corporations always prevail or that the agencies are mere tools of the corporations. Such is clearly not the case. Rather, the problem is one of relative influence. Regulatory agencies were themselves supposed to promote the public interest in what should be inherently an adversary proceeding. Instead, all too often they conceive of themselves as partners with industry—usually as the end result of a long process of political intervention by the industry. Thus, it is left to a handful of public-interest lawyers and other citizens' groups to aggressively pursue the interests of consumers and the public interest generally. In terms of corporate political power, this situation represents a significant victory. At the very least, corporations have the political and economic muscle to prevent intervention by the government in many instances. At most, they can harness the legal authority of the government to their own economic and political ends. If they do not call all the shots, their success rate is high enough to pose serious problems.

Notes

1. Gabriel Kolko, *The Triumph of Conservatism: A Reinterpretation of American History, 1900–1916* (New York: Free Press, 1963).
2. Cited in Marver Bernstein, *Regulating Business by Independent Commission* (Princeton: Princeton University Press, 1955), p. 265.
3. Ibid., pp. 74–102.
4. Samuel Huntington, "The Marasmus of the ICC: The Commission, The Railroads, and the Public Interest," *Yale Law Journal* 61 (1952), pp. 467–509.
5. *New York Times*, December 31, 1969, p. 1.
6. *Washington Post*, August 16, 1974, p. A1.
7. The 1962 law required that new drugs must be proven *effective* as well as safe. Prior to that, new drugs required only clearance as to their safety. Hence, the FDA had to go back and review drugs cleared prior to 1962 to ensure their efficacy.
8. U.S. Congress, Senate, Select Committee on Small Business, *Competitive Problems in the Drug Industry*, hearings before the Subcommittee on Monopoly, 91st Congress, 1st sess. (1969), pp. 5188–5248.
9. House Report No. 2284, 85th Congress, 2nd sess. (1958).
10. FDA Papers, October, 1969, p. 13. Cited in James Turner, *The Chemical Feast* (New York: Grossman, 1970), p. 20.
11. William Chapman, "Kirkpatrick 'Surprised' by Butz FTC Role," *Washington Post*, October 27, 1973, p. A2.
12. Ibid.
13. Study by Victor Kramer and James Graham of the Institute for Public Interest Representation, quoted in the *Washington Star*, November 6, 1975, p. A18.
14. Walter Rugaber, "Industry Groups Pay for Travel of ICC Members," *New York Times*, August 24, 1969, p. 1.

15. Ibid., p. 50.
16. See, for example, Morton Mintz, *By Prescription Only* (Boston: Houghton Mifflin, 1967).
17. Ibid., pp. 129–30.
18. Louis Caldwell, "The Standard of Public Interest, Convenience, or Necessity as Used in The Radio Act of 1927," *Air Law Review* 1 (1930), pp. 295–96.
19. Quoted in "Informal Bargaining Process: An analysis of the SEC's Regulation of the New York Stock Exchange," *Yale Law Journal* 80 (1971), p. 811.
20. Ibid.
21. Erwin Knoll, "Dial M for Money," *The Progressive*, January 1970, pp. 24–28. This summary draws heavily from Knoll's account.
22. Ibid., p. 26.
23. See Stephen R. Barnet, "The FCC's Nonbattle against Media Monopoly," *Columbia Journalism Review*, January–February 1973, pp. 43–50.
24. Roger Noll, *Reforming Regulation* (Washington: Brookings Institution, 1971), p. 18.
25. Fox-Smythe Transportation Company Extension Oklahoma, 106, ICC 1. Quoted in David Hemenway, "Railroading Antitrust at the ICC," *The Monopoly Makers*, Mark J. Green, ed. (New York: Grossman, 1973), p. 144.
26. Hemenway, *op. cit.*, p. 145.
27. Ann F. Friedlaender, *The Dilemma of Freight Transport Regulation* (Washington: Brookings Insitution, 1969), p. 98.
28. Economic Report of the President, January 27, 1966; Milton Friedman, *Capitalism and Freedom* (Chicago: University of Chicago Press, 1962); Mark Green and Ralph Nader, "Economic Regulation vs. Competition: Uncle Sam the Monopoly Man," *Yale Law Journal* 82 (1973), p. 871.

PART THREE
Corporations as Governments

5
The Corporation and Public Policy

In the preceding chapters, we discussed the influence and impact of corporations on the government. The actual importance of that influence, however, is not so much the effect it has on the government but on the country as a whole. Thus, the kind of corporate power we have been examining is a power that is exercised *through* the government. [When corporations participate in the political process in the formal institutions of government, they are political entities. Yet they are political entities even when viewed apart from the government. They are private governments in their own right—governments whose policies have as direct and significant an impact on citizens as the policies of formal governments.

In spite of the great impact of corporations, most discussions of corporate power end up by treating corporations as essentially private nongovernmental entities whose private policies incidentally have social impact. While there has been a good deal of analysis of potential remedies of corporate power, much less attention has been focused on the precise nature of the impact of corporate power. Of course, there have been many attacks on corporate power, but there has been little fundamental analysis of the actual content of that power. The basic analytic problem in assessing the impact of giant corporations is that both critics and apologists for corporate power work within a relatively narrow conception of the nature of public policy. Even though critics such as Ralph Nader, Morton Mintz, and Jerry Cohen[1] advance the notion of the corporation as a private government analogous to the state, they do not pursue this line of reasoning to its logical conclusion: If corporations are private governments or are completely analogous to public governments, what is the nature of the policies of such organizations? In contrast to the prevailing view of this matter, it will be argued here that those policies must be seen as public policies. It is only by asserting and analyzing their public character that the full impact of corporate power can be assessed and adequately reformed.

Defining Public Policy: The Boundary Between Public and Private

Although political scientists profess to be interested in the exercise of power in society, their definitions of public policy are rather limited. Different scholars use the term *policy* differently, and there is some disagreement over the content and scope of governmental actions that can be called *policy;* but there is fundamental agreement that public policy is something that *government* does. A typical definition states that public policy "consists in authoritative or sanctioned decisions by governmental actors."[2] But what about the actions and decisions of private organizations—labor unions, corporations, associations, and so on? It is generally agreed that such bodies have policies, but these are not public policies.

There is, however, a paradox in this approach that equates government policy with public policy. While political scientists draw a clear line between public policy and private policy, there is no similarly clear line between governmental (public) organizations and nongovernmental (private) organizations. Indeed, for many years now it has been recognized that there is a real blurring of the distinction between public and private organizations. This discussion of the private-public boundary is particularly relevant to our consideration of corporate power. Much of the discussion of this question concerns corporations, and, increasingly, the public character of the giant corporation is acknowledged. For example, Robert Dahl argues that large corporations are political entities, and he asserts that "it is a delusion to consider [the great corporations] a *private* enterprise. General Motors is as much a public enterprise as the U.S. Post Office."[3] (The fact that the Post Office has been transformed into the semiprivate U.S. Postal Service only underscores Dahl's point.)

There are several aspects to this blurring of boundaries between governments and corporations. First, there is such extensive cooperation between governmental organizations and nongovernmental organizations that it is difficult to know where one ends and the other begins. The defense procurement policies instituted by Secretary of Defense Robert MacNamara in the 1960s are an extreme but good example. Weapons systems were developed through the cocqual cooperation of the Pentagon and "private" industry. While MacNamara succeeded in establishing firmer civilian control of the military, Seymour Melman notes that "this result . . . was achieved by methods that also established an industrial management of unprecedented size and decision-power within the federal government. One result is that it is no longer meaningful to speak of the elites of industrial management, the elites of finance, and the elites of government and how they relate to each other. The elites have been merged in the new state-management."[4] Thus, corporations that are nominally private may be so dependent on defense business that they are in fact contracting agencies of the Department of Defense. For example, from 1960 to 1967 the top three defense contractors were Lockheed Aircraft, General Dynamics, and McDonnell-Douglas, whose defense business constituted 88, 67, and 75 per cent of their sales, respectively. Furthermore, much of the defense establishment is not even privately owned. The Joint Economic Committee of the Congress found that, as of 1967, $2.5 billion worth of industrial production equipment owned by the government was being used by defense contractors.[5]

The phenomenon of the intertwining of corporations in government programs is not limited to defense. During the Johnson administration, for example, government-sponsored job-training programs were provided by private corporations. Morton Grodzins has shown that the interconnectedness of public and private sectors may be even greater at the local than at the national level. In many small localities, private businesses and associations perform a variety of functions in cooperation with or instead of local government agencies.[6] Also, new forms of enterprise have evolved, which straddle whatever distinctions there may be between governmental and nongovernmental. Comsat—the communications satellite used for television and message transmission—and Amtrak—the government-supported attempt to revive passenger trains—are two prominent examples.

A second feature of boundary blurring is the impact and nature of actions taken by nongovernmental entities on their own. As Robert Dahl notes, the large corporation by its decisions may "cause death, injury, disease, and severe physical pain . . . impose severe deprivations of income, well being, and effective personal freedom . . . exercise influence, power, control, and even coercion over employees, customers, suppliers, and others."[7] It is this line of argument we will pursue more extensively in the following chapters.

A third aspect of the boundary problem is the direct role of private interests in making government policy. This policymaking role is based on the delegation of governmental functions to private groups—groups that are essentially unaccountable to many of those affected by the policy decisions they make.[8] For example, bar associations, which are simply supporting auxiliaries of corporate power, maintain a government-permitted monopoly, perform the governmental function of professional licensing, and certify lawyers as officers of the court.

A final aspect of the blurring of the public-private boundary is more fundamental and more controversial than the others. This is the alleged dominance of private elites in public life—roughly the American variant of traditional Marxist conception of the state as the executive committee of the ruling class. Rather than explaining in detail the arguments of C. Wright Mills and others, we will simply state that the power elite model holds that effective power in communities is actually held by a ruling class rather than by elected officials responsible to a widely dispersed plurality of interests.[9]

The elite is not necessarily conspiratorial, nor completely cohesive, but it does have a nexus of interests to which the formal government normally responds. Thus, although public policy does emanate from the government, the *decisions* behind those policies are reached by the elite acting with and through the government. An interesting variant of the power elite theory has been put forth by Peter Bachrach and Morton S. Baratz.[10] According to their conception, the power of elites to influence policy should not be measured solely in terms of their positive actions toward their objectives that may lead to victory in a controversy but also by their ability to keep that controversy from surfacing in the first place. Achieving a "nondecision" in an area where an interest group wanted no change is as much a demonstration of influence as if that group had fought in a public controversy and won. Thus, through a blurring of the boundaries between public and private, elite nongovernmental groups are seen as leaving their imprint on public policy.

"Nondecisions" as Corporate Influence

It can be seen that we are left with a paradox. On the one hand, it is readily acknowledged that in many instances there is no clear distinction between governmental and nongovernmental organizations. On the other hand, public policy is viewed as emanating exclusively from the government. But how can this be a useful conception when, in many instances, it is not clear what a government is? The answer must be that the prevalent definition of public policy as government policy is limited and unrealistic. The problem—and the solution—can be seen in relation to the nondecision argument of Bachrach and Baratz, who view nondecisions as issues on which the political structure of the community begs off because of anticipated reactions from the nongovernmental power structure. The result is a nondecision by government. This leaves aside the crucial point that the nondecision is only a nondecision *by the government*. Decisions on the issue (or nonissue) may still be made by nongovernmental bodies. Decisions are made and, cumulatively, there is a policy—a policy that may, in many instances, be *public* policy. For example, air pollution may be a non-issue in a community, and when there is no effective government regulation, decisions regarding air quality are left to the local polluter. In the case of a large city with many polluters, no one makes the decision. The resultant policy about pollution is established by the "tyranny of small decisions." But in the case of the single industry, town, or region, real and visible decisions about pollution levels are in fact made unilaterally.[11]

The involvement of government and private groups in public policymaking may be viewed as a continuum. At one end, private groups serve only to advise or influence the government to make policy. This is the kind of corporate involvement discussed in the preceding chapters. Farther down the continuum, there is a mix of public policymaking by governmental and nongovernmental organizations, such as when businesses participate in the planning and implementation of urban-renewal programs. At the other end of the continuum, in the absence of government decisions, powerful nongovernmental groups may be important sources of public policy. Particularly prominent among such nongovernmental policymakers are large business corporations. Before turning to a more detailed examination of public policymaking by corporations, it is also necessary to analyze not only who makes public policy but to analyze the nature and content of public policy.

The Components of Public Policy

Many definitions of public policy are based on or are consistent with the theoretical work of the political scientist David Easton. It is therefore useful to take Easton's concept of government and public policy as a starting point in our examination of the components of public policy. Easton writes that a policy "consists of a web of decisions and actions that allocates values,"[12] and public policy consists of the outputs of the political system—the authoritative allocation of values for society. Furthermore, inherent in the nature of authoritative outputs is that members of the political system "consider or are compelled to accept [them] as binding."[13]

We can readily accept these three components of public policy:

authority, binding decisions, and allocation of values for society. The question is whether these criteria must be or are limited to the outputs of the formal government.

Allocation of Values

Allocation of values is a relatively simple concept; it may be defined as the distribution of "goods, services, honors, statuses, and opportunities."[14] Taking a comprehensive view, we also include *costs* in the definition of allocations—in this case the allocation of societal burdens. With this comprehensive view, subsidies, taxes, a military draft, public offices (both substantive and honorary), welfare, medical care, education, and many other values may all be policy outputs—values that are allocated by the political system.

Easton cautions that the proper scope of political science (and, implicitly, public policy) includes not all allocations—since this would make it hopelessly unwieldy—but only those that are authoritative and that are societywide.[15] Easton notes that there is a variety of organizations and institutions whose members accede to their authority—churches, employers, and so on. Yet the policies of such organizations are not public policies because they are not authoritative for the whole of society. While Easton acknowledges that many government policies apply only to some people or regions within a society, he argues that their effects are nonetheless distinct from similarly limited effects of *private* group policies because as government policies they are accepted as authoritative by all members of society.[16] We will deal with the question of authority below. At this stage, the important point is that a public policy must be an allocation of values, but that allocation need not apply equally to the whole society. Indeed, it may even have a very narrow scope of application as long as it is authoritative.

Authority and "Bindingness"

In Easton's model the authorities are, by definition, the government, and he is very explicit about the role of government in making public policy (rendering outputs)—it is, by definition, a

completely exclusive role: "Fundamental to the present concep-
tualization of outputs is the idea that they consist of a stream of
activities flowing from the authorities in a system. It is the fact that
they are produced by the authorities that distinguishes them as
outputs."[17] However, when we move from who the authorities are
to what the authorities do we see that the case for equating public
policy with government policy is less clear. The function of authorities in a political system is to produce outputs—that is, to make
public policy. As we have seen, Easton argues that the authorities
are the exclusive producers of outputs. This, however, is not the
only characteristic of outputs.

Inherent in the character of authoritative outputs is the fact that
they are binding. Citizens must regularize their behavior as specified by the particular output—pay taxes, pay the minimum wage,
and so on. Like the definition of *public,* the binding nature of policy
is usually conceived of as stemming from the government—from
the *binder.* Public policy is binding because it stems from the government. We are told by Easton and others, however, that a distin-
guishing characteristic of government is that it makes binding
policy. Thus, we are left with the circular conclusion that outputs
are binding only because they are governmental, and they are
governmental because they are binding. If, however, we view the
"bindingness" of policy from the perspective of the affected
citizens—the "bindees"—we can begin to construct a more comprehensive and realistic view of public policy. From this broader
perspective, a policy is authoritative for society if it is binding,
regardless of the source of the policy.

The essence of binding policy is the absence of effective choice
by the affected party. A's policy is binding on B if B must regularize
his behavior to the dictates of A's policy regardless of B's own
preferences in the matter. A policy may be binding through two
situations. First, it may be enforced by sanctions after the fact. For
example, I file an income tax return and pay taxes even though I
do not want to because the policymaker (in this case the federal
government) will punish me if I do not. In this case we have
physical freedom but legal compulsion. I can act in a way contrary
to the binding policy, but it is irrational for me to do so because I

would then be punished. We can call this type "sanction binding-ness." The second type is one in which I do not even have the option of resisting the binding policy. Once I am sentenced to jail, my freedom is eliminated, and by physical coercion the state does with me what it will in accord with its binding policy. Physical coercion and violence are not the only implements of this kind of binding policy. All that is required to qualify is the removal from the bindee of all options of resistance. For example, I do not have the option of not paying income taxes which have already been withheld from my paycheck. The government, acting through my employer, has removed that option. This kind of bindingness we can call "situational bindingness," since the total situation is con-trolled.

The question now is whether nongovernmental entities can em-ploy either or both of these kinds of binding policies. The answer is clearly yes. For example, the New York Stock Exchange may punish individual violators of Exchange regulations by prohibiting member firms from employing them for a specified period of time. Just as in the case of government, a corporation may thus cause an individual to act against his own preferences or face the more unpleasant alternative of a severe deprivation of values—a sanction little different in effect from a judicially imposed fine. Of course, the sanctions of a corporation are less likely to be physical, but the economic sanctions represent a coercive force as powerful as a judicially imposed fine or an attachment of wages or assets by a governmental unit.

The second kind of binding policy, situational bindingness, is even more pervasive as an element of nongovernmental policymak-ing. This largely includes many externalities of corporations. En-vironmental degradation is probably the most obvious and perva-sive example of situational bindingness. For example, the citizens of Gary, Indiana, suffer a binding deprivation of health and aesthetic values due to the air pollution emanating from the plants of U.S. Steel. They may consider this a worthwhile tradeoff for employment and prosperity, but they are nonetheless bound by the policy outputs (pollution) of the industry. Similarly, all citizens of large urban areas suffer the binding policy outputs of automobile pollution. The point to be emphasized is that the pollution, to continue the example, does not simply occur as a spontaneous act of God. It is, rather, the result of identifiable decisions by corporate officials. In short, it is a policy made by those officials—officials who must be considered as part of "the authorities" in the political system. Furthermore, it is not always clear just who are the authorities in a political system. When we say that a member of the school board in Sheboygan, Wisconsin, is part of the authorities but that the president of General Motors is not, we cannot go very far in understanding government or corporations.

Corporations as Public Policymakers

Our argument to this point has been that nongovernmental entities can and do make public policies. The purpose of establishing that point is to emphasize that we are not dealing only with incidental impacts of corporations on society but with a situation in which corporations can affect citizens directly in the same way that governments do. Thus, this theoretical digression points out not only the inadequacy of prevailing definitions of public policy but also the inadequacy of our prevailing conceptions of giant corporations. The following chapters will pursue this line of argument and examine the kinds of policies formulated by corporations.

So that the discussion of corporate public policy can proceed with order and clarity, it is useful to differentiate among different types of policy. Since political scientists belatedly recognized that the political process differs among different policy areas, a number of typologies of public policy have been offered.[18] While it is tempting simply to use an existing typology, the problem with doing so is that existing policy categories are all based on the assumption that only governments make public policy. To get past this limitation, the discussion of corporate policymaking will be framed in a more general and abstract framework of public policy that is relevant to the policies of both corporations and governments.

We can call the first group of corporate policies *resource transfer*. This category includes all binding allocations of material goods and their costs and benefits. This combined category thus recognizes that all allocations of goods are actually transfers of goods and carry with them costs (extractions) to pay for those allocations. The second category is *regulatory* and has much the same meaning as that utilized in our application of the term to government policy. Regulatory policies entail direct control over personal or group conduct and the manipulation of environmental conditions affecting society.

In summary, it has been argued that public policy, defined as a binding allocation of values, is not the exclusive province of government but is also promulgated by powerful nongovernmental organizations—particularly giant corporations. This concept is important in order to understand the overall political role of corporations. Chapter 1 examined the nature of the corporation and its need to control its environment—an environment dominated by the government. Chapters 2, 3, and 4 analyzed the means by which corporations influence that governmental part of their environment. The following chapters of this section take an even broader perspective, covering corporate efforts to achieve stability in the total social and economic environment. It is these latter efforts that culminate in the making of public policy by corporations. In order to control the environment, corporations necessarily implement policies that are binding on large numbers of citizens. Corporations not only seek to influence governments in their environment, but they also act as governments to influence the broader environment.

The following two chapters will elaborate on the meaning of resource transfer and regulatory policies as they analyze corporate public policymaking in terms of those two categories.

Notes

1. Morton Mintz and Jerry Cohen, *America, Inc.: Who Owns and Operates the United States?* (New York: Dial Press, 1971).
2. Robert Salisbury, "The Analysis of Public Policy: A Search for Theories and Roles," in *Political Science and Public Policy*, Austin Ranney, ed. (Chicago: Markham, 1968), p. 152.
3. Robert Dahl, *After the Revolution?* (New Haven: Yale University Press, 1970), p. 120.

4. Seymour Melman, *Pentagon Capitalism* (New York: McGraw-Hill, 1970), pp. 13–14.
5. U.S. Congress, Joint Economic Committee, *Economy in Government Procurement and Property Management* (1968). Cited in Melman, *Pentagon Capitalism*, p. 79.
6. Morton Groadzins, "Local Strength in the American Federal System: The Mobilization of Public-Private Influence," in *Continuing Crises in American Politics*, Marian D. Irish, ed. (Englewood Cliffs, N.J.: Prentice-Hall, 1963).
7. Robert A. Dahl, "A Prelude to Corporate Reform," *Business and Society Review* 1 (Spring 1972), p. 18.
8. See, for example, Grant McConnell, *Private Power and American Democracy* (New York: Knopf, 1966).
9. C. Wright Mills, *The Power Elite* (New York: Oxford University Press, 1956). See also Floyd Hunter, *Community Power Structure* (Chapel Hill: University of North Carolina Press, 1953) and Jack L. Walker, "A Critique of the Elitist Theory of Government," *American Political Science Review* 60 (June 1966), pp. 285–95. For an affirmation of pluralist theory in the community power debate, see Robert Dahl, *Who Governs?* (New Haven: Yale University Press, 1961). See also Nelson W. Polsby, *Community Power and Political Theory* (New Haven: Yale University Press, 1963) for a concise summary of the leading community-power studies and a lucid analysis of the issues.
10. Peter Bachrach and Morton S. Baratz, "Two Faces of Power," *American Political Science Review* 56 (December 1962), pp. 947–52, and "Decisions and Non-Decisions: An Analytical Framework," *ibid.*, 57 (1963), pp. 632–34.
11. Cf. Matthew Crenson, *The Un-Politics of Air Pollution* (Baltimore: Johns Hopkins University Press, 1970).
12. David Easton, *The Political System*, 2nd ed. (New York: Knopf, 1971), p. 130.
13. David Easton, *A Systems Analysis of Political Life* (New York: Wiley, 1965), p. 352.
14. Gabriel A. Almond and G. Bingham Powell, Jr., *Comparative Politics: A Developmental Approach* (Boston: Little, Brown, 1966), p. 198.
15. Easton, *Political System*, pp. 131–34.
16. Ibid.
17. Easton, *Systems Analysis*, pp. 205–06.
18. On the utility of policy differentiation, see Theodore J. Lowi, "American Business, Public Policy, Case Studies, and Political Theory," *World Politics* 16 (July 1964), pp. 677–715 and Lewis A. Froman, Jr., "The Categorization of Policy Contents," in Ranney, *Political Science and Public Policy*, pp. 41–52.

6
Corporate Resource Transfer Policy

The corporate quest for hegemony stems from a need to forestall threats in the environment. In the previous chapters we have seen how corporations deal with their governmental environment. In this and the following chapter we will analyze the corporate attempt to stabilize the economic environment. Just as the political system cannot be left to chance, the business system surrounding each corporation must be anticipated and influenced to the greatest extent possible. The business environment includes other business organizations, consumers, labor, sources of capital, and products ranging from natural resources to finished goods. Additionally, there are such intangibles as technological development and the intensity of competition. No corporation of any consequence would last long if it did not base its plans on an accurate assessment of the business environment, and such planning is essential for the progress of the firm and the economy as a whole. Beyond this planning, large corporations seek to influence their economic environment, just as they do their political environment. Research and development programs are examples of constructive efforts to affect the future environment.

There is a point where the corporate attempt to influence the economic environment becomes a political problem. This point is reached when the giant corporation's understandable desire to control its environment extends to making policies that have a binding effect on large numbers of people—public policies as discussed in the previous chapter.

In terms of its impact on citizens, the most pervasive form of corporation-made public policy involves resource transfer—the extraction and allocation of material values. The very purpose of corporations is to transfer resources by procuring, producing, and distributing goods and services. However, only a portion of these transactions constitute public policy. The distinction between actions that consitute public policy and those that do not is not always a precise one; it lies in the degree of control a particular corporation exercises over its transactions. When others are confronted with corporate decisions that are binding on them, public policy may be said to have been made. Basic to that control is the dominance by giant corporations over their various markets and over the economy as a whole—a dominance noted by economists as the degree of economic concentration.

Economic Concentration

The term *economic concentration* refers to the proportion of assets and economic activity controlled by the leading firms in the economy or in a specific industry. In particular, there is *market concentration* which refers to concentration within particular markets—the percentage of a particular industry (automobiles, home appliances, processed foods, and so on) accounted for by the leading firms. Secondly, there is *aggregate concentration*, the amount of economic activity in the entire economy that is accounted for by a small number of firms. In examining the political role of corporations, economic concentration is of great importance for two reasons. First, a high degree of concentration, particularly market concentration, may provide the power for corporations to make binding policy for society. While high concentration does not by itself definitely connote the making of public policy, it appears to be a necessary precondition for the exercise of that power. Second, a high degree of aggregate concentration raises, at the very least, the same disturbing implications for a democracy as a similarly high concentration of political power would. Therefore, it is useful to discuss in general terms the nature and consequences of economic concentration before proceeding to some specific instances of corporate resource transfer policies. In this section we will discuss primarily aggregate concentration—a politically relevant indicator of raw or potential social power.

In spite of the platitudes celebrating the diversity and competitiveness of the American economy, there is in fact a high degree of economic concentration. Moreover, aggregate concentration has increased over the past twenty years. Of the total manufacturing assets in the United States, the 100 largest manufacturing corporations controlled 39.7 per cent in 1950. By 1972, that share had risen to 47.6 per cent. Indeed, most of the country's manufacturing assets are in the hands of the 200 largest corporations that held 60 per cent in 1972—a jump from 47.7 per cent in 1950.[1] These aggregate figures give only a rough outline of the state of concentration in the American economy. Even more revealing are the concentration ratios used by economists.

The concentration ratio indicates the percentage of sales accounted for by the top few firms in a particular industry. Thus, a four-firm ratio refers to the proportion held by the top four, an eight-firm ratio refers to the proportion held by the top eight, and so on. In his major study of economic concentration, economist John Blair utilizes four-firm concentration ratios to measure the extent of concentration in various industries.[2] Using data for 1963, Blair found that 33.3 per cent of all manufacturing output in the United States was in highly concentrated industries (those with a concentration ratio of 50 per cent or more), while 34.4 per cent of manufacturing output was in moderately concentrated industries (ratio of 25 to 49 per cent), the remainder, only 32 per cent, was in unconcentrated industries. Furthermore, the concentration ratios for particular market areas are even higher than the overall ratios for the country as a whole.

Periods of Merger Activity

The extent of concentration in our economy did not simply occur as the result of natural forces, nor even as a process of rewarding the most efficient enterprises—although that claim is no doubt comforting to the modern captains of industry. In fact, the modern face of concentration has come about as a result of shrewd, but not necessarily efficient or socially beneficial, business practices—particularly mergers. Mergers have long been a popular route to economic power in the United States. From the turn of the century on, there have been three significant periods of merger activity in the United States. The period from 1898 to 1902 gave birth to 2,653 important consolidations. By 1904, when the Supreme Court forbade monopolistic mergers in the *Northern Securities* case, the trusts controlled 40 per cent of the manufacturing capital in the United States. In the years preceding the Great Depression, 1925–1929, there was a second wave of mergers—4,583 in all. These were smaller mergers fueled by stock promotion, which came to a sudden halt with the stock market crash in 1929. These two merger movements were either vertical (companies acquiring related suppliers or customers of their primary business) or horizontal (companies acquiring competitors). Nearly 70 per cent of the mergers in the 1926–1930 period involved direct competitors. The Celler-Kefauver Act of 1950 challenged the largest of these mergers between competitors, and consequently the third merger movement was of a different kind.

The third wave of mergers started in 1955 and peaked in 1969. In 1967, 1968, and 1969 the merger movement reached all-time peaks; an average of over 3,500 mergers occurred *annually*. Overwhelmingly, the mergers in this period were conglomerate mergers—the acquisitions of firms in unrelated industries, the original firm becoming only a holding company for dozens of companies in diverse fields. By 1968, 89 per cent of all mergers were conglomerate in nature.[3] The late 1960s were the heydays of the merger movement. Conglomerates were heralded as the wave of the future—promising great efficiency and riches to stockholders and not subject to antitrust action. In fact, the bubble burst quickly, as it always had before; earnings stopped growing, and the formerly romantic entrepreneurs of the go-go years were frantically retreating in an effort to bail out themselves and their companies. But the legacy of conglomeration is very much with us and continually results in a high economic and political cost.

The broadest social cost of the conglomerates is reflected in the significant increase in aggregate economic concentration that resulted from the merger movement. The merger craze involved not small businesses combining to become big, but big businesses combining to become giants. In 1966, there were 99 mergers designated as "large" by the Federal Trade Commission—large meaning that the acquired firm had assets of at least $10 million. In 1967, there were 167 large mergers, with total acquired assets of $9.1 billion; and in 1968 the figure had grown to 201 large mergers with total acquired assets of $12.8 billion.[4]

Furthermore, a relatively few large companies accounted for a sizable portion of all the large mergers. Thus, companies with assets of $250 million or more acquired 37 per cent of the total number of acquired companies and 56 per cent of all the acquired assets.

The merger activity significantly intensified the state of concentration and changed the map of American business. Between 1962 and 1968, 110 of *Fortune*'s 500 largest industrial corporations disappeared as independent companies. From 1948 to 1968, the largest number of mergers took place among acquired companies that had assets from $10 to $100 million. In fact, had no such mergers taken place, by 1968 there would have been at least 50 per cent more independent businesses in this size range than actually existed by that date.[5] Given that decimation of independent companies, there can be little doubt that conglomeration has caused an increase in economic concentration, and Federal Trade Commission figures document the increase. The share of assets held by the 200 largest manufacturing corporations increased from 42.4 per cent in 1947 to 60.9 per cent in 1968. Of that 19 per cent increase, more than 15 per cent was due to merger activity and only 5.2 per cent due to internal growth.[6] In short, there has been a substantial decline in the pluralism of American economic life as a result of the major merger waves of the twentieth century—particularly the merger mania of the 1960s. This raises several important questions: Why has there been this dramatic wave of conglomeration, and why was it permitted? What have been the benefits? What have been the costs? These questions can be considered together as we look at the arguments offered in defense of conglomerates.

Defending the Conglomerates

While no one overtly claims that it is inherently desirable to concentrate wealth, numerous justifications have been offered to argue that there are considerable offsetting benefits—mostly economic efficiency and the greater economic good for society. One frequently offered defense of corporate mergers is that it is primarily sick and dying firms that are acquired by dynamic, lifegiving enterprises that can instill vigor and sound management into businesses that would otherwise disappear. This argument, however, simply does not square with the facts. FTC figures show that firms acquired in the peak period of 1967–68 were about average in terms of their profitability. Indeed, about half of the big manufacturing and mining firms acquired in 1967–68 had a profit rate greater than their industry average.

Regardless of what went before, conglomerate managers in the 1960s were fond of chanting breathlessly about *synergism*—the idea that the whole is more than the sum of its parts. It was argued that, through some mysterious combination of central management and decentralization—all bubbling along with the propelling magic of systems analysis—the various components of multidivisional, multiproduct corporations would be more efficient and profitable than the same companies run as independent businesses. Although during the first years of the 1960s conglomerate boom companies such as Litton Industries and Gulf and Western did post spectacularly rising earnings (and stock prices), the boom was not to last forever. By the early 1970s, major problems could be seen in the conglomerates—and they were not all due to the vagaries of the stock market. Corporations such as Litton, Ling-Temco-Vought, and "Automatic" Sprinkler were cited by the FTC report on mergers as having losses due to significant problems inherent in controlling large conglomerates. As the FTC report concluded:

. . . An examination of the profitability of merger-active firms reveals that they are not significantly more profitable than firms growing internally. While a few conglomerates did exceptionally well in earlier years, their recent performance indicates that they are not immune from ordinary management problems.[7]

Furthermore, although the leading conglomerates in the mid-1960s appeared to post spectacular increases in earnings, much of this performance was actually due to questionable accounting practices. For example, one study demonstrated how, using only "generally accepted accounting principles," firms with identical profits can be shown to have net profits ranging from $38,000 to $1,076,000, with six different amounts in between.[8] While the wildest disparities in accounting practices have been curbed since the heyday of "funny money" during the conglomerate boom, any accountant worth his fee can still induce substantial variation in the earnings of a corporation, depending on what he wants to show.

If conglomerate mergers were not truly more efficient, why did the merger wave have such momentum? One important reason was precisely the accounting shenanigans discussed above, in combination with a highly receptive stock market. There is a great variety of accounting devices enabling merger-active companies to report substantial increases in earnings per share without improving operating efficiency. As earnings per share of conglomerates increased year after year, stock prices increased ever more rapidly. Since most mergers were based on exchanges of stock (the owners of an independent company received conglomerate stock in exchange for relinquishing the assets of the company), the ever-increasing stock prices of the conglomerate enabled them to acquire more and larger companies. Conglomerates have a great potential for *seeming* to improve the performance of the firms they acquire, using accounting devices to portray a rapid growth in earnings per share. For example, AMF (American Machine Foundry), after acquiring John Morrell & Company, shifted from conservative to liberal accounting methods for depreciation and inventories, thereby converting what would have been a decline in earnings to a reported increase of $.74 a share.[9] Such apparent gains further increased stock prices, made more acquisitions possible, and the cycle repeated itself—until the stock market plummeted.

Another major reason for conglomerates can be found in the vagaries of the human psyche. It is simply more prestigious and more lucrative to be the head of a big company than a little company. The bigger the corporation and the more diversified it becomes, the greater is the span of control (power) of the men at the top. Beyond the positive accumulation of power involved in conglomeration, there is also an element of security. Proponents of conglomeration have claimed that, by diversifying a corporation, they prevent the old problem of having all their eggs in one basket. If one product or service has economic problems, the resulting losses affect only one division of a company, and the firm as a whole is protected by its diversity. All this may be true—although whether we should protect firms from the rigors of competition is another matter. What is more to the point is that it is not only or even primarily the firm as a whole that is protected; it is also the conglomerate chief. A lieutenant whose platoon is wiped out is in big trouble, but a general who loses only one platoon during an engagement is on safe ground. The same principle holds for the successful conglomerate chieftain. If the Arizona Widget division of Consolidated Consolidation, Inc. suffers losses, that is a problem primarily for the head of the division. It is *his* head that will roll, not that of the conglomerate chieftain.

Finally, another factor behind conglomeration was that government policy, through the Internal Revenue Code, encouraged mergers. The Federal Trade Commission concluded that "the tax laws create a significant institutional bias in favor of merger activity. Rather than exerting a neutral influence, current tax laws actually subsidize mergers." The key feature of the tax laws favoring mergers is that there is no federal tax on the sale of a business when that business is exchanged for stock. The accumulated value of a company can be sold without anyone having to pay a capital-gains tax. Of the 411 large mergers between 1963 and 1968 for which information is available, about 85 per cent of them were tax free. In almost all of these mergers, the acquiring firms paid a significant premium over the pre-merger market value of the acquired firm. Nonetheless, under Section 368 of the Internal Revenue Code, no capital-gains taxes had to be paid because payment was made by stock rather than cash. Thus, there has been a real incentive to sell out to a larger company that can exchange its own stock rather than to a new set of people who would continue the corporation as an independent entity and who would pay for it in cash.[10]

Effects of the Merger Movement

Thus, the real sources of the great conglomerate wave of the 1960s are to be found in imaginative, although legal, accounting practices, the vagaries of the stock market, the tax laws, and the forces of personal ambition. The supposed benefits of greater efficiency and profitability are seen to be illusory, and, if anything, they are contrary to the facts, as former "glamour" companies like Litton and Ling-Temco-Vought found themselves in real financial trouble. What the American economy was left with, therefore, was a substantial increase in economic concentration with no real societal gain. Quite the contrary—we have experienced an absolute decline in business pluralism. The conglomerate movement resulted in greater and greater economic decisionmaking power gravitating toward fewer and fewer hands. It was certainly not the only cause of concentration, but it did add to an already overconcentrated economy. Indeed, even when concentration in a given industry remains unchanged by conglomerate mergers, competition can still be undermined. John Blair has argued that this will result if, fearing retaliation by a large conglomerate, smaller single-line producers hold back from initiating competitive moves. According to Blair:

. . . Competition will also be lessened if rival conglomerates, encountering each other in a number of different industries, forbear from competing with each other in any one of them. And potential competition may be lessened if a company with the resources and ability required for internal expansion makes its entrance into an industry by acquisition rather than by building new plant capacity.[11]

Of equal importance are the political implications of the merger movement. As is discussed throughout this study, the line between economic and political power is a tenuous one indeed. Although we have strayed far from the ideal, our constitutional structure was established with the dispersion of power as a major goal— separation of power, checks and balances, and federalism. As we will argue in greater detail in Part Four, the distribution of economic power should be viewed in the same terms. For political reasons, if for no others, the concentration of economic decisionmaking power insulated from checks and accountability is a situation to be avoided for the same fundamental reasons as those that apply to political power: concentration of power tends to reduce political accountability and is thus an assault on fundamental democratic values.

Of course, even in pursuit of democratic values there is a trade-off between the necessity of limiting power and the necessity of governing. Indeed, this is a fundamental dilemma of any democratic regime as Madison noted in *The Federalist,* No. 51:

. . . In framing a government which is to be administered by men over men, the great difficulty lies in this: You must first enable the government to control the governed; and in the next place oblige it to control itself.

Similarly, in the economic sphere there can be little doubt that large-scale enterprise is essential for our overall economic welfare. It is not particularly useful, therefore, to urge a return to a mythical state of pure competition composed only of tiny enterprises. Economic values should not be entirely subordinate to democratic values—even if they could be. But it is a far cry from the necessity of realizing economies of scale in modern economic life to sanctioning severe reductions in political/economic pluralism. Thus, while economic values need not be controlling in our evaluation of economic concentration, they are relevant. We have already seen that the claims of the virtues of conglomerates were wildly overblown. More importantly, conglomerates and the leading firms in highly concentrated industries generally have imposed significant and substantial economic costs on society. Their leverage in imposing those costs is commonly known as *market power.*

As defined by economist William Shepherd, "market power is the ability of a market participant or group of participants . . . to influence price, quantity, and the nature of the product in the marketplace. Acquired and rationally exercised, market power may yield during its duration the commercial rewards of high and risk free profits, as well as a wider range of social and political advantages."[12]

Thus, market power resulting from economic concentration is not only an economic phenomenon but a political one. Market power is at the core of the ability of giant corporations to execute resource transfer policy. In the remainder of this chapter and the next, we will deal with the various components of resource transfer policies—starting with corporate market power over price, quantity, and the design and quality of products.

Administered Prices

Just as taxation by public governments is the most pervasive form of government policy, in terms of its impact on the largest number of citizens, so too is taxation by private industry the major mode of corporate resource transfer policy. The notion of taxation by private organization is not a novel conception. Thurmond Arnold noted that "taxation by industrial organizations is a pleasanter way of paying tribute than taxation by government." Arnold argued sarcastically that the distinction was a convenient myth:

. . . No one observed the obvious fact that in terms of total income of an individual it made no difference whether his money went for prices or taxes. Men believed there was a difference because prices were automatically regulated by the laws of supply and demand. If any great corporate organization charged too much, in the long run it would be forced out of business by other corporations which did not charge so much. This might not be true if the corporation had a monopoly but our antitrust laws protected us from anything like that.[13]

While not all pricing policies need be considered as private taxation, giant corporations can effect such taxation through a system of administered prices. Rather than setting prices in reaction to competitive pressures expressed through the "law" of supply and demand, some corporations in highly concentrated industries are able to exercise considerable (although not unlimited) discretion in setting their own prices. This kind of situation, resulting from a market in which a few competing producers predominate, was described by Gardiner Means:

. . . (1) Prices tend to be administered, and not sensitive to short-run changes in demand and supply. (2) Competing producers tend to set the same prices or maintain the same price differentials over considerable periods of time. (3) There is apt to be one producer who is looked to as the leader in making price changes. (4) Prices tend to be set in terms of long-run considerations and not in terms of the short-run variations in demand and supply factors which dominate prices set by competition.[14]

The antitrust Subcommittee of the Senate Judiciary Committee concluded in 1958 that administered pricing was the general situation in the steel industry. Despite wide fluctuations of demand over time, steel prices rose steadily through the 1950s. The situation contrasts sharply with the price of scrap metal where the selling market is composed of many small firms.[15] In the steel industry, U.S. Steel is the price leader, and the other companies have historically matched U.S. Steel price rises to the penny.[16] As Gardiner Means points out, the setting of administered prices is not an unlimited power. U.S. Steel cannot set prices at *any* level it chooses. There are vaguely defined lower and upper limits. But, as Means says, "the price leader in steel operates within an area of pricing discretion such that within a significant range it can set one price rather than another."[17] In this situation, the price leader is exercising the same kind of pricing power exercised by a governmental agency in the case of a regulated industry. There, too, the power is not unlimited; rather, it is utilized within reasonable lower and upper limits. In both cases a binding resource transfer is effected by a public policymaker. The public policy role of the administered price leader was implied in the statement of U.S. Steel chairman Roger Blough before the Senate antitrust subcommittee when he stated: "I commend to the thoughtful consideration of this committee the question of whether or not our price action was responsible and in the public interest."[18] While there is considerable disagreement as to whether administered prices lead to excessive or exorbitant profits, the point remains that such a system consists of unilateral price setting in a regulated price structure. Just as it is public policy when the Civil Aeronautics Board sets airline fares, so too is it public policy when U.S. Steel sets steel prices.

It should be noted that there is a lively controversy over the impact of administered prices and the relationship between economic concentration and inflationary prices. Some economists argue that prices in concentrated industries have not risen more than average compared to less-concentrated industries.[19] It is fair to say, however, that all the evidence is not yet in. Given the high degree of aggregate economic concentration, it is not altogether clear what constitutes an "unconcentrated" industry. There is also the important political problem that average levels of concentration or price increases may conceal other important dimensions of economic performance, such as the availability, choice, and quality of products. That is, that regardless of overall trends, the market power of particular industries may lead to important areas of public policymaking by corporations. In the following two sections, we will examine such corporate policymaking in the areas of health policy and energy policy. These areas have been chosen for analysis because of the importance of corporate decisionmaking in those areas and the universal impact of those decisions. In order to demonstrate the sources and manifestations of corporate power, we will develop these cases in considerable detail.

Health Policy: The Pharmaceutical Fix

Within the area of health policy, we will focus on the pharmaceutical industry—one of the most significant areas of resource transfer through administered prices. Increasingly, health care is being regarded as a vital and legitimate area of governmental policymaking. Within the total health-care system, major decisions about the price and availability of drugs are made by a relatively small group of manufacturers. At the retail end, prescription drugs are selected by the physician, and their availability is controlled by the government. The consumer needs the drug but has no effective choice and is usually in no position to shop for alternatives. We can therefore conceive of this system of administered pricing as a health tax on citizens, since the distribution and sales of prescription drugs have a direct and completely binding effect on consumers. One indication of the amount of economic resources being transferred is the fact that in 1971 American consumers spent an estimated $4,367,381,000 on prescriptions purchased at retail pharmacies alone—not including the amount spent by hospital patients, public health agencies, and other institutional consumers. The amount of money changing hands, to say nothing of the vital importance of the product, makes these transactions clearly significant. The political importance of the drug trade, however, is not based simply on the volume of sales or the need for the product. Rather, in the context of political power, our concern is focused on the discretionary power of the industry. How much power do individual pharmaceutical corporations have over the amount consumers must pay for drugs? In short, how much market power do the major drug firms have?

Since market power results from lack of competition, the first step is to see to what extent the drug industry is concentrated. At first glance, it would appear that it is amazingly unconcentrated. Its main trade association, the Pharmaceutical Manufacturers Association, consists of 136 members, only half of which are small businesses. Dr. C. Joseph Stetler, president of the PMA, proudly asserted that there is an extremely low degree of concentration in the drug industry, since no single company accounts for more than 7 per cent of total domestic prescription sales.[20]

There is, however, a major flaw in the PMA's denial of market concentration: the market for drugs is not industrywide. Economists normally define markets by geographical or product classes, and the actual markets for drugs are defined by much narrower therapeutic categories into which different drugs fall. There are different categories of prescription drugs that are not substitutable—antibiotics or diuretics, for example—and in certain of these drug categories there may be a very high degree of market concentration. The relevant markets are thus defined by therapeutic class rather than by the industry as a whole. By this standard, there is indeed a high degree of concentration.

A pattern of specialization has emerged among the large firms so that, within each product type, there is domination by a small group of firms. These positions of leadership with therapeutic categories have also remained stable over time.[21] Moreover, the top firms in the industry have been able to dominate a large number of different markets. Thus, William S. Comanor, a Harvard economist, found that in a group of twenty therapeutic markets the industry's five leading firms accounted for 56 to 98 per cent of the output in each market. As Comanor noted: "It is within these markets that decisions on prices are made, and given such concentration ratios, we should not expect individual firms to disregard their own impact on market parameters. It is on this basis that market power has been achieved."[22]

One of the characteristic indices of industries possessing market power is the existence of high profits relative to other industries. In this respect, the drug industry looks powerful indeed; it has consistently had unusually high profits. The table below shows the return on equity of the drug industry compared to all manufacturers, for the period 1961–1971. The drug industry has consistently been first or second in profits.

Related to high profits, of course, are high prices, and most observers believe that profits in the drug industry result from the lack of price competition. What is too high? Particularly for products with the vital importance of pharmaceuticals, it is difficult to be precise. Nonetheless, a couple of examples illustrate pricing practices that are not uncommon in the industry—practices that, by any standard, lead to prices that are "too high." For example, under an exclusive arrangement, Miles Laboratories produced kits for prediagnosing mental retardation in infants for about $6 each and sold them for $262.[23] Similarly, in a show of extraordinary market

Returns on Equity and on Sales, Industry Medians, 1961-1971

	RETURN ON EQUITY			RETURN ON SALES		
Year	All industry (%)	Drug industry (%)	Rank	All industry (%)	Drug industry (%)	Rank
1961	8.3	15.8	2d.	4.2	10.5	2d.
1962	8.9	16.2	2d.	4.2	10.5	2d.
1963	9.1	14.7	2d.	4.4	10.6	1st.
1964	10.5	16.3	1st.	5.0	10.8	1st.
1965	11.8	18.0	1st.	5.5	10.3	2d.
1966	12.7	18.4	1st.	5.6	10.2	2d.
1967	11.3	18.0	1st.	5.0	9.6	2d.
1968	11.7	17.9	1st.	4.8	9.0	2d.
1969	11.3	19.1	1st.	4.6	9.2	2d.
1970	9.5	15.5	2d.	3.9	9.3	2d.
1971	9.1	15.1	2d.	3.8	9.1	2d.

SOURCE: Statement of Willard F. Mueller, Director, Bureau of Economics, Federal Trade Commission, in *Drug Industry Hearings* (1967), pt. 5, p. 1827.

power, the international quinine cartel tripled the price of quinine in the 1960s.

Same Drugs, Different Prices

Even more to the point are instances of differential prices for the same drug. Hugh Douglas Walker asserted that "the most pointed evidence that large firms in the drug industry possess market power is that for products which are therapeutically homogeneous, they are able to charge higher prices than those charged by smaller firms."[24] This manifestation of market power is pervasive in the drug industry. For example, prices for the drug reserpine (used widely for control of high blood pressure) vary widely according to the size of the firm producing it and whether the drug is sold under a brand name or under its generic name. Thus, 72 small firms sold reserpine for an average of $5.66 per thousand tablets under the generic name; 20 small firms sold it at $14.89 per thousand under a brand name, and five large firms sold it under a brand name at an average price of $35.96 per thousand.[25]

The phenomenon of differential prices directly reflects on the lack of competition in the drug industry. In a price-competitive market, one normally expects to find that firms selling drugs at several times the prices being asked by other manufacturers would fare very poorly. In practice, however, drug companies have little to fear from competitors selling identical drugs at far lower prices. For example, among the companies selling the sedative sodium secobarbital, Eli Lilly & Company offers it under the brand name Seconal at $18.30 per thousand—more than three times the price of most competitors' tablets. One might expect that the market for the drug would be divided among several firms and that Lilly would face strong price competition. But, according to Lilly's own figures, it accounts for approximately 95 per cent of all retail sales of sodium secobarbital and approximately 90 per cent of the institutional market.[26]

Not only are there great price differentials between brand name and generic drugs, but there are also price differentials between brand name drugs sold in the United States and the same brand name drugs sold in other countries. The table shows the domestic and foreign price differentials for three widely used antibiotics. It should be emphasized that these price differences pertain to the same drug manufactured by the same company. In nearly all cases, the price in the United States is considerably higher than the price overseas—this despite the fact that the drugs were manufactured in the United States.

The drug industry defends these practices by citing differences in wage rates, distribution costs, price and wage controls, taxes, import duties, currency revaluations, and sources of raw materials. These arguments fall apart, however, in light of the fact that U.S. drug manufacturers sell drugs to *domestic* wholesalers at different prices depending on where the drug is to be used. If the domestic wholesaler states that the drug will be shipped overseas, his price may be up to 50 per cent lower than if he were to sell it to domestic users.[27]

One novel justification for differential prices discriminating against American consumers was offered by W. H. Conzen, president of the Schering Corporation: "the living standards and purchasing power of people abroad differ greatly from those in our own country."[28] In other words, they charge what the traffic will bear. In fact, U.S. drug companies face more competition abroad than at home, and it is these competitive pressures that keep foreign prices lower. Conversely, it is the market power of the manufacturers that is responsible for saddling American consumers with high drug prices. To return to the earlier question of when drug prices are "too high," it is clear that at the very least prices are too high when the same product is available at a much lower price in other countries or in our own country under generic names.

Drug Companies and Advertising

A major adjunct to the market power of major drug houses is the sheer bulk of their advertising. Although the industry as a whole is unusually profitable, some of the larger firms are well above the average, and advertising plays a major part in their success. According to Federal Trade Commission data presented by Willard

Selected Antibiotic Prices in the U.S. and Eight Foreign Countries, January 1970

PRICE TO DRUGGIST, BRAND NAME, AND MANUFACTURER

Generic name	U.S.	Aust.	Brazil	Can.	Eire	Italy	N.Z.	Sweden	U.K.
Ampicillin (250 mg.)	$21.84 Polycillin, Bristol	$20.48 Penbritin, Bristol	$41.95 Polycillin, Bristol	$22.18 Ampicin, Bristol	$9.31 Pentrexyl, Bristol	$19.15 Sintopenyl, Aesculapius	$11.30 Penbritin, Beecham	$16.58 Pentrexyl, Bristol	$8.23 Penbritin, Beecham
Erythromycin (250 mg.)	$26.12 Erythrocin, Abbott	$14.51 Erythrocin, Abbott	$11.92 Pantomicina, Abbott	$25.04 Erythrocin, Abbott	$8.56 Erythrocin, Abbott	$24.57 Eritrocina, Abbott	$10.88 Official price	$19.21 Erythromycin, Abbott	$10.02 Erythrocin, Abbott
Tetracycline HCl (250 mg.)	$5.34 Achromycin-V, Lederle	$9.79 Achromycin-V, Lederle	$4.22 Achromycin-V, Cyanamid Quim do Brasil	$12.64 Achromycin-V, Lederle	$3.42 Achromycin-V, Lederle	$10.84 Achromycina, Cyanamid	$13.78 Achromycin-V, Lederle	$13.89 Achromycin-V, Lederle	$5.04 Achromycin-V, Lederle

SOURCE: "Domestic and Foreign Prescription Drug Prices" by Edmond M. Jacoby, Jr. and Dennis L. Hefner, Department of Health, Education, and Welfare. Presented by Senator Gaylord Nelson, U.S. Congress, *Congressional Record*, 92nd Congress, 2nd sess., p. 32934.

Mueller, the five major companies with advertising outlays over $50 million in 1966 had an average rate of return of 29 per cent during 1961–1965; those who spent between $10 million and $50 million on advertising had an average profit of 19.7 per cent; and those spending less than $10 million made a profit of 17.3 per cent.[29]

The drug industry argues that their heavy promotional expenditures enable them to maintain a system of mass production of drugs in great volume, with resultant savings to consumers. However, actual experience belies this contention. For example, the tranquilizer chlorpromazine was introduced in 1954 by Smith, Kline and French under the brand name Thorazine. The price to pharmacists was then $6.06 per hundred tablets. By 1965, because of the usefulness of the drug and also because of a heavy promotional campaign, sales of the drug had skyrocketed. By the drug firms' theory, the virtues of great volume sales should have reduced the price. In reality, the 1965 price was still $6.06 per hundred. Only in 1969, when other tranquilizers were in effective competition for the market, was the price of Thorazine reduced.[30]

Nonetheless, it is important to understand the role of pharmaceutical advertising—because it tends to increase rather than decrease prices. One of the reasons advertising campaigns are so important for drug companies is the virtual absence of price competition. Thus, firms that seek a big share of the market are unable to increase their sales or profits by offering identical quality drugs at lower prices. Physicians have no incentive to seek lower prices— they don't pay for prescriptions. To gain the attention of doctors and to get them to switch from one brand to another usually requires a firm to mount a major promotional campaign. Since access by price competition is effectively closed, the only way to get a market share is to conduct a successful promotion to capture the doctors' attention. This, in turn, spurs firms that are already in the market to increase their own advertising and promotional activity. This type of promotional competition, of course, has the effect of driving prices up, while creating further barriers to price competition.

Indeed, the issue of barriers to competition is an important component of the ability of corporations to make binding allocation of resources—in this case the consumer's health dollars. In fact, there are substantial barriers to the entry of new firms into particular therapeutic markets. As evidence of these barriers, William Comanor stated:

. . . In a free market economy, high profit rates, which are not accounted for by differences in rates of growth of demand or by the degree of risk, will not persist for a prolonged period of time in the absence of factors which restrict the entry of new firms. If high rates of return in an industry exist, new firms will enter the market, and this will generally have the effect of driving prices down to more competitive levels. High prices and profits suggest, thereby, that specific factors are present which restrict the entry of new firms.[31]

Needless to say, the drug industry does not publicly admit that their high profits are due to entry barriers. Rather, they advance a list of noble, but ultimately unconvincing reasons for their prices and profits. Probably the most common justification is grounded in the expenses and value of new drug research: "at generic level prices, we cannot have new discoveries. At generic level prices we will stifle research and the development of new medicines, and soon we will have neither the new drugs nor the generics."[32]

In fact, however, large price differentials exist even when high-price companies did no research on a particular drug. For example, CIBA Pharmaceuticals developed reserpine under the trade name Serpasil, and sold it for $39.50 per thousand tablets. The same drug, under their own trade names, was sold by Parke Davis for $33.96, by Upjohn for $33.58, and Lilly for $15.75. These large firms, however, had done no research on the drug and were simply selling it under a license from CIBA. In contrast, five smaller licensees were selling reserpine at less than $1 per thousand.[33]

Furthermore, research expenditures are not impressively high in any event. In 1971, the research expenditures of the major firms ranged from 4 to 11 per cent of sales—with eight of the largest companies spending 6 per cent or less. These research outlays hardly justify price differentials that sometimes range up to a factor of 30.[34]

Indeed, the major drug companies may actually spend more

money on advertising than they do on research. Although reliable precise figures are impossible to come by, estimates of the amount spent on promotional activities in 1968 range from $434 million to more than $1 billion (according to an estimate by the Social Security Administration). By contrast, in 1971 the major drug firms spent less than $700 million on research. The promotional expenditures can also be compared to the $977 million spent for all educational activities by American medical schools. Thus, in terms of the allocation of medical-related resources, the amount allocated to hucksterism weighs heavily.[35]

Not only does the industry exaggerate its research effort, but the direction and nature of that effort has also been called into question. Much research is not oriented to actual product improvement or new breakthroughs but toward acquiring patent protection for drugs that are basically imitative in nature. Thus, whatever risk there is, is not caused by the perils of basic research but is simply related to marketing strategies of no real social benefit. As Dr. Henry Steel pointed out:

. . . In order to make the greatest profits per drug it is usually necessary to be first in the market, otherwise the advertising cost of wresting the market away from the first (and also heavily advertised) drug is disproportionately great. Hence the motivation to devise new drugs. But at the same time, the new drugs found by others must be rapidly copied, so that the costs of research, both primary and imitative, come to mount up. And the fact that everyone is trying to copy and/or improve everyone else's product leads to an overly rapid rate of product obsolescence and an artificially induced "risk" of short commercial life for the average product.[36]

In addition to research, the industry frequently claims that their high profits are justified by the risks they take and their need to attract capital. Dr. Willard Mueller of the Federal Trade Commission, however, observed that "large drug companies should have little difficulty obtaining adequate capital should they choose to go into the market for it. Actually, however, their profits are so large that drug companies seldom need to go to the capital market for equity capital."[37] Furthermore, the Department of Health, Education, and Welfare Task Force on Prescription Drugs also concluded that "the exceptionally high rate of profit which generally marks the drug industry is not accompanied by any peculiar degree of risk, or by any unique difficulties in obtaining growth capital."[38]

Drugs and the Patent System

In short, the high prices and profits of the industry are not induced by market forces; rather, they are a unilateral assessment of administered prices on the American public. They constitute a binding assessment and therefore are an exercise of political power. Similarly, a major source of the market power of the large firms derives from political institutions—in this case the patent system for drugs. The United States is practically alone among advanced industrial nations in allowing unlimited patents for drugs. Patents for pharmaceuticals are treated no differently from patents for chemicals, machines, electric pencil sharpeners, or any other commercial product—in spite of the fact that pharmaceuticals are a vital product leaving the consumer little choice but to pay up or remain ill. While there is general agreement that it would not be wise to eliminate drug patents altogether, there is also considerable sentiment to restrict the exclusivity and unlimited use of patents in the industry.

The relationship between prices and patents can first be seen in the case of penicillin—on which there was no patent. As penicillin became widely available, there were many firms selling the drug; intense price competition developed, which forced prices down. It became apparent that purchasers would notice price differences among identical products sold by various manufacturers, and this experience was a great incentive to make use of the patent system in introducing new products. By obtaining patents, product standardization could be prevented—at least for a time. Thus, drug firms relied on patents, followed by advertising, to prevent the development of standardized products and to get a substantial share of the market before the patent ran out. The overall impact of the system did not create tight monopoly positions; even patented drug products are frequently substitutable. But the use of unrestricted patents did prevent price competition between identical chemical products from developing as it had in the case of penicillin.[39]

Generic vs. Brand-Name Drugs

To say that the present use of the patent system leads to higher prices implies that it is possible for drugs manufactured by different companies to be identical. Thus, the issue of patents is closely related to the entire question of generic-name drugs versus brand-name drugs. The generic name of a drug is simply the standardized name, and the trade or brand name denotes a particular form of the drug made by a particular manufacturer. Thus, Seconal is the trade name for Lilly's version of sodium sccobarbital. Either under license or after patents have expired, a particular drug, with a single generic name, may be sold under dozens of different trade names. It is the trade name that is dominant in current American medical practice. We will discuss the medical effects of drug-promotion activities in relation to prescription-issuing by doctors in a later chapter. For now, it suffices to note that approximately 90 per cent of prescriptions written by physicians specify a particular brand-name product. Most states have so-called "antisubstitution" laws that require pharmacists to dispense only the particular brand prescribed and not the same drug under its generic name—potentially at a lower price. Thus, the patient is almost always given a prescription with a trade name, and it is only that trade-name drug he can buy.

The reliance on trade names is both a manifestation and a major source of the continued market power of the large drug firms. In their extensive and costly promotional campaigns (estimated at up to $3,000 per doctor annually), large firms advertise drugs under their trade names. The flood of advertising displaces generic names and leads to a proliferation of names for a single product. For example, the tranquilizer meprobamate may be prescribed alone or in combination under the trade names Apascil, Calmiren, Cirpon, Ecuanil, Equanil, Harmonin, Mepantin, Miltown, Probamyl, Sedasil, Viobamate, and twenty other trade names. The efforts of the drug firms' promotion activities are geared toward establishing brand-name loyalty among physicians so that they become accustomed to prescribe a particular medication only under a trade name. There is no doubt that those efforts have been successful. The proliferation of brand names itself encourages reliance on a particular brand by creating confusion and complexity. It is impossible for doctors to keep up with the flood of brand names. They have enough to remember without trying to be conversant with each of the estimated 7,000 brand names on the pharmaceutical market. The bulk of the information they get comes through advertising and in self-defense they come to rely on particular drugs.[40]

The pharmaceutical industry readily concedes that physicians rely on brand names. The Pharmaceutical Manufacturers Association (PMA) contends that, by using trade names, it is easier for doctors to identify the manufacturer of a product than by using generic names, and that doctors use brand names as reliable short cuts to overcome the complexity of choosing the right drug for a particular condition. But these arguments are extremely weak. First, the complexity of prescribing is in no small part *caused* by the proliferation of brand names for identical products. Second, even assuming that doctors do rely and should rely on particular firms as proof of product quality, there is an easier way: doctors could simply prescribe by generic name and specify the manufacturer whose product is to be used. Incredibly, the PMA contends that it is easier for doctors to specify the manufacturing source of drugs in their prescriptions by brand name rather than by naming the manufacturer of a particular formulation.

In fact, the sole purpose of identifying drugs by trade names is to enhance the effects of the costly promotional and advertising efforts of the drug firms. The proliferation of names only serves to create confusion for prescribing physicians, leading them to rely upon the names of products with which they have become familiar. These products are the ones that have been actively promoted by the drug companies. Drug names are thus part of the advertising program of the large firm.

This kind of promotional activity ultimately leads to increased costs for consumers. The advertising itself ultimately becomes part of the price of drugs, and, as we have seen, those expenditures are not trivial. Perhaps more importantly, the promotional system effectively prevents competition and the potential for lower prices. As Dr. Solomon Garb has observed:

. . . The use of these private product names prevents the operation of a free competitive market in drugs. Few if any physicians can keep up with all these names, let alone the prices of each product. Let us suppose that Equanil sold for 50 per cent less than Miltown. A doctor accustomed to prescribing Miltown would be unlikely to change, if he did not know that Equanil was essentially the same thing, producing exactly the same result, but cheaper.[41]

Thus, in a situation in which product comparisons are obscured by dozens of trade names, doctors cannot readily take price differentials into account. The promotional system has a further anticompetitive effect. The dominance of the trade-name system maintains the dominance of only those few firms in particular therapeutic markets that can afford the heavy promotional expenses. And, once established with a giant share of the market, smaller firms are hard-pressed to penetrate the veil of advertising. What competition there is revolves around advertising claims and trade-name repetition, and that kind of competition only popularizes particular trade names and strengthens the use of trade names in general. The system therefore makes price competition ineffective, and consumers have no choice but to pay the price unilaterally determined by the large drug firms.

Is there an alternative to the present system of drug promotion and the great market power of the large drug firms? Critics of the industry, such as Senator Gaylord Nelson, argue that drugs should be prescribed by their generic name so as to allow consumers to buy the lowest price product from their pharmacists. Since no one advocates sacrificing quality simply to reduce prices, the basic issue is whether the purity and effectiveness of pharmaceuticals is guaranteed only by the trade-name system or whether greater reliance on generic drugs can be had with no sacrifice in drug quality. And behind this issue is the question of generic equivalence—whether a drug sold under its generic name by one manufacturer is actually the same as the same chemical formulation sold under a trade name by another manufacturer. In other words, is all aspirin (or reserpine, etc.) the same? Although the answer to the question of whether the same drugs are the same may seem obvious, in fact there is considerable controversy over just this issue, and the issue is more complex than it first appears.

The drug industry maintains that there are real and important differences among drugs from different manufacturers. Their position was succinctly put by Joseph Stetler of the PMA: "You can have equivalency in terms of equal content of the drug, and you may have chemical equivalency, but this is not the whole problem. You have to determine whether or not the drugs act the same way in the patient."[42] The PMA steadfastly maintains that drugs sold under generic name do not guarantee the same biological effect in patients (level of drug in the blood, speed of absorption, and so on) or the same clinical effect (providing the desired response to the patient's illness): "Although two drug products may contain, or are supposed to contain, the same amount of the same active ingredient, this provides no assurance that both products will produce the same clinical effect in any particular patient."[43] Thus, the PMA maintains that government regulation and existing drug standards such as the United States Pharmacopeia do not give complete assurance that two products will perform equally in patients. For this assurance, it is necessary to rely on particular trade-name products.

The PMA, however, is hardly a disinterested witness. As noted above, the trade-name system is an inherent part of the lucrative system of promoting pharmaceutical sales. Thus, the doubts that the big firms shed on the quality of generic drugs can be viewed as part of that promotional system. By advancing the proposition that quality is only guaranteed by using brand names, the reliance by doctors on brand-name products is further enhanced and there is greater acceptance of trade-name products and advertising.

In fact, there is practically no evidence that generically equivalent drugs are not the same in their clinical effect—the most crucial indicator. Although the PMA put together a list of 501 references dealing with the influence of manufacturing formulation on drug effectiveness, a review by the Food and Drug Administration found that there were only two or three references that demonstrated a statistically significant lack of clinical equivalency—and in one case the differences were without any practical clinical importance.[44]

Furthermore, as the director of the National Formulary pointed out, "from a technical standpoint, there is really no such thing as complete 'drug equivalence' . . . even if we compare two batches of the very same drug product of a single firm."[45] Thus, while there may be rare instances of clinical nonequivalence between chemically identical drugs, this may also occur among different batches of the same brand-name product.

In general, then, the issue of clinical nonequivalence has been blown out of proportion and put in a misleading perspective by the big drug firms. Responsible observers do not claim that chemically identical drugs will *always* behave the same in patients and that all the evidence on the subject is conclusive. However, as the Task Force on Prescription Drugs concluded: "Lack of clinical equivalency among chemical equivalents meeting all official standards has been grossly exaggerated as a major hazard to the public health."[46] Thus, it would seem that the burden of proof is on the major firms to show that the present system of trade-name prescribing, which rewards them so handsomely, is a guarantee of anything other than their own profits and market power.

The economic stakes involved are great. While generic-named drugs are not always less expensive than brand names, they usually are—sometimes by a huge amount. For example, ampicillin is available from a generic-name manufacturer at $4.70 per hundred 250 mg. capsules. The same dosage and quantity under the brand name Polycillin is $14.85 and as Penbriten for $14.54. Penicillin G can be had for $1.45 per hundred under its generic name, but Squibb charges $10.04 per hundred for the same dosage under the name Pentids 400.[47] An even more glaring comparison can be seen by looking at the price differentials between generic- and trade-name drugs made by the same company. Despite their claims that trade-name drugs are more reliable than their generic counterparts, the major companies themselves distribute drugs under their generic names, and there are great price differences even between identical drugs sold by the same company. For example, the City of

New York paid $15.63 per thousand for 50 mg capsules of Bena-dryl purchased from Parke Davis, but paid the same company $3.00 for the same quantity of the same drug under its generic name, diphenhydramine.

Attempts at Reform

There has recently been some progress made to reform the drug promotion and prescribing system. In November 1974, the De-partment of Health, Education, and Welfare announced plans to implement a policy whereby only the lowest available price for particular drugs would be paid in such federally funded programs as Medicare and Medicaid. Under HEW plans an approved list of drugs to be prescribed by generic name would be drawn up, and the burden of proof would then be on physicians to justify any prescriptions for those drugs that specified a more expensive brand name.

Nonetheless, the individual consumer who fills his prescription at his neighborhood pharmacy is still subject to the enormous market power of the big drug firms. For those millions of consum-ers the power and policies of a few large drug corporations are manifested as a binding allocation of health dollars—from the consumer to the corporation. Just as citizens might be taxed by governments in return for health services, so too are consumers taxed by the market power of the drug firms—a tax they pay in the form of needlessly high prices on their pharmaceuticals. Just as with a government tax, this is a binding form of public policy.

Natural Resources

Up to now we have been discussing the transfer of resources in terms of private taxation and other allocations of money. Another major and increasingly important component of resource transfers is the control and allocation of natural resources by giant corpora-tions, particularly the energy conglomerates. Ironically, the less-developed countries of the world are ahead of the United States in recognizing the threat to their sovereignty posed by corporate control of their natural resources. They realize, as we do not, that the control of natural resources is an integral part of the authoritative allocation of values—in this case natural wealth. While the development of resources may be more efficiently handled by private business, this does not dispose of the problems of political power and accountability that go along with such private control. Therefore, in this section we will examine the control of energy-related natural resources as a case of public policymaking by corporations. The energy crisis in general and some of its specific manifestations, such as the gasoline shortage in 1973-74, have highlighted the impact of the looming corporate presence of the oil industry. The issue was cogently laid out in 1973 by Senator Philip Hart:

. . . This thing we call the "energy crisis" didn't creep up on the industry. Four years ago, representatives of the industry during import quota hearings of this subcommittee, laid out effectively their projections of increased demand and the shortage of domestic supply to fill it. . . .

The obvious question—and one more and more members of Congress are asking today—is how, with the increased demand forecast well in advance, these competent businessmen came up so short in supplies right now?

The most harsh critics are at least inferring that some kind of conspiracy brought on the shortages. The less harsh critics are complaining that the industry is gaining great competitive advantages by "taking advantage" of the crisis. . . .

But there is another possibility: The structure of the industry itself.[48]

Petroleum Control and Cooperation

The key word to describe the structure of the petroleum industry is *control*. In the first place, the industry is concentrated, and the degree of concentration has been increasing. The eight-firm ratio of concentration in crude oil production increased from 43.8 per cent in 1960 to 50.5 per cent in 1969. In 1969, the top four firms alone accounted for 31 per cent of all domestic crude oil production. The estimates of their control over the proven reserves of domestic oil show an even greater degree of concentration. The top four controlled 37 per cent in 1972, and the top eight controlled 64 per cent.

The degree of concentration in oil refining is even greater. In 1972 there were 129 refining companies, but 58 per cent of American refining capacity is controlled by eight companies: Exxon, Standard Oil of Indiana, Texaco, Shell, Standard of California, Mobil, Gulf, and ARCO. Of course, these figures can be read two ways. It can also be argued, and the oil companies do vigorously argue, that eight companies accounting for 51 per cent of crude oil and 58 per cent of refinery operations hardly constitutes control by a unified industry. This assertion, however, conveniently overlooks the fact that the big eight do not compete against each other in the nation as a whole. As John Blair pointed out with regard to economic concentration generally, the actual concentration in regional markets is usually higher than overall concentration, and the majors do tend to concentrate their refinery product in particular regions.[49] Furthermore, as we shall see presently, the relationships among the majors are characterized far more by cooperation than competition.

The structure of control is even more dramatically shown by the structure of the companies themselves. Here, the key word is *integration*. The majors are all completely vertically integrated, that is, they control petroleum production from the oil well through the refining process all the way to retail sales. Indeed, the pattern of economic concentration in the oil industry is even more clearly seen in light of vertical integration. The top eight oil refiners are also the top eight crude-oil producers. This integration is important because it removes potential competitive pressure to offset the anticompetitive effects of economic concentration. That is, if the refineries were highly concentrated, but in different hands than the crude production, there could still be pressure to drive domestic crude-oil prices down. Such downward pressure on prices would also benefit the smaller refiners, which are particularly disadvantaged in relation to the integrated major oil companies.

The majors vigorously defend vertical integration in the name of efficiency and good business. Thus, Exxon extolled the virtues of vertical integration in a charming little advertising allegory entitled: "What does Dinwiddy's Diner have in common with Exxon USA? Vertical integration, that's what!" In it, the man from Exxon patiently explains economic integration to the enterprising Mr. Dinwiddy, an independent restaurateur. It turns out that Dinwiddy grows his own produce, raises his own livestock for slaughter, has his own truck bring his own raw food to the diner, prepares it fresh, and so on. The Exxon man, having found a brother in commerce, points out that Dinwiddy's Diner is vertically integrated—just like Exxon: "You grow food, harvest it, transport it, process it, distribute it, and sell it. That's vertical integration." "By golly, I guess you're right," Dinwiddy exclaims. The Exxon man and Dinwiddy go on to note that lots of industries have fully integrated companies—such as steel, agribusiness food processors, and electronic companies—just like oil. Gee whiz, they seem to exclaim together, why do those nasty critics pick on the oil industry for vertical integration?[50]

Let us hope that Dinwiddy's cooking is better than his economic knowledge or his common sense. First of all, no industry is more fully integrated than oil. The majors extend all the way from raw material extraction "downstream" to retail sales of the finished product. Dinwiddy's would have been much more like Exxon if it were a chain of thousands of restaurants that not only grew their own food but also grew and controlled the supply of raw food to other restaurants as well. One suspects that Dinwiddy wouldn't be too thrilled to compete against Howard Johnson's if Dinwiddy also had to buy his own produce and meat from Howard Johnson's. Yet it is precisely this situation that prevails in the oil industry today. As the major firms proudly point out, there are about fifty integrated oil companies and a greater number of independent refiners and independent marketers of refined oil products. What is not so widely touted is that the majors not only have complete control over their own integrated operations, they also have tremendous leverage over the rest of the industry—control that they use to their considerable advantage by discriminating against the independent segment of the industry.

For example, although the big eight majors produce over half the total American refinery product, the independent gasoline marketers received only 1.6 per cent of their total purchases from these eight firms. The other big integrated firms, however, provided 43 per cent of the total purchased by the independent marketers. As the Federal Trade Commission noted: "It appears that the eight largest firms have avoided market forces in their policy of limited dealings with independent marketers."[51] Furthermore, the majors below the top eight act as "buffers" between the big eight and the independent marketers. In 1971, the second eight had net purchases of 96 million barrels of gasoline from the eight largest majors and made net sales of 91 million to the independent marketers. Thus, while the big eight do not sell to independent marketers directly, they can still impose shortages on them by reducing sales to the smaller majors.[52]

It is not only the independent marketers that must contend with having their resources controlled by the biggest majors. The independent refiners are in an equally disadvantageous position. Indeed, their position is so competitively disadvantageous that it is exceptionally difficult for potential firms to enter the refining industry—despite the demonstrated need for new refining capacity. One defining characteristic of an uncompetitive industry is high barriers to entry in that industry, and such barriers certainly exist in the oil industry as a whole. The most obvious barrier to entry is the high cost of the physical plant required. But even for firms that might be able to raise the required capital, there are other obstacles. There are substantial risks related to an independent refiner's ability to establish a dependable supply of crude oil. Independent refiners traditionally have had to depend on the majors (who are their competitors) for access to crude because the majors directly own substantial amounts of crude and also because they control most of the remainder—primarily through their control of oil pipelines. The alternative to this dependence is to enter the industry as an integrated firm, an option that raises the required capital costs to impossibly high levels. Thus, the status quo of limited competition prevails, and the majors continue to control this vital national resource.

One very important factor in maintaining dominance over the smaller firms is that the oil pipelines are mostly owned by the majors. The great pipelines are the vital conduits through which crude and refined oil flow many hundreds of miles from the wellhead to refineries and from there to various storage depots. Since they are regarded as a means of interstate product transportation, the pipeline rates are regulated by the Interstate Commerce Commission. Nonetheless, the technological requirements related to the pipelines are such that the majors owning the pipelines are still able to discriminate against independent refiners. The ICC has, during its recent history, not been noted for holding shipping rates down. On the contrary, the rates approved by the ICC may be well above the competitive cost of shipping oil. For the majors, an excessively high pipeline rate is no problem. They own the pipelines and simply transfer funds internally from one department to another. The independents, however, must incur a real cost paid out for the excessive charge. Furthermore, the majors can exclude or limit flows of crude to independent refiners by requiring minimum-size shipments, granting irregular shipping dates, limiting available storage space for oil awaiting shipment at pipeline terminals, and by other assorted delaying or harassing tactics.[53]

The Oil-Depletion Allowance

The majors' control over oil occurs not only in the absence of effective government regulation, but it actually has been enhanced by previous government policies—in particular, the oil-depletion allowance and oil-import quotas. The depletion allowance was widely regarded as simply one of the largest gifts from the Treasury to giant corporations. The allowance permitted a firm producing crude oil to deduct 22 per cent of the total revenues received from producing crude oil. The official rationale for this loophole was that the extra money created an additional incentive for oil exploration and drilling—an assumption that is completely unproven. Although all crude-oil producers got the depletion allowance, it conferred a far greater advantage on the integrated majors than on any other segment of the industry. Regardless of whether the depletion allowance created an incentive for drilling, as alleged, it in fact created an incentive for integrated oil firms to seek high crude prices (which it charges its own refineries) and low prices and profits from refinery operations. The integrated firms benefited because the depletion allowance reduced the tax on the high profits from crude production, while the refinery profits—which are kept low because of high crude prices—are not subject to the same tax deduction. Of course, the independent refiners who must buy oil from other sources were severely disadvantaged. While the depletion allowance was eliminated for the major firms in 1975, its effects on the structure of the industry linger on.

There has long been some government-imposed quota system on the sale of crude oil. Until the 1950s, a system of state quotas of crude oil prevented excess competition in the industry. This action by the states was particularly effective because Texas, Louisiana, and Oklahoma were states observing the quota system at a time when they accounted for nearly all of the domestic production. But by the late 1950s, other states and the Mideast became important sources of supply. Such an increase in supply naturally placed downward pressure on prices and, equally importantly, threatened control over the supply by the majors. Consequently, starting in 1959, mandatory federal import quotas were placed on oil and continued until 1973.

The quota policy was the most important instance of federal intervention in the petroleum industry. In order to exercise monopoly power, firms must be able to control the supply of their product. By severely limiting crude-oil imports, one of the chief sources of competitive supply was curtailed. The domestic integrated firms thus operated in an environment in which their domestic prices were protected against large-scale alternative supply sources. Thus, public policy (which they had considerable influence in establishing) enabled the majors to enjoy the effects of a tight oligopoly situation without actually having to conspire to get it.

The current absence of oil-import quotas somewhat alleviates the dependence of the independent refiners on the integrated majors and thus lessens an important barrier to entry into the refining business. In the past, however, the major oil companies have always been able to induce the federal and state governments to prevent excess supplies of crude. While it seems strange to worry about excess supply in these oil-tight times, from the standpoint of the majors any substantial amounts of crude beyond their immediate control would be considered excessive. Any potential entrant into the refining industry would therefore have to assume that the majors, with the help of the government, could easily reassert control over conditions of supply.

In short, the major firms have consolidated their market power through various exclusionary tactics. As the FTC concluded:

> These firms basically attempt to sharply limit the supply of crude available to independent refiners and refined product available to independent wholesalers and retailers. This is accomplished by minimizing use of formal market sales and thus avoiding flows of product from within the majors' vertically integrated structure to the market. It is also accomplished through control of pipelines, exchange agreements, processing agreements, and price protection coupled with price wars. An elaborate network of devices to deny independents access to product has been erected. The resulting system endangers existing independents, makes new entry difficult or impossible, and yields serious economic losses to American consumers.[54]

Competition Among the Majors

But what about competition among the majors? After all, many economists claim that, even in an oligopolistic industry, competition among giant firms can still yield benefits of efficiency, low prices to consumers, and so on. In theory and in some other industries this may be so, but it is simply not the case with oil. The industry is characterized far more by cooperation than competition. Thus, there is cooperation between the majors in owning and operating the pipelines—the very system which is a major exclusionary device employed against the independents. The bidding on government oil leases also demonstrates cooperative action. Oil leases for offshore government land are sold through presumably competitive bidding. However, oil firms commonly submit joint bids on those leases. The result is a small number of bidders for each lease. Because of the existing concentration within the industry, this practice by the petroleum giants is extremely anticompetitive and further bolsters their control over oil resources. Furthermore, with respect to Alaskan oil and gas leases, firms that were partners in joint bidding for one tract tended not to compete with their former partners in joint bidding for other tracts.[55]

To recapitulate, the oil industry operates much like a cartel with fifteen to twenty major firms. They exercise great market power and benefit from federal and state policy, enabling them to promulgate public policies of their own. The major firms clearly have enormous power over the amount and the allocation of supply. The next question is how they have used that power.

Withholding the Supplies

One important piece of evidence of the use of that power was uncovered by a survey conducted by the Consumer Subcommittee of the Senate Commerce Committee. According to subcommittee chairman Frank Moss, activities by the oil companies "made whatever scarcity there was far worse than it need have been and much more severe in some areas of the country than in others."[56] Strong evidence was uncovered of "mass withholding of winter fuels, diversions of supply from one area of the country to another, and inexcusable failures to produce"—policies all traceable to the power of the major integrated oil companies.

One of the most significant instances uncovered by the subcommittee was the severe shortage of heating oil in the upper Midwest during the winter of 1972–73. The upper Midwest is supplied by refineries on the Gulf Coast that ship oil through the Explorer pipeline connecting in Tulsa to the William Brothers pipeline, which runs up through the Midwest. The Gulf Coast refineries also connect to the huge Colonial pipeline, which runs up the East Coast. In 1972, the major refineries increased their shipments up the East Coast, through Colonial, by an amount far in excess of what would be expected based on past experience—an increase of about 9 million barrels compared to a normally expected increase of no more than 4.5 million. Furthermore, almost 2 million barrels remained under Colonial's control, undelivered, by the end of the 1972–73 winter. Additionally, during the winter 9 million barrels were delivered into tanks along the Colonial pipeline. Thus, during the winter more than 11 million barrels of home heating oil were withheld.

It was not as though this oil were not needed elsewhere. At that time there was a growing severe shortage in the Midwest—a shortage that became clear by December 1972. It was not a shortage of absolute supply; it was a shortage of delivered oil. Deliveries to the Midwest from the Explorer pipeline ran more than 20 per cent below that forecast by Explorer shippers less than twelve months earlier. As Senator Moss pointed out, "Some time between the end of 1971 and the fall of 1972, shippers who were originally going to supply the Plains States, changed their minds. How each shipper could have decided independently for this change is beyond my comprehension." At the same time, deliveries through the Colonial pipeline up the East Coast increased 50 per cent in December and 15 per cent in January 1973.

Could this misallocation have been just a fluke resulting from misjudgments by the major oil companies acting independently? This is hardly likely. Colonial is owned by ten majors, who have representatives on its board of directors. They thus have access to the projections and actual shipments of all shippers and could not have avoided knowing about the excess supply situation. Indeed, even after oil-import quotas were abolished in January 1973, freeing the East Coast to bring in all the oil it wished, supply through the Colonial increased 15 per cent over the previous year. At the same time, it could hardly have been a coincidence that the shippers to the Plains States simultaneously reduced supply or ceased sales altogether and continued to do so, even in the face of a serious shortage. In short, due to a lack of competition among the majors and what must have been a tacit understanding among them, home-heating oil that normally would hve reached the upper Midwest was withheld and channeled instead into storage tanks along the eastern seaboard.

The heating-oil episode demonstrates the misallocation of resources caused by the majors. There was probably not an absolute shortfall during the period in question. In fact, there is a good deal of artifice about the "energy crisis" in general. Oil is indeed a finite and depletable resource, but it is by no means clear that there is any shortage of available reserves in the ground. What is clear is that the price has risen dramatically. While it is convenient to put all the blame on the Organization of Oil Exporting Countries (OPEC), that cartel has been willingly served and aided by the big eight international majors. M. A. Adelman, a leading expert on petroleum economics, has argued that, through their high degree of concentration and vertical integration, the majors serve as "tax collectors" for OPEC. That is, the oil companies, not the producing nations, are the actual sellers of oil. Because of the companies' tight control over the distribution network (through vertical integration), they have no incentive to do anything but pass on to consumers the taxes levied by the OPEC countries. They do what the OPEC countries could not do alone: they control sales and prevent price undercutting that would otherwise occur.[57] They are therefore not only private governments, but private governments serving the interests of our adversaries.

Regardless of the total supply situation there has been a shortage of finished petroleum products. According to the Federal Trade Commission, several crucial factors behind the domestic supply shortage are directly traceable to the structure and policies of the American oil industry.

First, there has been a decrease in the production of domestic crude oil. Because foreign crude is high in sulfur and many refineries are unable to handle this type of crude, they must depend on supplies of domestic crude. The major firms, however, have prevented many independent refineries, particularly those in the Midwest, from obtaining sufficient supplies of "sweet" crude. As a result, such refineries have been running far below capacity. Second, the majors have behaved collectively as a classical monopolist would; that is, they have increased profits by restricting output. Their collective behavior has been characterized as cooperation rather than competition. Finally, in spite of their advanced capacity for economic forecasting, the majors did not expand refinery capacity sufficiently to meet demand. To be sure, the spokesmen for the majors blame this problem on the opposition of environmentalists and the barriers of new environmental controls. However, now that import controls have been removed, the majors have suddenly overcome those problems and have announced plans to build new refining capacities.[58]

The issues of refining capacity and oil industry forecasts are important ones and should be emphasized. As Senator Henry Jackson noted:

. . . One major cause of the shortage which should not be overlooked or minimized is the Nixon Administration's incomprehensible and foolish reliance last summer on the clearly incorrect and self-serving recommendations of major oil companies that import controls should be maintained; that refined products should not be imported; and the assurance that refinery capacity would be adequate to meet all demands for petroleum products over [the] next year.[59]

Thus, Texaco's board chairman wrote to the director of the Office of Emergency Preparedness in July 1972 opposing an increase in the import quota for finished petroleum products. He stated that there is "sufficient refining capacity available in the United States to meet anticipated demand for clean products over the balance of this year."[60] These "self-serving recommendations" of the industry raise serious questions. If industry estimates were deliberately misleading, a clearly illegal conspiracy exists. If the estimates were simply unintentional errors offered in good faith, the situation is hardly less serious. One of the basic arguments in defense of the giant integrated firms is that they offer the most efficient means of production and distribution of petroleum. But if their forecasts were so far off the mark (and this was even before the Arab oil embargo of late 1973), there is simply no rationale for society's permitting these huge aggregations of economic power to continue to control our resources with the consequent costs to important values of pluralism and economic competition.

The Trend to Energy Diversification

The problem of concentration and giantism in the oil industry is seen even more starkly in the trend to energy diversification by the major firms. Indeed, the term *oil company* is no longer adequate to label giant concentrations of resources that are properly regarded as energy conglomerates. Particularly since 1965, an increasing number of oil companies has expanded into the production of energy resources other than oil. By 1970, of the 25 largest oil companies, 18 had interests in oil shale, 11 in coal, 18 in uranium, and 7 in tar sands. The greatest area of expansion has been into coal and uranium production. Thus, as of 1972, four of the largest 15 coal companies are now oil company subsidiaries, and coal production by oil companies accounts for 20 per cent of the total output. In uranium milling, oil companies account for about 40 per cent of domestic uranium-milling capacity, and the former oil company Kerr-Mcgee is the largest single uranium producer in the country.[61]

This diversification has serious negative effects on potential competition in the energy field. While there has always been competition among different fuels, modern technology makes possible a far greater degree of substitutability (and hence competition) between fuels than was ever present before. Thus, electricity is substitutable for any fuel for most purposes. Oil shale and coal compete with crude oil and can be used to produce synthetic gas to compete with natural gas. Consumers could potentially benefit from the greater availability and downward price pressure inherent in a market with more-or-less interchangeable competing products. So it can be readily seen that increasing control under the same roof of substitutable energy resources prevents this potential from being realized.

The oil industry argues that they are simply achieving greater efficiency because they can take advantage of their existing technological expertise in exploiting other natural resources. The hunt for uranium does indeed require many of the same geological skills utilized in the oil exploration. Similarly, oil shale and tar sands can provide a hedge against future shortages of crude oil. However, as energy economist Bruce Netschert argues, the move by oil companies into the production and marketing of coal for conventional uses (as opposed to using coal as a product to manufacture synthetic fuels) bears no such relation to traditional oil company activities. While the mining of uranium might call for the expertise of oil companies, the same is not true in regard to advanced stages of uranium milling and marketing.[62]

Implications of Fuel Conglomerate Policy

The present and potential effects of the expansion of the energy conglomerates present serious problems for America's energy future. First, there is a strong upward price pressure on all fuel markets in the face of an energy crisis. While competition among fuels might act as a counterweight to exert downward price pressure, the energy conglomerate that controls competing fuels certainly has no incentive to reduce prices. Instead, a price increase in any of its fuels is very much to its advantage.

A second problem concerns the relationship of the energy conglomerates to electric utilities that are both their fuel customers and their energy competition in supplying other industries. The energy companies are unregulated (except for natural gas), and vis-à-vis electric utilities they have greater flexibility to adjust prices and profits. The energy companies also supply the fuel needed to generate electricity and can thus influence the production costs of their major competitor.

Finally, as Bruce Netschert suggests, there is a potential chilling effect on innovation:

. . . How can the public be sure, for example, that the emergence of synthetic fuels industries will occur at the pace which economic circumstances would, under free market forces, dictate? It could well be that the self-interest of certain companies with dominant positions, if not of the industry as a whole, would call for delaying the inauguration of a synthetic fuel industry in order to protect existing investments in crude oil and natural gas.[63]

In short, despite the self-serving claims of greater efficiency and a superior capacity to satisfy the nation's energy needs, excessive conglomeration has all the potential for creating even greater inefficiencies and misallocations of resources. The real impact of energy conglomeration is horizontal integration—controlling more and more potential competitors. Combined with vertical integration, this phenomenon leads to a degree of control over our energy resources that in other nations would be allowed only for the government. In fact, the degree of control exercised by the giants of the oil industry readily qualifies them as private governments—

governments that are making public policy by cooperatively allocating energy resources. Even if their policies were entirely efficient and benevolent, such unified control is fundamentally perilous to democratic values. But what is even worse, that power has been exercised in such a way as to exacerbate shortages and increase prices for consumers throughout the United States. Thus, the economic problems inherent in the energy crisis can also be traced to the political problem inherent in a system of allowing private governments to formulate and carry out public policy.

The Beneficiaries

The other side of resource transfers of money concerns the question of *to whom* the resources are transferred. There is a definite redistributive resource transfer whereby money is allocated to top executives of giant corporations. When members of congress raised their own pay and that of top bureaucrats in 1975 by only 5 per cent, there were anguished howls from many taxpayers and critics, who rightly saw this money coming out of their own pockets. Yet, in many ways compensation of major corporation executives is also a form of taxation on the public. It is figured in as a normal business expense and is thus passed along in prices. It is ultimately the retail consumers of all products, from toasters to automobiles, who are assessed a tax to pay these salaries. Of course, these privately levied taxes are quite small and represent only a fraction of product costs.[64] Nonetheless, to the fortunate executives, this represents a significant resource transfer. For example, despite their firms' dismal record in foreseeing the nation's urban transportation needs, the board chairmen of the big three auto firms had to struggle along on an average compensation of $833,000 in 1973.[65]

The creation of such incredible disparities of wealth in society must be recognized as a public policy—one formulated by corporate governments and financed through taxation on customers and on stockholders.[66] That such payments result from a private assessment is evident from several factors. First, the amounts involved are so exorbitant as to far surpass any reasonable incentive to attain and perform well in the job. Second, in many instances executive compensation continues to rise even when corporate income remains static or declines.[67] Finally, the salaries are, in effect, set by those who receive them. Although the boards of directors formally approve salaries and are themselves chosen by the stockholders, the theory of stockholder control was shown to be a myth at least as far back as the famous work of Berle and Means.[68] In summary, top-level executive compensation represents a public policy of subsidy to an economic elite financed by a system of taxation on consumers and shareholders. The system is similar to any other subsidy. Only the identity of the policymakers is different.

Notes

1. U.S. Bureau of the Census, *Statistical Abstract of the United States: 1974* (Washington, D.C., 1974), Table 799, p. 487.
2. John M. Blair, *Economic Concentration: Structure, Behavior and Public Policy* (New York: Harcourt Brace Jovanovich, 1972), pp. 13–14.
3. U.S. Federal Trade Commission, Staff Report, *Economic Report on Corporate Mergers* (Washington, D.C., 1969), p. 61.
4. Ibid., p. 43.
5. Ibid., p. 47.
6. Ibid., p. 192.
7. Ibid, p. 118.
8. Sidney Davidson *et al.*, *An Income Approach to Accounting Theory* (Englewood Cliffs, N.J.: Prentice-Hall, 1964), p. 564.
9. "Conglomerate Earnings: Credibility Gap," *Wall Street Journal*, July 24, 1969, p. 16.
10. FTC *Report on Corporate Mergers*, p. 142–43.
11. U.S. Congress, Senate, Committee on the Judiciary, *Economic Concentration*, hearings before the Subcommittee on Antitrust and Monopoly, 91st Congress (1969–70), pt. 8, p. 4890.
12. William Shepherd, *Market Power and Economic Welfare* (New York: Random House, 1970), pp. 3–4.
13. Thurmond Arnold, *The Folklore of Capitalism* (New Haven: Yale University Press, 1937), p. 263.
14. Gardiner Means, *Pricing Power and the Public Interest: A Study Based on Steel* (New York: Harper & Brothers, 1962), p. 20.
15. U.S. Congress, Senate, Committee on the Judiciary, *Administered*

Prices, Steel, Report of the Subcommittee on Antitrust and Monopoly, 85th Congress, 1st sess. (1958), pt. 8, pp. 18–22.

16. Ibid., p. 14–15.
17. Means, *Pricing Power*, p. 43.
18. U.S. Congress, Senate, Committee on the Judiciary, *Administered Prices*, hearings before the Subcommittee on Antitrust and Monopoly, 85th Congress, 1st sess. (1957), p. 214.
19. See, for example, J. Fred Weston and Stanley I. Ornstein, eds., *The Impact of Large Firms on the U.S. Economy* (Lexington, Mass.: D.C. Heath, 1973).
20. U.S. Congress, Senate, Select Committee on Small Business, *Competitive Problems in the Drug Industry*, hearings before the Subcommittee on Monopoly, 90th Congress, 1st sess. (1967), pt. 4, p. 1416. (Subsequently referred to as *Drug Industry Hearings*.)
21. *Drug Industry Hearings*, statement of Dr. Leonard Schifrin, pt. 5, pp. 1893–94.
22. William S. Comanor, "Research and Competitive Product Differentiation in the Pharmaceutical Industry in the United States," *Econometica* 31 (November 1964), p. 380.
23. *Washington Post*, June 19, 1965, p. 3.
24. Hugh Douglas Walker, *Market Power and Price Levels in the Ethical Drug Industry* (Bloomington: Indiana University Press, 1971), p. 25.
25. Ibid., p. 26.
26. *Drug Industry Hearings*, pt. 3, p. 991.
27. Statement of Senator Gaylord Nelson, *Congressional Record*, 93rd Congress, 1st sess. (1972), July 9, 1973, pp. S12781–82.
28. *Drug Industry Hearings*, pt. 2, p. 645.
29. Ibid., pt. 5, pp. 1822–23.
30. Milton Silverman and Philip Lee, *Pills, Profits, and Politics* (Berkeley: University of California Press, 1974), p. 51.
31. *Drug Industry Hearings*, pt. 5, p. 2050.
32. Ibid., statement of W. H. Conzen, pt. 2, p. 662.
33. Ibid., pt. 3, pp. 911–12.
34. Ibid., Summary, p. 31.
35. Silverman and Lee, *Pills, Profits*, pp. 54–55.
36. *Drug Industry Hearings*, pt. 5, p. 1932.
37. United States Congress, Senate, Select Committee on Small Business, *Task Force on Prescription Drugs: Report and Recommendations*, prepared by the U.S. Department of Health, Education, and Welfare (Washington, D.C., 1968), p. 19.
39. *Drug Industry Hearings*, statement of Dr. William Comaner, pt. 5, p. 2055.
40. Ibid., statement of Dr. Solomon Garb, pt. 2, p. 530–31.

41. Ibid., pt. 2, p. 526.
42. Ibid., pt. 4, p. 1367.
43. Ibid.
44. Ibid., statement of Dr. Philip R. Lee, Assistant Secretary for Health and Scientific Affairs, Department of Health, Education, and Welfare, pt. 9, p. 3726.
45. Ibid., statement of Dr. Edward Feldman, pt. 1, p. 413.
46. *Drug Task Force Report*, p. 27.
47. These are all 1973 wholesale prices compiled from industry price lists. Statement of Senator Gaylord Nelson, *Congressional Record*, 93rd. Congress, 1st sess. (1972), June 11, 1973, pp. S10820–23.
48. U.S. Congress, Senate, Committee on the Judiciary, *Competition in the Energy Industry (Gasoline and Fuel Oil)*, hearings before the Subcommittee on Antitrust and Monopoly, 93rd Congress, 1st sess. (1973), p. 2.
49. Blair, *Economic Concentration*, pp. 13–14.
50. *Exxon USA*, Third Quarter, 1974, pp. 8–10.
51. U.S. Federal Trade Commission, *Investigation of the Petroleum Industry*, prepared for the Permanent Subcommittee on Investigations, Committee on Government Operations, U.S. Senate, 93rd Congress, 1st sess. (1973), p. 10.
52. Ibid.
53. Ibid.
54. Ibid.
55. Walter J. Mead, "The Competitive Significance of Joint Venture," *Antitrust Bulletin* 12 (Fall 1967), pp. 841–46.
56. U.S. Congress, Senate, Interior and Insular Affairs Committee, *Market Performance and Competition in the Petroleum Industry*, hearings, 93rd Congress, 2nd sess. (1973), pp. 5–15. The following account is based on Senator Moss' findings.
57. M. A. Adelman, "Is the Oil Shortage Real? Oil Companies as OPEC Tax Collectors," *Foreign Policy* 9 (Winter 1972–73), pp. 69–107.
58. FTC *Report on the Petroleum Industry*, pp. 38–39.
59. Jackson letter to Lewis Engman, chairman, Federal Trade Commission, May 31, 1973, in FTC *Report on the Petroleum Industry*, p. v.
60. Ibid.
61. Bruce Netschert, "The Energy Company: A Monopoly Trend in the Energy Markets," in *The Energy Crisis*, Richard S. Lewis and Bernard I. Spinrad, eds. (Chicago: Educational Foundation for Nuclear Science, 1972), pp. 73–74.
62. Ibid., p. 75.
63. Ibid.
64. In the years 1947 to 1956, compensation of officers and directors of

U.S. Steel ranged from 1.2 to 2.4 per cent of net income. For Bethlehem Steel the range was higher—from 2.8 to 4.3 per cent. *Administered Prices Report*, pp. 109–110.

65. Based on figures in *Business Week*, May 4, 1974, p. 59.
66. Stockholders come out considerably worse than customers. Compensation for officers and board members ranged from 3 to 13 per cent of dividends in the steel industry. *Administered Prices Report*, pp. 109–10.
67. Ibid., p. 109.
68. Adolf A. Berle, Jr. and Gardiner C. Means, *The Modern Corporation and Private Property* (New York, 1932, 1968).

7
Corporate Regulatory Politics

Regulatory policies involve the direct control of conduct. The regulatory organization places limits on the freedom of regulated individuals and groups. In the context of public governments, regulation is a widespread and well-known activity. For example, the Civil Aeronautics Board and the Interstate Commerce Commission ultimately determine the prices charged by the segments of the transportation industry under their control—and the agencies even determine who may enter the industry. Regulatory agencies such as the Consumer Product Safety Commission also determine the form in which certain products may be sold and may even ban certain products outright. While there are immediate and direct relationships between regulator and regulated, there is also a wider range of indirect, societywide impacts inherent in those relationships. That is, the regulatory agency, backed up by its coercive power, has an immediate and direct impact on an industry when the agency mandates the conditions under which firms can sell their products and services. But there is also a regulatory effect on consumers who can buy those products and services only as offered under the terms of the regulatory mandate. For example, the airlines are clearly regulated when they have to go to the CAB for approval of their fares and routes. But airline passengers (and potential passengers) are thereby also regulated; they must pay what the CAB decides and have a choice of airlines completely limited to those approved by the regulatory agency.

As we have seen in Chapter 4, regulation does not proceed in a political vacuum. Regulation is a two-way process in which the regulators and the regulated each try to control the other's behavior; and regulatory outcomes are usually heavily influenced by the regulated industries. Indeed, as Marver Bernstein notes: "In the light of the concept of private government, regulation becomes a struggle between public and private governments to write the rules of conduct for regulated industries and industrial practices."[1] Although Bernstein was addressing himself to the influence of private governments in initiating and implementing policies *through* the regulatory agencies, the same principle applies even in the absence of decisions being made by regulatory agencies and even in industries that are not heavily regulated by the government. The fact is that, in concentrated industries, binding regulations are commonly in force. Sometimes these regulations originate with the federal or state governments—with varying amounts of influence from the regulated industries. But these regulations may also be unilaterally imposed by the leading corporations in nominally unregulated industries.

Drawing from the continuum of public policy (see p. 112), there is also a continuum of the regulatory policy category. It runs from regulation promulgated by the government to regulation promulgated by industries free of government restraint. Thus, regulatory policy toward a particular industry may contain a mix of particular regulatory decisions independently laid down by government agencies and corporations. Furthermore, corporate regulatory decisions have a direct impact on the targets of regulation and an indirect impact on a much wider public. As with resource transfer policy, regulatory policies of corporations are backed by market power in concentrated industries.

Regulating Business by Business

While much of this book concerns the effects of corporate power on the average citizen, it must also be emphasized that a great deal of that power is directed toward small business, and that this, too, is a significant problem. A widespread type of private regulatory policy with significant impacts on small business and consumers is the framework established by manufacturers or parent corporations with retail distributors or franchise holders. This regulatory framework is particularly pervasive in the automobile industry. Until the passage of the Automobile Dealers Franchise Act (1956), auto manufacturers had complete control over their dealers and could terminate their franchises at will. Exhibiting one of the basic criteria of a government, they even had their own judicial system for adjudicating disputes between dealers and manufacturers. Needless to say, the manufacturers usually prevailed—a problem that led to the passage of the 1956 legislation. The auto manufacturers still have close control over their dealers, however; according to the representative of one large dealers association, the 1956 act has done little to lessen the regulatory power of the manufacturers. The automobile distribution system is still rigidly controlled by a regulatory-type framework.[2]

The heart of the system is the manufacturers' ability to determine who may become an automobile dealer. Unlike other retail businesses, the auto dealer must get a franchise from a manufacturer in order to sell automobiles. Usually, because a dealership is a highly lucrative business, the prospective dealer is in a highly unequal position vis-à-vis the manufacturer. The latter can choose from hundreds of likely prospects in granting franchises, but the prospective dealer can apply to only four domestic manufacturers. Furthermore, it is rare for a prospective entrant to have sufficient capital to acquire a dealership on his own. For the fortunate dealer who gains a franchise this is no problem—the manufacturer supplies needed capital and gains a financial interest in the dealership. The manufacturer thus selects dealers, partially capitalizes them, and imposes on the relationship a highly restrictive franchise agreement.

In restricting entry into the retail end of the business, auto manufacturers function as entry-controlling regulatory agencies such as the FCC and the ICC. Similarly, they impose a series of operating requirements on dealers who are allowed to go into business. These rules include the exclusive use of certain replacement parts supplied by the manufacturer, minimum sales quotas, and the disclosure to manufacturers of highly detailed financial information. And, as in some industries regulated by government, franchisees cannot sell their franchise except to an approved buyer. If the manufacturer has a financial investment in the dealership (an increasing trend), it also can exercise voting control. If we make the reasonable assumption that the retail selling of cars is a business distinct from their manufacture, automakers are in the enviable position of being able to control entry into and otherwise regulate another entire industry. This ability is normally, and correctly, thought of as public policy and is formulated and executed by a government. In this case, however, the "government" is an automobile manufacturer.

Business Regulatory Policies and the Consumer

The regulatory policies of corporations also have a variety of direct and indirect effects on consumers, particularly with regard to the conditions under which consumers are able to buy particular products of concentrated industries. Again, the auto industry is a good illustration. It is no secret that consumers generally are unhappy with the quality of new cars and of automobile repairs and service. Virginia Knauer, consumer adviser to President Ford, reported that problems with automobiles were the most frequent consumer complaint. Consumer complaints run the gamut from manufacturing defects to the inability of consumers to get consistently adequate service. It must be emphasized that these problems are not merely the normal problems inevitable with any complex machine or even the result of chronically dishonest repairmen. Rather, they result from the intentional policies of the automobile manufacturers—policies that make high-quality products and good service virtually impossible.

When a consumer buys a car, he or she may have the illusion that one is able to bargain with the dealer and that the sale is the result of a compromise reached by two equal bargainers. In fact, all that is being bargained about is the price of the car. All other conditions of the sales contract—delivery date, penalties to be applied if the car is unfit, warranties, or future service—are imposed on the buyer in a take-it-or-leave-it fashion. Thus the so-called sales contract is a contract only in the loosest terms. In legal terms, it is a contract of adhesion: it is binding on the customer but, in effect, not very binding on the manufacturer, who has designed it to be as difficult as possible to enforce against himself and who simply imposes it as a set of terms for the buyer. Even if an automobile literally falls apart before the customer has driven a mile away from the dealership, the customer may have to go through expensive and burdensome litigation in order to get redress.

Consumers and Car Warranties

The problems are seen first in the warranty situation. The Federal Trade Commission contended that the automobile industry has been promising the public defect-free cars through sales promotions, advertisements, and, most importantly, warranties.[3] For example, a 1962 advertisement for Chrysler Corporation cars proclaimed: "NOW! 5-year/50,000 MILE WARRANTY! Another first for Chrysler! Engineering leadership has resulted in an extended warranty on the power-train of the 1963 Chryslers." Another ad, in *Fortune* magazine, asserted that the new warranty was "the result of the highest engineering and production standards, combined to give . . . another great auto 'first.'" In fact, the new warranties were Chrysler's response to its own sagging sales and declining share of the market. Chrysler did provide extended protection of those parts of the car that almost never break down anyway; but the warranty was primarily a sales device—an effective one as Chrysler sales shot up 40 per cent the following year. Moreover, the FTC concluded that

. . . the car buyer has been led down a primrose path. With the possible exception of the initial expansion of coverage to 1 year/12,000 miles, warranty extensions have had no correlation with quality or developments in engineering and manufacturing. A defect-free car has not been provided. The warranty has simply been used as a gimmick to sell cars.[4]

Automotive warranties are part of the profitable product-regulation policies of the manufacturers. This can be seen in several aspects of the warranty system. First, cars are far from being defect-free, as promised. There are problems of poor design and even poorer quality control. A study of quality control on the assembly line by the Roscoe Pound American Trial Lawyers Foundation found that "often, less than one-tenth of 1 per cent of the component parts are even spot checked by inspectors."[5] Furthermore, defects that result from this carelessness are often not corrected by the car dealer's predelivery inspection. Dealers receive an inadequate allowance from manufacturers, and they tend to give a car only a cursory inspection before turning it over to the customer. They may give it no preparation at all except for a car wash. This chain of indifference is clearly reflected in the experience of car buyers. A survey of members of an association of executives responsible for company-owned cars reported that approximately 30 per cent of their autos required some warranty-covered repairs—half of which were attributed to poor predelivery preparation. A Consumers Union survey found that 80 per cent of the respondents reported some warranty work, and about one-third of new cars were delivered in an unsatisfactory condition.[6] Thus, the implied promise of defect-free cars has not been kept. But what about the warranty itself? Does it provide a remedy for the consumer?

Although warranty coverage expanded during the 1960s in terms of the number of miles and years of ownership covered, in the 1970s the 5-year/50,000-mile warranty is a thing of the past, and all the manufacturers have retrenched. Although the length of coverage was heralded as the major factor in warranty coverage, it was actually rather trivial. In fact, the usual automobile warranty *limits* rather than expands the rights of consumers vis-à-vis the automakers. If there were no express warranties issued, the purchasers of cars would be protected by the "implied warranty of merchantability" of the Uniform Commercial Code operative in 49 states. The code provides for standards of fitness that products must meet—expansive standards that would provide a high measure of protection. Automobile warranties that consumers are forced to accept are, however, legal documents that substitute a highly conditioned and limited express warranty for the UCC implied warranty of merchantability. Even though current warranties are shorter and simpler, auto warranties are still devoted entirely to limiting the manufacturers' and dealers' liability.

But surely, it might be objected, the warranty provides some protection. After all, nearly everyone has had some warranty service on his automobile. Unfortunately, here again, the consumer is systematically shortchanged. Instances of consumers being cheated are so common that there are even terms insiders use to describe the variety of swindles. There is, for example, the "wall job" whereby the car is parked next to a wall—where it stays unrepaired; there is the "sunbath" treatment whereby the customer's car is parked in the sun until it is returned to him. Although car manufacturers claim that warranty problems are not serious and not the subject of much consumer complaint, a survey by the National Association of Fleet Administrators belies that claim. It was found that only 53 per cent of warranty work was handled satisfactorily and that 26 per cent of all warranty work required repeat visits.[7]

But what does this have to do with corporate power? We are so accustomed to the image of the shady car dealer or repair man that terms such as *used-car dealer* are loaded with derogatory images. However, while there is certainly a fair number of dishonest people in the automobile service business, it is the enormous market power of the manufacturers over the dealers that creates poor service on warranties and routine repairs. Indeed, a 1970 study by William Leonard and Marvin Weber asserted that the relationship between automakers and dealers was tinged by "criminogenic market forces." They argue that

. . . what appears to the public as unethical or criminal behavior on the part of dealers and mechanics represents "conditioned" crime, or crime stimulated by conditions over which the dealer or mechanic has but little control. Perhaps a better phrase would be "coerced" crime since it results from the coercion of strong corporations whose officers can utilize the concentrated market power of their companies to bend dealer and mechanic to serve company objectives."[8]

Automaker Emphasis on Sales

A major factor inducing auto dealers to provide poor service on warranty and other repairs is the automakers' heavy emphasis on sales. While it may seem strange to criticize auto manufacturers for encouraging sales, the point to remember is that sales are stressed far more than service and *at the expense of service*. Dealers may lose their franchise for not meeting high sales quotas, but they almost never face a similar threat for poor service. As Betty Furness has stated, the manufacturers regard service as an "unwanted step-child." One economist who has studied the automobile business extensively stated: "The realities of the situation are that Detroit's income derives largely from the sale of automobiles to dealers and only slightly from dealers' service to customers. . . . Consequently, the manufacturer looks to the dealer principally for sales; and service becomes—to use an industry expression—a 'necessary evil.' "[9]

Thus, all the incentives offered the dealers are for sales, not service. While manufacturers blithely claim that their dealers must offer good service in order to induce customers to buy future cars of the same make, in fact just the opposite is true. Poor service hastens the time when the consumers must buy another car. Since there are so few manufacturers, it does not matter if the disgruntled Chevrolet owner buys a Ford as his next car. Another motorist, angry at his Ford dealership, will switch to Chevrolet. The vice-president for marketing of Ford Motor Company admitted as much: "At the moment the automobile industry is trading dissatisfied customers."[10]

While the emphasis on sales hurts all phases of automobile service, it most directly affects warranty service. When a customer gets a defect repaired under warranty, the auto dealer making the repair is reimbursed from the manufacturer. However, all manufacturers maintain a rate schedule that pays the dealers less than they make doing regular repair; dealers are also allowed a smaller profit on parts than they get from regular service. Although dealers are usually reluctant to admit that the service they offer is inadequate, the policies imposed on them by the manufacturers inevitably lead to the consumer being the big loser. As stated by the National Automobile Dealers Association:

. . . Inevitably undercompensation by the manufacturer must lead to some degree of limitation on the dealer's ability to perform warranty work. . . . This limitation may be expressed in one of two ways. Either work will not be performed completely up to the standards of cash work, or some form of avoidance of warranty work will be practiced.[11]

Dealers also complain they are not given a sufficient allowance from manufacturers for preparation of cars for delivery. Thus, the lack of quality control on the assembly line is usually not remedied by the dealer but is passed along to the consumer, necessitating warranty work, which is also inadequate—all due to the policies imposed by the giant automobile corporations.

Product Manipulation

Regulatory policy established through corporate market power also includes *product manipulation*—regulating consumer choice by manipulating and limiting product availability. Products can be made available only in certain forms, sold only when other products are purchased, or manufactured in such a way that consumers will soon have to buy additional products from the manufacturer in order to keep the original investment working.

Once again, the automobile industry provides concrete illustrations of policymaking power manifested in the inability of consumers to buy a nonfragile car. Until very recently, automobiles were designed as though they were intended to be mounted on a pedestal rather than driven in traffic. The Insurance Institute for Highway Safety conducted crash tests on 1969 model cars and found that the average damage sustained by four full-sized sedans crashed against a barrier cost $200.28 to repair. The speed was five miles per hour, roughly the speed of a man walking. At ten miles per hour the crash damage jumped up to $652.46.[12] A basic problem was that the bumpers, rigidly attached to the automobile body, were worse than useless—not only did they not protect the car, but they caused part of the damage. Finally, in 1973, automobiles were equipped with front and rear bumpers that could sustain minor impacts without crumbling. But it should be emphasized that functional bumpers were forced on the auto manufacturers by federal regulation. Automakers abandoned their decorative and expensive-to-replace bumpers only under the coercion of law, although the technology had been in existence for a long time. In fact, automobiles in the 1920s and 1930s had sturdier functional bumpers than cars in the 1960s. The auto companies simply deprived the consumer of choice in the later cars and imposed the costs on drivers through the higher insurance rates needed to pay for damage to flimsy cars. Federal automobile bumper standards corrected only one aspect of automobile flimsiness, however. Automakers still utilize vast expanses of difficult and expensive-to-repair sheet metal as well as easily damaged steering and control mechanisms.

But why would the automobile companies do anything but build the finest quality cars they could? After all, their advertising proudly points out all the quality features in their products. Automobile executives repeatedly claim that they must build durable cars to gain customer acceptance. Clearly one factor is cost. No one seriously proposes that cars must be built that would sustain *no* damage in a crash. Even if such a vehicle were possible, its cost would be prohibitive. But there is a great difference between no damage and excessive damage, and the basic reason why cars are built to sustain excessive damage is found in the market for replacement parts. Unlike maintenance parts such as spark plugs and air filters, major replacement parts (fenders, door panels, and so on) must be purchased from manufacturers. Although no separate profit figures are available for parts, the cost of replacement parts suggests that the profits must be substantial. For example, a 1969 Chevrolet Impala had a list price of about $3,500. However, it would cost $7,500 to buy all the parts that go into that car—and that would be completely unassembled! The labor to assemble them would be at least another $7,500 for a total cost of $15,000, or more than four times the list price of the car.[13] Thus, auto manufacturers realize enormous markups on parts sold to dealers for replacement, and, because there is no competitive market, consumers have no alternative source of these parts. In 1976, the Federal Trade Commission charged General Motors with monopolizing the replacement parts business, but it will probably be years before the case is settled.

The warranty and replacement-parts situations illustrate the binding policies of product manipulation possible in a highly concentrated industry. Automobiles in most sections of the country are virtual necessities. Not only is the price administered by the manufacturers in the first instance, but the conditions of sale and continued performance of the product are also forcefully and unilaterally imposed by the manufacturers. The economic concentration of the industry combines with the essential role of automobiles in our transportation system to render this consumer problem a political problem of corporate public policy.

A Policy Mix: The Drug Industry

As we argued earlier in this chapter, regulatory policy frequently results from a mix of governmental and nongovernmental decisions. Furthermore, the precise mixture may change over time. Thus, policy regarding automobile safety was the almost-exclusive province of the automobile industry until federal legislation in 1966 made it a subject of government public policy; after that time policy resulted from both government and industry decisions, with the government being the dominant partner. In the previous chapter, the system of administered pricing in the prescription drug industry was discussed. Of equal importance is the regulatory framework surrounding the drug-prescribing system.

The outer bounds of the system are set by the Food and Drug Administration, which is responsible for clearing new drugs for safety and efficacy. The FDA also has authority over specific therapeutic claims and warnings about side-effects in prescription-drug advertising and in the package inserts accompanying drugs—both of which, incidentally, the consumer rarely sees. But FDA regulation in this area is not comprehensive or complete. Drug manufacturers are required only to make no misrepresentations about the use and effects of their products; they need not go beyond these minimum regulations and tell the whole truth—to give, for example, data on comparative price and efficacy. It may appear to strain credulity to expect business firms to tell their customers that substitute products may be better and cheaper, but we raise this issue only to emphasize that government requires manufacturers to supply very little information. In terms of public policy, the disclosure of certain information *is* affected by the decisions of a federal agency—the Food and Drug Administration—but the bulk of the decisions about information is left to the industry. Thus, the overall regulatory system is composed of a public-private mix, and it is therefore relevant to assess the quality of pharmaceutical information.

In theory, the physician is very knowledgeable about all facets of prescribing medications—especially their relative effectiveness for various illnesses. In practice, the physician's objective and scientific sources of information are greatly limited. There is general consensus that medical school training on drug therapy is inadequate; in any case, the rapid proliferation of new products would quickly outdate specific medical-school drug education. There are postgraduate programs to keep physicians abreast of new developments in pharmacology, but these programs are few in number and reach only a small fraction of practicing physicians. While many large public hospitals maintain their own drug formularies to provide objective information on the drugs of choice for particular conditions, the average physician in private practice has no comparable source. In fact, as Dr. Philip Lee, the former Assistant Secretary for Health and Scientific Affairs of the Department of Health, Education, and Welfare, pointed out: "Most of the drug information received by practicing physicians comes from the advertising and promotional activities of drug companies—from printed and graphic advertisements and from drug salesmen known as detail men."[14] So, in terms of the actual regulated drug-information system, industry sources dominate. While such a situation is not necessarily bad, the dominance of self-interested purveyors of information in so crucial an area of health policy is nonetheless fraught with hazard. These hazards are clearly seen when we examine the specific sources and quality of information provided to physicians.

One of the most well-known and widely used sources is the *Physician's Desk Reference*. It is distributed free of charge to doctors, and it includes listings of drugs from most of the large manufacturers, together with their uses and side-effects. However, this publication is financed by the drug firms that buy space in it to list their drugs. It is actually a series of advertisements—often useful and informative advertisements, but advertisements nonetheless. Furthermore, the *Physician's Desk Reference* does not give comparative cost information for the doctor who might want to be cost-conscious on behalf of his patients; nor, of course, does it provide any comparative critical information about the relative efficacy of drugs. In the view of Dr. Harry Williams, professor of pharmacology at the Emory University School of Medicine, the *PDR* is typical of industry-supplied information in that it lacks comparative data. With regard to the information available to doctors, Dr. Williams further noted: "It might be said that the physician has available to him the scientific literature and can make his judgment about the relative value of drugs from the literature. This is just not so—the physician does not have the time."[15]

Beyond listings in the *Physician's Desk Reference,* the drug industry shapes the information reaching the physician through even more explicitly commercial means. There are, of course, advertisements in professional journals such as the *Journal of the American Medical Association,* as well as ads taken in so-called "throwaway" magazines provided free to physicians for the purpose of pushing commercial messages. Until 1955, the American Medical Association required that claims made in the advertisements carried in its *Journal* had to be cleared by the Association's Council on Drugs. However, that requirement was dropped when the *Journal* began losing a good deal of advertising revenue to journals that didn't observe that nicety. Thus, for all practical purposes, organized medicine does not intercede in the policy system of providing pharmaceutical information.

A more direct source of information consists of the drug salesmen, known as detail men, representing the individual pharmaceutical firms. As salesmen with a product to push, they are hardly unbiased sources of information. Beyond that problem, their education and training (most have no formal education in pharmacology or medicine) hardly qualify them to provide therapeutic guidance to physicians. Furthermore, unlike written advertising, the kind of representations that detail men make to physicians cannot be monitored or regulated. Indeed, there have been instances in which detail men, either on their own or under direction from their companies, have exaggerated the worth of their products or even downplayed side-effect hazards.

While some observers minimize the effect of drug advertisements, there is considerable evidence that promotional materials have a major impact on physicians' medical decisions. In the first place, it is hardly likely that drug companies would spend vast sums on advertising were they not getting a good return on that investment. More significantly, many surveys have shown that most doctors are first induced to prescribe a new drug not by a scientific report but by advertisements or the presentations of detail men.[16] According to a study in California carried out for the Social Security Administration, there was a dramatic difference in attitude toward the use of mood-altering drugs (tranquilizers or antidepressants), depending on the physician's source of information. Physicians who relied primarily on detail men were more likely to accept the use of mood-altering drugs in social situations as being legitimate and to believe that they should not be thought of only as a last resort. On the other hand, physicians who preferred medical journals as primary information sources were more reluctant to accept drug use as a legitimate treatment for mood disturbances resulting from the stresses of everyday living. The latter group were less likely to prescribe tranquilizers or amphetamines to relieve common stress.[17]

A major policy problem resulting from the drug promotion system is that promotional activities can lead to excessive use of drugs for minor conditions. As indicated in the example above, this phenomenon is particularly true with regard to tranquilizer advertisements that stress the use of drugs for what are really minor adjustment problems. The enormous emphasis on peddling pills for every problem is seen strikingly in the drug companies' own advertising copy. Thus, the tranquilizer Librium was promoted for use by young women in college who faced the following situations:

. . . today's changing morality and the possible consequences that her new freedom may provoke acute feelings of insecurity. Her newly stimulated intellectual curiosity may make her more sensitive to and apprehensive about unstable national and world conditions. Exposure to new friends and other influences may force her to re-evaluate herself and her goals. She may be excessively concerned over competition—both male and female—for top grades; unrealistic parental expectations may further increase emotional tension. The new college student may be afflicted by a sense of lost identity in a strange environment.[18]

It would be hard to find a college student in the country who wouldn't qualify under these criteria for tranquilizers. The Sandoz company, in a similar vein, promoted its tranquilizer Serentil "for anxiety which comes from not fitting in—the newcomer in town who can't make friends and the organization man who can't adjust to altered status with his company, the woman who can't get along with her new daughter-in-law." What is even more disturbing than the rather cavalier "pill for every problem" orientation of such advertisements is the fact that, in sound medical practice, tranquilizers such as Serentil should be intended only for patients suffering from *severe* anxiety and tension and usage should be closely monitored by a physician. Indeed, so potent are such drugs that the Food and Drug Administration required the Sandoz company to run corrective ads stating that Serentil was approved only for serious psychiatric disorders and should not be used for commonplace problems. But, as with false advertising generally, the advertisements presumably had an impact and an effect that lingers on.

Beyond the immediate impact on medical practice from this stress on mood-altering drugs, there is also a more diffuse effect on society as the drug firms lend their own considerable weight to the drug culture of the young. As Dr. Mitchell Rosenthal, director of the Phoenix Programs in New York City, stated:

. . . We are all advised in the advertisements sponsored by the drug companies not to suffer pain or discomfort, however mild, for more than a few seconds. . . . Yet we scold our young people when they do not wish to "face reality" and turn to drugs.[19]

Nor is this mere supposition. Several studies have shown a strong positive relationship between the use of mood-altering prescription drugs by parents and the use of illicit drugs by their children. In families in which parents use tranquilizers or amphetamines, there is a far greater likelihood that children will use illicit drugs such as LSD, marijuana, and heroin.[20]

In summary, the heavy promotional activities of the major drug firms should be regarded as regulatory policy to the extent that the commercially supplied information is substituted for impartial scientific data. The outer bounds of the information system are set by the Food and Drug Administration, but within those bounds, corporation-made policy prevails. Furthermore, this situation has led to serious problems of drug abuse—both with regard to legally prescribed drugs and to use of illegal drugs by children and teenagers. Thus, policymaking power is not only utilized by the drug firms, but it is utilized irresponsibly.

The Environment and Regulation of Social Costs

Private regulative policy also involves all those activities that promote or adversely affect individual welfare—binding allocations *or deprivations* of values such as life, health, and pleasure. This includes governmental policies such as food and drug regulation, occupational·safety, pollution control, and the like. Let us take the case of pollution control.

It is clearly public policy when a government requires the installation of various pollution-abatement devices, either in industrial plants or in automobiles. It is also public regulatory policy when an industry unilaterally decides to install or *not to install* such devices. This is precisely what happened in the case of the automobile industry. There was not even the problem of a "nondecision": the four auto manufacturers formulated a public policy of not developing and installing pollution-abatement devices. In 1955, they agreed to a cross-licensing arrangement on antipollution devices. As later adduced by a federal grand jury, the arrangement consisted of agreements: (1) not to publicize competitively any solution to the problem of automobile emissions; (2) to adopt a uniform date for the announcement of the discovery of any control device; and (3) to install such devices only on an agreed date.[21]

The industry enjoyed a virtual monopoly of policymaking in this area until 1964, when California approved four emission-control devices and, in accord with a previous California law, required the installation of qualifying devices on all 1966 cars sold in the state. Although the Automobile Manufacturers Association in February 1964 had stated that the devices would not be ready until the 1967 model year, the grand jury found that the auto companies had in fact already developed devices when the AMA resolution was issued. In any event, the automobile manufacturers managed to comply with the California requirement in 1966, their previous protestations notwithstanding. Nonetheless, the conspiracy resulted in no voluntary development and installation of antipollution devices between 1954 and 1967. As the Antitrust Division noted in its summary of the grand jury investigation, the evidence proved

. . . the existence of an industrywide agreement and conspiracy among the auto manufacturers, through AMA, not to compete in the research, development, manufacture and installation of motor vehicle air pollution control devices for the purposes of achieving interminable delays, or at least delays as long as possible. The cross-licensing agreement was used as a cover and focal point of the conspiracy.[22]

The case was eventually settled by a consent decree.[23]

Just as the Clean Air Amendments of 1970 was a public policy placing maximum limits on polluting automobile emissions, the 1955 agreement among the manufacturers was a public policy in the opposite direction. The only difference is that the former was a policy of the federal government, while the latter was a policy of private governments. They both, however, were public regulatory policies.

The Buffalo Creek Disaster

At times, the deprivation of values can be truly disastrous, as was demonstrated in Buffalo Creek, West Virginia, on February 26, 1972. That day, after a heavy rainfall, a mountain of slag and waste containing at its top a 14-acre lake collapsed and sent a 30-foot-high wall of mud cascading down to the valley below. As a result, nearly 5,000 residents were left homeless and 125 persons died. The slag heap had been deposited as part of coal-mining operations by the Buffalo Mining Company, a subsidiary of the Pittston Company, one of the nation's largest coal producers. Two days after the disaster, a spokesman for another Pittston subsidiary admitted to reporters that "the responsibility is Pittston's in the long range. I would say the refuse pile is our responsibility." The Pittston Company, however, quickly denied any responsibility. A Pittston official stated that the flood was an act of God and that there was nothing wrong with the pile except that it was "incapable of holding the water that God poured into it."

In fact, the disaster was a classic example of corporate rather than divine irresponsibility. The slag heap was a violation of the 1969 Coal Mine Health and Safety Act, which prohibits bodies of water on such refuse piles. In 1966, the Buffalo Creek slag heap was one of thirty-eight singled out by the United States Geological Survey as hazardous; a USGS geologist predicted topping and breeching of the bank in the event of a heavy storm. The U.S. Bureau of Mines ignored the violations, under the convenient fiction that the slag heap was a dam and not a refuse pile. The Pittston Company ignored the warnings altogether, apparently deciding that the risks were acceptable.[24] In doing so, the corporation was making regulatory policy for the people in the valley—a policy that ultimately proved a disastrous deprivation of welfare.

It may be objected that the preceding examples are unfair because they are the worst cases and may not be at all typical. Indeed, the cases of the auto emission conspiracy and the destruction at Buffalo Creek are extreme; at the very least, they raise questions of legality. Although it is possible to catalog other examples of gross environmental damage, the point of such dramatic examples is to demonstrate the extremes to which the current mix of public and private regulatory decisions can take us. To the smog-choked people living in the Los Angeles basin during the period in which pollution control technology was withheld, it is little comfort that the exercise of corporate power to which they were subjected was not typical.

Pollution and Externality

There is a more fundamental point to be made, however, and it revolves around the concept of the *externality* of which pollution is a classic example. An externality is any indirect or secondary effect of a transaction that affects people not involved in that transaction. For example, noise suffered by people living near airports is an externality of air transportation; water pollution is an externality suffered by people living downstream of paper or chemical plants; and so on. Not all externalities are negative. For example, we all enjoy the delicious aroma coming from a bakery, and we all profit when other individuals get innoculations against contagious diseases. Public policy, however, must be concerned with externalities that are negative and objectionable. Until very recently, the costs of economic transactions were stated only in dollar terms; all transactions were seen as contributing equally and unambiguously to our gross national product. Although precise measures have yet to be developed, there is now more concern for the externalities of such transactions—externalties that must be accounted as *social costs*. This new emphasis on social costs stems from a belated recognition that our national (and international) welfare consists of more than the economic value of our commerce.

While the "horror stories" presented here—and also available in abundance from other accounts—may be extreme, they differ only in degree from the prevailing tendency in private enterprise. That tendency is to externalize social costs. An enterprise causing the externality has basically two options: it can contain the externality to the greatest extent technically possible (for example, purify its waste material, install noise abatement devices, and so on), or it can simply pass the externality along and impose (externalize) its cost on to society. Without government intervention, there is little doubt what most enterprises choose to do. Why incur a cost when you can readily make someone else incur it? In terms of pure economic rationality, the man at the top is no doubt correct in deciding to maximize his own profits by shifting his costs to society. However, the costs that society must bear are substantial indeed.

Air and water pollution are probably the most noticeable and troublesome negative externalities imposed on society by industrial enterprise. Roughly half of our total air pollution (by weight) comes from motor vehicles. While each of the millions of cars and trucks on the road is thus a source of pollution, the amount of pollution is largely determined by the design characteristics of the vehicles—determined, that is, by the handful of manufacturers who cling tenaciously to the present design of the internal combustion engine. Vehicles are the major sources of carbon monoxide and hydrocarbons and also produce a considerable proportion of nitrogen oxide pollution. The other major pollutants in the air are sulfur oxides and particulates which come mostly from the burning of coal and oil. In 1971, various industrial processes were responsible for 50 per cent of the total particulates in the air and 21 per cent of the total hydrocarbons. Electric utilities alone accounted for 62 per cent of the total sulfur oxides emitted.[25] There is no completely agreed-upon level at which pollution is suddenly dangerous. Much depends on such factors as the weather and the health of individuals. But in substantial amounts, these pollutants are always unpleasant to breathe and are frequently dangerous—particularly to people with heart and lung disorders. Furthermore, levels that are known to be dangerous often prevail. The Environmental Protection Agency estimated in 1972 that 43 per cent of the U.S. population live in areas where EPA danger levels for sulfur dioxide are exceeded.[26]

The problem of water pollution may be even more serious, and it is more directly traceable to industrial sources. Water pollutants include biodegradeable materials, such as sewage, that consume oxygen in water; when the amount of material exceeds the capacity of the body of water to break it up, all oxygen is consumed, and the affected lake or stream "dies"—it can no longer sustain aquatic life. There are also nonbiodegradeable pollutants, such as inorganic chemicals and heavy metals including mercury, cadmium, and others. These materials reach the water through mining and manufacturing operations, oil fields, agricultural processes, and natural sources. Many of them are toxic to fish life and probably harmful to humans. Perhaps the most troublesome group of pollutants are synthetic organic chemicals such as pesticides, synthetic industrial chemicals, and the wastes from their manufacturers. These materials resist conventional waste treatment processes and are highly persistent in the water. That is, the natural breaking down of organic materials in the waterways either does not occur or occurs so slowly that these chemicals enter our food chains through absorption by plants and animals. The scope of the problem is truly awesome. While the hazards from mercury or cadmium in the water are well known, that is just the tip of the iceberg. In fact, little is known about the estimated 12,000 potentially toxic chemicals now used in industry. And the situation is getting worse as an estimated 500 new chemicals are produced each year.[27]

The danger from this industrial garbage in our water can be seen dramatically in light of the specific hazards posed by pollutants. There is growing recognition that many or most human cancers are probably caused by chemical carcinogens in our air, water, and food. There is also evidence that water-borne chemicals are responsible for birth defects and long-range (and irreversible) genetic damage. While there are known hazards, such as mercury poisoning, the hazards not yet completely known may be even more serious. As Barry Commoner argued:

. . . Like the sorcerer's apprentice, we are acting upon dangerously incomplete knowledge. We are, in effect, conducting a huge experiment *on ourselves*. A generation hence—too late to help—public health statistics may reveal what hazards are associated with these pollutants.[28]

Industry is responsible by far for most water pollution in the United States. While both municipal wastes and industrial wastes together are the greatest sources of waste discharges into the nation's water, nearly half of the municipal waste consists of waste products from factories in urban areas.

The more than 300,000 water-using factories in the United States discharge nearly four times as much oxygen-consuming wastes as all residences connected to sewer lines in the United States.[29] More than half the total volume of industrial wastes comes from four industries: paper, organic chemicals, petroleum, and steel. To restate the problem in political terms, through their decisions on pollution-control operations and investment, a relatively small number of corporations have an enormous impact on public health—a policy area of vital importance.

Federal Policy in Pollution Control

Of course, in recent years the federal government has become increasingly active, and it now clearly dominates the environmental policy area. But it must be stressed that the new federal role still leaves a substantial amount of discretion in the hands of corporate officials. This can be seen when we examine the basic themes of the relevant federal legislation. Under the Clean Air Amendments of 1970, the Environmental Protection Agency is directed to set standards of air quality and to require that the states prepare implementation plans in accord with them. The legislation also directs EPA to set standards for particularly hazardous emissions and to set standards to be followed by all new industrial plants. Thus, the law is addressed both to general air-quality standards and, in a more limited way, to specific sources of pollution. Additionally, specific emission standards for automobiles were set. The Water Pollution Control Act Amendments directed that standards be set for individual plants that discharge water-borne wastes and required a permit system for discharges from both industrial and municipal sources.

Superficially, the laws look impeccable, but in practice they are not completely workable. Both laws rest on the notion of setting absolute limits on pollutants. But what happens when an industry cannot meet the standards (or claims it cannot)? The answer is exemplified by an EPA decision in September 1973 to lower the standards for sulfur dioxide emissions from power plants. The acting EPA administrator unhappily noted that the choice had been "this or nothing or a shutdown" of power plants unable to meet EPA standards. The same situation has prevailed with regard to automobile emissions. Faced with automakers' claims of inability to meet the legally established limits, the standards have been modified and deadlines successively delayed.

Similarly, in the case of water pollution, federal and state agencies confront the unhappy dilemma of shutting down plants unable to meet waste discharge standards—not an attractive or realistic option at a time of high unemployment—or allowing them to fall below the standards. Beyond that problem, the outreach of the law still allows industries to discharge their wastes (externalize their costs) onto society; the laws only place limits on the amount of waste they can dump in the air and water. While the law sets a goal of *no* water-borne waste discharge by 1985, it is highly doubtful whether this is technologically possible. Furthermore, the goal is economically prohibitive: the cost of eliminating 90 per cent of the water pollution in the United States may be equalled by the cost of removing the remaining 10 per cent to achieve *totally* pollution-free water. Indeed, a study by the Brookings Institution and Resources for the Future concluded: "The 1985 zero-discharge goal strikes us as so unrealistic that it hardly deserves discussion."[30]

The preceding discussion does not mean that pollution control laws are not desirable nor that industry should be let off the hook. The point is that, despite the formal pronouncements of the laws, *in practice* corporations will still be allowed freely to pass on costs to society. The laws have improved the situation from what it was prior to 1970, but a basic problem of public policy still remains. In the process of externalizing environmental and other social costs, policy decisions are being made by industries. It is irrelevant whether such costs are inevitable or even whether people would be willing to pay higher taxes or prices to reduce environmental damage. The essential point is that corporations are able to impose a cost on society in terms of directly depriving people of certain welfare values such as health and aesthetic enjoyment. At one time such decisions were undertaken unilaterally by corporations. Now, under a variety of federal and state laws, government sets the outer limits. But within those limits, corporations still decide on the extent to which they impose social costs. Thus, industries that are major contributors to the overall pollution level can be seen as participating on the same level as government agencies in the regulatory decisions affecting public health and welfare.

Alternative Pollution-Control Plans

Although reform proposals will be discussed more fully in Part Four, it should be noted at this point that there are alternative strategies of pollution control that can remedy both the environmental and political problems inherent in the currently prevailing approaches. The most widely advocated alternative is a system charging fees to industries discharging wastes into the environment. The fees would be greater than the cost of removing a substantial proportion of the pollutants. Therefore, there would be a clear economic incentive for industries to seek the most efficient means of reducing their pollution. The government could monitor such a fee system as readily as it monitors industries under current regulations; but there would be a great advantage in that the system would be free of the rigidities inherent in a more-structured "thou shalt not pollute" regulatory system. Such a procedure could most readily be established, for example, in the form of effluent charges for the more than 50,000 major industrial sources of water pollution. For a variety of reasons that go beyond our present analysis, an effluent-charge system could substantially reduce the overall cost of pollution control to society while maintaining a high standard of environmental quality.[31] Beyond that, this alternative strategy has the substantial public-policy benefit of ending the corporations' ability to treat society's air and water as their free dumping ground. Costs could no longer be externalized to society but would be borne by firms as a cost of doing business (and passed on to customers in the cost of the product). By imposing a system of fees, government agencies, rather than corporations, would be dominant in the making of environmental public policy.

The Workers: Paying the Price

One of the most insidious areas of corporate regulatory policy is occupational health and safety. Although we have a comfortable public image of vast improvements from the days of sweatshops and child labor, for millions of American workers conditions at the present time are bad enough. According to a 1972 presidential task-force report, occupational diseases kill as many as 100,000 workers annually and disable at least 390,000. Accidents on the job are responsible for more than 14,000 deaths and 2.2 million disabling injuries every year. Furthermore, these statistics are widely regarded as low estimates of the actual incidence of occupational deaths and disabilities; diseases such as lung cancer may not appear until after the worker has stopped working, and accidents on the job are widely underreported.

Just as with environmental protection, corporations have tried to shift the onus of responsibility to the victims—in this case the workers. Industrial accidents are commonly seen as the fault of workers, without acknowledging that the workplace itself may not be safe. In opposing an occupational health and safety bill in 1968, a spokesman for the National Association of Manufacturers said:

> . . . The human factor is one of the most important causal elements involved in any accidental occurrence. . . . Each employee must be motivated through training, education and supervision to understand and to want to perform work safely. This desire must come from within—it cannot be imposed through the threat of civil or criminal sanctions against the employer.[32]

Thus, slogans such as "Safety is everybody's business" and "Safety pays" are common.

Moreover, the diffusion of responsibility goes beyond slogans. For example, in many plants that work with such substances as beryllium and asbestos—whose dust is highly toxic and/or carcinogenic—management provides workers with respirators to wear instead of installing better ventilation and dust-suppression devices. The respirators are cumbersome and extremely uncomfortable, particularly in the high heat inside the plants, which is also caused by poor ventilation. Since the hazards of the air they breathe in the plants has been unknown or little understood by workers until it is too late, it is hardly surprising that most workers quickly discard their respirators—a folly not discouraged by corporations since management does not want to raise embarrassing questions about just how hazardous internal plant environments may be.

As to just how dangerous conditions really are in certain industries, the facts are shocking in the extreme. Although industry prefers to talk about occupational safety in terms of accidents, the problem of long-term health hazards may be even more severe. Among instances of severely disabling occupationally caused illnesses are the following:

1. Deterioration of the nervous system in workers in the Columbus Coated Fabrics division of the Borden Company caused by

something in the fumes in the poorly ventilated air—the exact culprit was not located.

2. Beryllium disease, an incurable condition involving severe loss of lung function, coughing, and extreme weight loss, in workers at the plants of the Beryllium Corporation and other beryllium mining and processing operations.

3. Cancers of the lung, scrotum, kidneys, larynx, pancreas, stomach, and blood (leukemia), among steel workers who work around coke ovens.

4. Lead poisoning among workers in the lead refining plants of American Smelting and Refining Company and the Anaconda Company.

Moreover, in all these and many other instances the industries in question consistently denied that health hazards existed. They either claimed that only a few workers were particularly susceptible to the hazards or that adequate precautions were being taken in the plants. How did they know? Their own well-paid medical consultants told them so, despite abundant independent medical evidence to the contrary.[33]

The documentation could go on and on, recounting how thousands and perhaps millions of American workers are exposed to conditions causing cancer and a variety of diseases of the nerves and lungs. But the stark realities of the situation can perhaps be best grasped by looking at the tragedy befalling Americans at the individual level. In her moving study of occupational health, *Muscle and Blood,* Rachel Scott recounted her visit with the family of one worker who had beryllium disease:

We could hear someone at the front door. *"Daddy's home!"* cried Jackie, Ferdinand's ten-year-old son, running into the kitchen and out again. Several minutes passed before Ferdinand appeared and sat down at the table. He leaned over, supporting himself with his forearms on the table, breathing in deep gasps, sucking the air through his mouth.

"Hi, how did it go?" his wife asked.

"Okay, I'm tired," he said, ending the statement with an apologetic laugh. "I'll get my wind."

His wife looked at him. "He walks up the stairs and he gets . . ." She shook her head; her voice was tight. "I . . . I was saying . . . last night, he woke me up when"—Ferdinand was coughing now, a dry rapid cough—"when the pain pills wore off . . . he gets a lot of pain . . . he was moaning and all, until they took effect again and he fell asleep. I couldn't go to sleep anymore. I was through."

Ferdinand was still coughing. She reached for his arm and squeezed it, then withdrew her hand self-consciously. "I don't know," she said. "If . . . if we could, I'd like to try another climate, or something. I'll go to Australia if we have to."

"We're going to the Fiji Islands," he said gently, smiling at her. "I'm going to find a nice island someplace where nobody's ever been. A store to buy food in. Her and the kids 'n somebody to talk to, I guess. That's all, I guess." He sat gazing at her. A large handsome man with soft dark hair and a serious face except for his long, almost comical nose, he looked younger than his forty-three years.

"We try to keep the kids' spirits up," said Mrs. Ferdinand, "because they get downhearted, you know, from being in so much. The only thing that bothers them is, their daddy's sick, and they want him to get better. And they can't understand why . . . why we have to do without so much just because he got sick. Why is it that because he got sick we can't afford to do anything or buy things. They do a pretty good job though. They're good kids."

"Yeah," agreed Ferdinand, "we got good kids."[34]

For permitting the conditions that crippled Mr. Ferdinand and other workers, the Beryllium Corporation was fined by the federal government the amount of $298—hardly an incentive to maintain a decent work environment.

Safety as a Cost of Production

Hazardous working conditions exist not because corporate chieftains are sadistic but because they really do not think about it too much. Safety is regarded as just another cost of production, and, like all other costs, there is a relentless drive to hold it down. Rachel Scott quotes industrial hygienist Ray McClure, who told her:

. . . We've tried over the last twenty years to talk safety to employers and get them to be good, but as long as it costs money they're not going to do it. It takes money for maintenance, it takes money for safety and health. I don't think it's fair to have a slogan like "Safety pays." It doesn't. In most plants it just doesn't. It doesn't turn a profit.[35]

While it may be understandable for managers to be motivated more by profit than by employee welfare, the activities of some corporations have gone tragically and unforgivably beyond mere cost cutting; with the cooperation of doctors and government agencies, corporate officials have knowingly sacrificed workers. In the first place, there has probably never been a health hazard arising from working conditions or product use whose existence has not been denied by the corporations responsible for it. A worker at the Pittsburg Corning asbestos plant in Tyler, Texas (which was shut down because of its health dangers) recounted: "During that whole time, no one ever told me or anyone else I know that asbestos could harm you. Why, I can remember some of our supervisors saying it not only wouldn't hurt you, but was *good* for you. They even used to tell you you could *eat* it."[36] Official denials to the government and the public are usually more subtle, but no less deceitful. In hearings on a proposed standard for asbestos dust in plants, representatives for Johns-Mansville and other producers adamantly fought for a more permissive standard than independent scientists and physicians regarded as safe.

The mix of government and corporate-made regulatory policy is nowhere more evident than in regulation of occupational health and safety. Despite the clear intent of the Occupational Health and Safety Act, government officials have acquiesced in a regulatory system in which cost considerations have become paramount. While no regulatory scheme can realistically expect to achieve zero hazards or disregard all economic considerations, we can at least hope that the economic costs of a policy reflect more than corporate preferences. Yet there is evidence that, in worker safety, it has been primarily the corporations' dollar costs that have been considered, not the workers' or society's. For example, in 1972 the National Institute for Occupational Health and Safety recommended an asbestos-dust standard of two fibers per cubic centimeter of air. The Occupational Health and Safety Administration within the Department of Health, Education, and Welfare then contracted with the consulting firm A.D. Little to come up with an asbestos standard. This study was commissioned in spite of the fact that the National Institute's standard had resulted from several years of comprehensive study and was held to be technically feasible by the Secretary of Labor's own Advisory Committee on the Asbestos Standard.

It turned out, however, the A.D. Little study was an attempt to determine the socially acceptable risk of exposure to this hazardous substance—that is, how much society should be willing to pay to avoid loss of lives. This assessment was undertaken despite the clear language of the Occupational Health and Safety Act, which states that "each employer shall furnish to each of his employees employment and a place of employment which are free from recognized hazards that are causing or are likely to cause death or serious physical harm to his employees." So much for the law. In fact, the effective definition of "socially acceptable" turns out to mean acceptable to industry. As Sheldon Samuels of the AFL-CIO stated:

. . . Congress to the contrary, and throwing its Occupational Safety and Health Act to the winds, the executive branch of government has decided on its own that the cost to the employer of meeting any new occupational-health standard must fall within an economic range that is acceptable to industry.[37]

Not surprisingly, the A.D. Little study relied almost entirely on industry estimates in judging economic feasibility.

While it is tempting to write this episode off as just another of the corrupt foibles of the Nixon administration, there is a more fundamental point to be recognized. Industrial corporations consistently try and often succeed in regulating the health-related aspects of the work environment in ways that are economically attractive to themselves but devastating to their employees. With the help of an acquiescent government, some of the giant corporations are thus able to promulgate regulatory policy which has binding effects on the health of the workers. In those instances, the social cost of enterprise is completely borne by workers and, to an extent, we are all guilty of reaping the fruits of their sacrifice. Most of us live in comfort, enjoying products whose manufacture is literally killing workers. Nonetheless, while our comforts may unknowingly rest on the backs of the workers (who may also be unaware of the health hazards they face until it is too late), it is they who run the great industrial enterprises who allocate those risks. In the face of inadequate and unresponsive government enforcement of the law, the responsibility for making public policy in this area has fallen squarely upon the corporations themselves.

In conclusion, it should be noted that decisions about risk are made not only for employees but for consumers as well. A good example is automobile safety. Prior to the National Traffic and Motor Vehicle Safety Act of 1966, the question of automobile safety was left largely to the unilateral discretion of the automobile manufacturers. Their policy was that only minimal expenditures would go to automobile safety and that even low-cost devices such as effective restraint systems and collapsible steering columns would not be provided. Indeed, even so elementary a feature as safety glass was initially rejected by General Motors president Alfred P. Sloan, Jr. in 1929 because it would "materially offset our profits."[38] Such policies were followed even in the face of abundant evidence that safety glass would save a significant proportion of the 50,000 lives lost annually in crashes. As a result of new government policy, such devices were eventually mandated. It is an empty exercise in formality to say that the corporate decisions about auto safety were not public policy, while the government's decisions were. In both cases, the decisions had binding consequences for most citizens, and both constituted public policy.

Notes

1. Marver Bernstein, *Regulating Business by Independent Commission* (Princeton: Princeton University Press, 1955), pp. 277–78.
2. See U.S. Congress, Senate, Select Committee on Small Business, *The Role of Giant Corporations,* hearings before the Subcommittee on Monopoly, 92nd Congress, 1st sess. (1971), pt. 1., statement of Raphael Cohen, pp. 45–67.
3. U.S. Federal Trade Commission, *Report on Automobile Warranties* (1970), pp. 38–43. Reprinted in U.S. Congress, Senate, Committee on the Judiciary, *Automotive Repair Industry,* hearings before the Subcommittee on Antitrust and Monopoly, 91st Congress, 2nd sess. (1970), pt. 5, Appendix.

4. Ibid., pp. 69–70.
5. Cited by Donald Randall and Arthur Glickman, *The Great American Auto Repair Robbery* (New York: Charterhouse, 1972), p. 37.
6. FTC *Report on Automobile Warranties*, pp. 52–53.
7. Ibid., p. 64.
8. William Leonard and Marvin Weber, "Automakers and Dealers: A Study of Criminogenic Market Forces," *Law and Society Review* 4 (1970), pp. 407–24.
9. *Automotive Repair Hearings*, pt. 1, p. 14.
10. U.S. Congress, Senate, Committee on Commerce, *Consumer Products Guaranty Act*, Hearings before the Consumer Subcommittee, 91st Congress, 2nd sess. (1970), statement of John J. Nevin, p. 214.
11. FTC, *Report on Automobile Warranties*, p. 100.
12. *Automotive Repair Hearings*, statement of William Haddon, p. 3240.
13. *Automotive Repair Hearings*, statement of Arthur C. Mertz, p. 3247.
14. U.S. Congress, Senate, *Competitive Problems in the Drug Industry*, hearings before the Select Committee on Small Business, 90th Congress, 1st sess. (1967), pt. 9, p. 3713.
15. *Drug Industry Hearings*, pt. 2, pp. 460–61.
16. Milton Silverman and Philip Lee, *Pills, Profits, and Politics* (Berkeley: University of California Press, 1974), p. 50.
17. Milton S. Davis and Lawrence S. Linn, "Final Report: Patterns of Influence Among Pharmacists, Physicians and Patients," cited by Senator Gaylord Nelson, *Congressional Record*, February 21, 1973, pp. 4822–25.
18. Advertisement reprinted in U.S. Congress, Senate, *Advertising of Proprietary Medicines*, hearings before the Select Committee on Small Business, 92nd Congress, 1st sess. (1971), pt. 2, p. 824.
19. Ibid., pp. 558–59.
20. Ibid.
21. Memorandum reprinted in U.S. Congress, Senate, Select Committee on Small Business, *Role of Giant Corporations*, hearings before the Subcommittee on Monopoly, 92nd Congress, 1st sess. (1971), pt. 2A, Appendixes, Corporate Secrecy: Overviews, pp. 1662–89.
22. Summary cited in Mark J. Green *et al.*, *The Closed Enterprise System* (New York: Bantam Books, 1972), p. 257.
23. Although three of the four Justice Department attorneys on the case recommended both civil and criminal actions, Antitrust Division chief Donald Turner declined to ask for indictments. The grand jury wanted to issue indictments; it did not do so because it did not realize it could have done so even in the absence of a Justice Department request. A Justice Department civil suit was filed on January 10, 1969. In spite of protests from many congressmen and the state of California, the Justice Department under the leadership of Attorney

General Mitchell did not go to court but signed a consent decree with the auto industry in which the industry agreed not to further conspire to inhibit the development of antipollution devices without admitting it had done so in the first place.

24. Harry M. Caudill, "Buffalo Creek Aftermath," *Saturday Review,* August 26, 1972, pp. 16–17.

25. U.S. Bureau of the Census, *Statistical Abstract of the United States: 1974* (Washington, D.C., 1974), p. 179.

26. Council on Environmental Quality, *Environmental Quality, 1972* (Washington, D.C., 1972), p. 10.

27. U.S. Public Health Service data cited in David Zwick and Marcy Benstock, *Water Wasteland* (New York: Grossman, 1971), p. 8.

28. Barry Commoner, *Science and Survival* (New York: Viking Press, 1966), p. 28.

29. Council on Environmental Quality, *Environmental Quality—1970* (Washington, D.C., 1970), p. 32.

30. Allen V. Kneese and Charles L. Schultze, *Pollution, Prices and Public Policy* (Washington, D.C.: Brookings Institution, 1974), p. 63.

31. See Kneese and Schultze, *Pollution, Prices and Public Policy,* chapter 7 for a more detailed analysis of the economic rationale of a system of effluent charges.

32. Quoted in Rachel Scott, *Muscle and Blood* (New York: Dutton, 1974), p. 278.

33. Ibid., pp. 13–36, 60–70, 95.

34. Ibid., pp. 21–22.

35. Ibid., p. 4.

36. Paul Brodeur, *Expendable Americans* (New York: Viking Press, 1974), p. 100.

37. Ibid., p. 150.

38. *Role of Giant Corporations Hearings,* p. 402.

PART FOUR
Toward Political Accountability

8

The Problem of Securing Accountability

In the preceding chapters we have asserted that a number of societal ills can be traced to the great concentration of economic and political power currently residing in America's giant corporations. To restate the issue briefly, it was seen that, through their considerable financial and organizational resources, corporations have attained superior access and leverage in the political system. Through a combination of inadequate legislation and their own efforts, giant corporations have been able to influence heavily and even, at times, to control the regulatory agencies that were supposed to hold the reins in the name of the wider public interest. Even more troublesome, it was argued that corporations themselves have been the promulgators of *public* policy—either in concert with government agencies or unilaterally. Thus, our thesis all along has been that it is extremely shortsighted to limit our conception and analysis of public policy only to those policies emanating from governments or to view the activities of corporations only in terms of their impact on the economic system. It is equally important, however, not to go overboard in utilizing this broader conception of corporate power and public policy. For purposes of analysis and reform, there are limits to what can usefully be considered direct manifestations of corporate power and privately made public policy. Specifically, we urge three caveats.

The Limits of Corporate Power

First, not all the impacts of corporate enterprise upon citizens can be considered to be public policies of particular corporations or the result of corporate influence on the institutions of the government. Much of the impact of corporations on society is due to the social and economic consequences of modern technology, a pervasive capitalist ideology, and large-scale industrial organization. One must distinguish these generalized conditions from specific instances of corporate public policymaking. The line between specific policy and social environment sometimes may be vague, but it should be kept in mind. Furthermore, even with specifiable policies, the line between those that are purely private and those that are public is not precise. In this respect, the situation is analogous to the fuzzy line between public and private organizations. It is a matter of further research and analysis to attempt to establish more precise criteria of "publicness" for both organizations and policies.

Second, the thesis being advanced is not a conspiracy or a "power-elite" theory. We do not claim that there are *hidden* powerful interests pulling the strings of government or that government is nothing more than a reflection of powerful economic interests. Rather, we assert that, in addition to government policies that are influenced by the exercise of corporate power, a significant amount of public policy is made by corporations without even having to go through the formal institutions of government.

Finally, it is not contended that all the effects of corporate policymaking are evil. While we need not accept the conservative view that the only valid criteria for assessing business performance are economic, it should still be emphasized that large corporations do provide benefits such as goods, services, and employment. Most of this activity, however, does not constitute public policymaking. Corporate participation in the Urban Coalition and other such enterprises indicates that corporate policymaking can be beneficient and may coincide with the interests of other groups in society. Furthermore, the corporate policymakers have some economic limits on their power, and they might exercise self-restraint in using their political power. They cannot charge *any* price for *any* product; nor are they able to elect or depose a member of Congress whenever they want.

While these cautionary notes place some limits on the problem of corporate power, they do not dispose of the issue. As Morton Baratz argued, even though corporate policymakers may be benevolent and restrained in their exercise of power, "this is hardly a satisfactory arrangement for a society which places a high value on a decentralized power structure."[1] Baratz approvingly cites Peter Drucker who notes: "The important fact about 'enlightened despotism'—also the one fact 'enlightened despots' always forget—is that while it appears as enlightenment to those in power it is despotism pure and simple to those under it."[2]

This last point is at the heart of the problem. We would not countenance a totally nonelected, self-perpetuating oligarchy in government merely because many of its policies were beneficial. Corporations too have great social power and make public policy; and when they do, there is not even the formal accountability to the public required in government.

Thus, in considering the impact of giant corporations, the proper focus must be on political power and accountability. By now, that may appear to be an obvious proposition, but it is not uncommon for many people to blame certain of our ills on much broader abstract forces—especially science and technology. Consider, for example, the following statement: "Science and technology have provided society with enormous material benefits and a higher standard of living and health. Yet these benefits have been accompanied by alarming rates of resource consumption and new hazards to ecological systems and health."[3] This line is rather typical of the writing on the social effects of technology, and, at a superficial level, it sounds entirely unobjectionable. After all, it is not a startling revelation that our lives have been changed by the development and application of technology.

The maddening problem with this kind of pronouncement is

that it implies that science and technology, and hence their impact on human beings, are based on impersonal forces—forces that can only be controlled through majestic changes in our values and institutions. Thus, Jacques Ellul states: "It is useless to rail against capitalism. Capitalism did not create our world; the machine did."[4] Perhaps so. But to dismiss capitalism as currently practiced as being of little consequence is completely unfounded. Even more to the point, we can do something about the organization of capitalism, whereas we are unlikely to "undiscover" the automobile, nuclear energy, or the aerosal spray can.

When we seek change and control over our environment, we must aim at those institutions that make decisions relevant to those areas. Machines, or "technique" in Ellul's phrase, cannot be held accountable; corporations can and must be made so. It is not a question of humanity in the abstract controlling technology but of particular people in particular social entities making particular decisions. To claim more is to abandon hope of reform. This situation is analogous to the concept of "nondecisions"—a subject discussed at greater length in Chapter 5. Simply because a government does not make decisions in areas such as the environment does not mean that such decisions are not made. It only means that, when they are not made by the government, they continue to be made by other entities.

So far, this book has examined the kinds of decisions made by certain of those entities—large corporations—their sources of power in making those decisions and their impact on affected interests. We now turn to the means, present and potential, of holding corporations accountable.

Controlling the Corporation: The Gap Between Theory and Practice

In examining the present system of control of corporate enterprise, we can broadly divide the problem into internal control and external control. The problem of internal control concerns the question of who has ultimate power of decision within the particular corporate community. The problem of external control concerns the question of control exercised over the corporation as an entity by outside, societal forces. In both areas, there is a considerable gap between theory and practice—a gap that, by now, may be rather obvious but that nonetheless has great policy implications.

Shareholder Democracy

In theory, the large corporation is just a larger version of the corner grocery or hardware store, with some differences due to size and legal limitations. The stockholders collectively own the enterprise and set broad policy through their representatives on the board of directors. But unlike the small proprietor, the stockholders do not bear legal responsibility for the debts or other liabilities of the corporation. And, even though individually they own but a small fraction of the firm and even though their control is indirect, the stockholders are seen as owning and controlling; it is to them that the corporate officials are ultimately accountable. The stockholders are thus considered the effective electorate in a "shareholder democracy."

This convenient myth was dislodged over forty years ago by Adolf A. Berle and Gardiner C. Means in their classic treatise, *The Modern Corporation and Private Property.*[5] They observed first the implications of the wide dispersal of ownership:

As the ownership of corporate wealth has become more widely dispersed, ownership of that wealth and control over it have come to lie less and less in the same hands. Under the corporate system, control over industrial wealth can be and is being exercised with a minimum of ownership interest. Conceivably it can be exercised without any such interest.[6]

The essential point is that the concept of "ownership" means something completely different in the context of the giant publicly held corporation than it does in the small proprietorship. In the classical economic tradition of Adam Smith, inherent in private property was unity of ownership and control—a person both owned and controlled the disposition of his property. But in the large corporation with its multitude of "owners" (stockholders), the functions of ownership and control have become separated.

. . . This separation of function forces us to recognize "control" as something apart from ownership on the one hand and from management on the other. . . . . Since direction over the activities of a corporation is exercised through the board of directors, we may say for practical purposes that control lies in the hands of the individual or group who have the actual power to select the board of directors . . .[7]

And who does have the power and hence the control? The trend, pointed out by Berle and Means, and long since consolidated, is for corporations to be under management control, with stockholders having no real voice in choosing the board of directors. For most stockholders control is confined to a choice between voting for or against proxies chosen by management:

. . . In neither case will [the stockholder] be able to exercise any measure of control. Rather, control will tend to be in the hands of those who select the proxy committee by whom, in turn, the election of directors for the ensuing period may be made. Since the proxy committee is appointed by the existing management, the latter can virtually dictate their own successors. Where ownership is sufficiently sub-divided, the management can thus become a self-perpetuating body even though its share in the ownership is negligible.[8]

While the separation of ownership and control is well recognized and may even be old hat by now, the implications of this situation are still timely and weighted with significant implications for public policy. When we seek to determine to whom management is ultimately accountable within the legal corporate community, it turns out that management is actually accountable to management—to itself.

It might be objected that federal and state laws do provide some protection for stockholders by making management responsible for fulfilling certain legal obligations. Currently, there are three basic remedies available to stockholders.[9] First, the stockholders have voting rights and may displace the corporate management through proxy contests, mergers, or tender offers. While management has inherent advantages in presenting its case to stockholders, the law attempts to compensate for those bargaining inequities. Nonetheless, any attempt to displace a sitting management group is very costly and is far from a common occurrence.

Second, federal disclosure statutes require that management make periodic reports on performance. However, as we will see below, the problem of corporate secrecy is such that a substantial amount of useful information is never released. Finally, there are the federal securities laws relating to "insider trading"—stock transactions by management. Basically, management officials cannot utilize inside, undisclosed information in buying or selling the stocks they hold in the company they manage.

These rules, however, although they are broad safeguards against outright fraud by management, do not operate as a real mechanism of accountability. This trio of strictures, according to Yale law professor Marvin Chirelstein, "pretty much exhausts the efforts of law to promote responsibility in corporate policymaking."[10] The law provides only the broad outer limits of management discretion, and, as Chirelstein notes, "the legal weaponry is blunt and clumsy." Thus, management governs largely unencumbered by any workable mechanism of accountability to stockholders. At the same time, it claims for the corporation the same privileges that adhere to private property in the traditional sense—in which ownership and control are in the same hands. Management's use of rights inherent in an ownership interest that it does not, in fact, possess precludes effective accountability to stockholders. Whatever check on corporate power that might come from the stockholders is not currently realized.

The preceding discussion does not mean that stockholders and boards of directors have *no* effective power; in fact, the role of corporate boards may well be changing. For example, in 1976 the top two executives of Lockheed Corporation and the chairman and three top executives of Gulf Oil Corporation were ousted by their respective boards of directors in the wake of revelations of payoffs to foreign politicians. Nonetheless, it should be pointed out that these were scandals of extraordinary magnitude and that, moreover, payoffs by these corporations and more than a dozen others had gone undetected by board members for years.

Up to now, we have been discussing corporate management as a unified entity that acts with clear decisiveness. The problem of accountability, however, may be complicated further by the lack of such unity of action and the lack of complete internal control by the head of the corporation. The chief of the corporation may have as much trouble securing compliance to his wishes as governors, mayors, and even the President of the United States have in their areas of responsibility. The lower levels of bureaucracy within the corporation present the same problems of responsiveness as do public bureaucracies. Thus, corporations will not necessarily be instantly and effectively responsive, either to the consciences of managers or to market incentives.[11] This does not mean that no one can be held accountable. Rather, it means that the locus of accountability within the corporation is itself a policy problem. As Thomas Schelling notes: "For policymaking . . . the question becomes that of assigning or identifying responsibility at the socially expedient point, so that cognizant parties are able and motivated to act responsibly."[12]

Consumer Sovereignty

In classical economic theory, the primary mode of external control on corporations is the free competitive market ultimately regulated by "consumer sovereignty"—the notion that, by their collective decisions on what to buy and how much they are willing to spend, consumers actually dictate the policies of business corporations. Thus, the exercise of central authority is unnecessary. The classic statement of this system of self-regulation was the theory of Adam Smith who held that, when every person in a system of enterprise pursued his own self-interest, the greatest common good would result—as if the economy were guided by an "invisible hand." While the role of consumers pursuing their own self-interest was only one element of that invisible hand, for purposes of examining controls on the business firm it exercised a central role.

While resurrecting Adam Smith in 1976 may seem like setting up the flimsiest of straw men, the utilization of consumer sovereignty as a defense of corporate actions is very much alive and well in late twentieth-century American capitalism. From the tinseled gas-guzzling automobiles prevalent until recently to violence on television, the most common corporate justification has been consumer preference.

At this juncture in the book, there is little point in further dismantling the myth of consumer sovereignty; and, as a theory of external control, the notion can be dispensed with rather quickly. It will be recalled that, in Chapters 6 and 7, it was shown that giant corporations, far from responding automatically to consumer preferences, have considerable influence in determining prices, availability, quality, and safety of products. At this point, however, a cautionary note should be restated. The market power of giant corporations does not mean that consumers are totally without influence in their buying decisions. Contrary to some of the wilder analyses of corporate power, consumers are not blank slates totally manipulated by corporate advertising. It would be a pretty dismal view of human nature and intelligence to hold that consumers' buying decisions are wholly controlled by giant corporations. Some heavily promoted products do turn into expensive flops, the most notorious example being the ill-fated Ford Edsel in the 1950s. And it was, after all, massive consumer resistance to "full-size" cars that led Detroit, kicking and screaming, finally to reduce automobile size in the mid-1970s. But these are rather extraordinary cases, and they in no way vitiate the argument presented that there is very considerable market power present in highly concentrated industries. Thus, the conditions of sale, including such matters as warranties and service, were not affected even by the severe automobile sales slump in 1974–75. Indeed, only the relatively puny American Motors Corporation has even attempted to be competitive in the terms of warranty service.

To say that consumers have limited influence over the giant corporations is not to say they are similarly without influence in the total economy. In a provocative analysis, John Kenneth Galbraith argues that the economy is composed of two systems—the market system and the planning system.[13] The market system is composed of smaller enterprises in competitive industries; it is this component of the economy that is subject to consumer influence. But, as Galbraith argues, the market system is subservient to the other component of the economy—the planning system. The planning system is made up of large enterprises that require substantial amounts of capital and technology. Because of the great scope and size of the investments required, firms in the planning system strive to control their environment. An immense amount of planning is necessary; and there must be no surprises—least of all consumer preference. In the planning system, consumer preference is the factor to be manipulated, not corporate policy. Thus, in Galbraith's view, the role of consumer sovereignty is confined to a market system of small business that is subservient to and disadvantaged by the giant corporations of the planning system.

Moreover, even if consumer sovereignty did hold sway in the planning system, it would not act as an effective check against many of the basic problems posed by giant corporations. Consumer choice really has little bearing on problems such as pollution and occupational health. Although some observers are infected by the romantic notion that consumers can be induced to make their purchases with an eye to social conscience, this is not likely to serve as a check on corporate power. Indeed, since many of these abuses occur in basic industries such as mining and steel production, consumer choice could in no way exercise an external control. In short, the forces of the market system are not adequate to control the present economy, if indeed they ever were.

Control by the Public Purpose

Although the forces of the free market were once thought to function as an automatic system of regulation, the history of the corporation as a legal form shows that there was an earlier, more deliberate mode of external control. That control consisted of the responsibilities mandated for the corporation in return for the privilege of a government-granted corporate charter. The corporate form of organization in the United States loosely evolved from British antecedents and actually had its roots in the medieval merchant guilds, whose authority encompassed many of the functions now associated with civil governments. By the beginning of the seventeenth century, corporations were given private privileges enabling them to conduct business for profit in exchange for the undertaking of public responsibilities. At that time, civil government had already replaced corporate government in the regulation of domestic trade, but the state ceded to corporations the responsibility for foreign and colonial commerce and the privilege of trading in the name of the crown. Thus, corporations such as the British East India Company had royal charters that governed the terms of the corporation's existence. Gradually, through the next century, private legal rights associated with incorporation expanded in importance and overshadowed the notion of a primary public obligation.

From the very beginning of our history as a nation, the United States made use of the legal concept of the corporation. American law inherited from English jurisprudence the concept of the corporation as a franchise—a privilege granted by the sovereign power of the state. Indeed, most of the original English settlements in America were chartered companies of proprietary colonies. The essential nature of the privilege was that the corporation was a legal entity independent of its owners. It could hold property and exercise legal rights in its own name, and its owners had strictly limited liability. While British experience with corporations was directed to different ends, and our own evolving corporate law was shaped by early American needs and institutions, the one definite feature inherited from British law was the concept that a positive act of the sovereign governmental authority was necessary to grant corporate status. By its authority to grant that status, government was the original control on the corporation and the corporation was a legal creature of the state. This conception of the corporation in law was concisely stated by Chief Justice John Marshall in the *Dartmouth College* case:

. . . A corporation is an artificial being, invisible, intangible, and existing only in contemplation of law. Being the mere creature of law, it possesses only those properties which the charter of its creation confers upon it, either expressly, or as incidental to its very existence.[14]

Following from this rationale of the corporate charter, the early American corporations were enterprises vested with a direct public interest, such as turnpike and canal companies. By 1800, only 335 profit-seeking companies had been incorporated in the United States. Of these, 219 were turnpike, bridge, and canal companies; only six were manufacturing companies. Thus, the corporate charter also provided the privilege of a monopoly franchise similar to today's concept of public utilities. Charters in the United States were granted primarily by state legislatures, and every charter required a special legislative act. Through this process, the notion of the charter as a privilege for public purpose was kept alive. But soon, as more and more charters were requested, this notion faded. By the mid-nineteenth century, incorporation had become routinized through general incorporation laws by which companies were to be incorporated "for any lawful purpose." By 1870, the public-purpose theory of incorporation had vanished.[15] What this trend meant was that incorporation had shifted from a *privilege* bounded by certain public purposes to a relatively unencumbered *right* routinely dispensed by the states. With that shift, the obligation of the corporation to be accountable to the state and society diminished.

There is a basic dilemma of accountability inherent in the very nature of corporate enterprise as it has evolved. One of the major benefits of incorporation is that the corporation itself is a separate entity, and the corporate form limits the financial and other legal liabilities of the officials associated with the corporation. While corporate officers are certainly not immune from the reach of the law in the case of overt wrongdoing, as we have already noted, the legal remedies are blunt and clumsy. The kinds of legal sanctions that are available are adequate for abuses such as insider stock trading, bribery, fraud, and so on; but they do not readily lend themselves to the kinds of corporate decisions that have been discussed in the preceding chapters—decisions that nonetheless have very direct and significant social impacts. Since this privilege of limited liability is part and parcel of the corporate organization, the law of the corporation itself limits the actual accountability of corporate officials.

Up to now, we have discussed traditional economic and legal means of controlling corporate power and have found those wanting. Beyond those problems, moreover, there are more overt barriers to accountability. One of the major limitations on our ability to obtain corporate accountability stems from our lack of sound information about corporate activities—a subject to which we now turn.

Corporate Secrecy and Political Accountability

To obtain any effective system of corporate accountability, there is one vital precondition: information. The matter was concisely stated by President Theodore Roosevelt in his first message to Congress:

. . . Great corporations exist only because they are created and safeguarded by our institutions; and it is therefore our right and our duty to see that they work in harmony with these institutions. . . . The first requisite is knowledge, full and complete; knowledge which may be made public to the world.

Seventy years later, however, lack of knowledge still represents a primary barrier to accountability. The remainder of this chapter discusses the sources, manifestation, and impact of corporate secrecy.

Although it is tempting simply to charge that corporations are infected by secrecy simply because they have something evil to hide, there are more important and broader reasons as well. Indeed, secrecy by corporations stems from many of the same factors that produce secrecy in government agencies. Corporations are bureaucratic organizations, and, as Max Weber argued in his classic essay on bureaucracy, a preoccupation with secrecy is inherent in such organizations:

. . . Every bureaucracy seeks to increase the superiority of the professionally informed by keeping their knowledge and intentions secret. Bureaucratic administration always tends to be an administration of "secret session"; insofar as it can, it hides its knowledge and action from criticism.[16]

Secrecy is a source of power for an organization because information that might be useful to competing organizations is thereby withheld. Corporations, however, do not hoard information primarily for competitive reasons but because they feel it is essential to fulfill the larger goals of the organization. In the case of the corporation, control over information is seen as being necessary in order to pursue goals such as profit maximization or growth. Of course, a corporation, like any other organization, can carry secrecy far beyond the point at which it is merely helpful to the organization and becomes instead a liability for the broader public—and sometimes for itself as well.

There are several more specific sources of corporate secrecy. Some of the information that corporations wish to keep secret has been gathered at the behest of the government, which itself condones and supports corporate secrecy in the interest of preserving what it regards as fairness in economic regulation.[17] Advance publicity about investigations of potential violations in areas such as product safety, automobile recalls, and advertising might do great financial damage to companies that are later found to be blameless. Thus, information collected and produced by corporations as part of the regulatory process is kept confidential outside of the closed circle of corporate and government officials. In this respect, the role of secrecy is much the same as in preliminary law enforcement investigations generally.

Furthermore, the government's own requirements for information may themselves create new areas of corporate secrecy. Government regulations may require corporations to collect and maintain information in previously unrecorded areas such as data on racial employment, occupational safety, and waste management. Corporations then usually desire to keep such information confidential outside of the government agencies to which they must report, and they may have a legal right to the confidentiality of such data, as is true of information furnished to the Census Bureau. Thus, the reporting requirements of the government create categories of corporate information that subsequently become "secret."

Other factors also enter into corporate secrecy, especially considerations of legal liability with regard to product safety. Thus, automobile manufacturers had been especially secretive about automobile defects until legislation required specific public recall procedures. Such systematic data on product defects could be and have been used by plaintiffs in damage suits resulting from accidents allegedly caused by defective cars. Even at the expense of losing particular law suits, automobile manufacturers have sometimes withheld information of possible product defects.[18]

Corporate secrecy is also rooted in the competition characteristic of the private economy. Corporations overtly claim a right to secrecy based on the need to maintain a competitive advantage. Indeed, John Kenneth Galbraith regards control over information as the *sine qua non* of modern industrial organization.[19] Thus, in discussing more detailed disclosure of financial information, Thomas C. Mann, president of the Automobile Manufacturers Association, stated:

. . . The disclosure of detailed financial data by a company would enable competitors to determine its points of weakness and strength. The competitors could then avoid a competitor's strength and exploit his weakness. Detailed knowledge of a competitor's cost and profit data would, for example, assist a manufacturer in making decisions about his own production of a competitive unit. Accounting measures and procedures themselves are considered important managerial tools and proprietary in nature; release of detailed data through which these methods and procedures could be revealed would be, in my opinion, undesirable.[20]

Most economists would agree with Mann's assessment of the value of detailed information to competitors. However, as we shall see below, they tend to view disclosure as aiding competition in general rather than competitors in particular. Greater information is therefore seen as invaluable as a spur to competition that is salutary for the overall optimal efficiency of the economy. Thus, while greater disclosure may be disadvantageous for a particular corporation, it is socially beneficial. Corporate managers, however, are not so magnanimous about disadvantaging themselves in order to spur competition—regardless of how much they may honor competition in the abstract.

Finally, corporations may simply have things they want to hide for reasons of embarrassment, potential financial harm, or possible criminal prosecution. Only rarely are such factors acknowledged, however. Usually, secrecy in such cases is rationalized by claims of superior expertise and the need to place "isolated" embarrassing

facts "in perspective." For example, in response to first-hand un-
contested testimony regarding deliberate falsification of specific
test data on an aircraft brake manufactured by B. F. Goodrich, the
company's general counsel stated: "When you take data from several different sources, you have to rationalize among those data
what is the true story. This is part of your engineering know-
how."[21]

Manifestation of Corporate Secrecy

Since corporations have information that is properly kept confidential or which is of no consequence outside the organization, we
must first determine which kinds of information are of sufficient
public importance to warrant compulsory disclosure. In a working
paper prepared for a large-scale congressional investigation of
corporate secrecy by the Subcommittee on Monopoly of the Senate
Select Committee on Small Business, Senator Gaylord Nelson and
committee counsel Raymond Watts listed seven types of valuable
policy-relevant information controlled by corporations.[22]

1. Financial information about separate organizational, industrial,
   and geographical segments of a business and the interrelationships of the segments.
2. Information on industrial and natural resources ownership and
   control.
3. Product information needed by or valuable to consumers.
4. Information on new discoveries and on how and why decisions
   are made to market or withhold new products and technologies.
5. Information about government procurement and government
   contracts.
6. Environmental impact information.
7. Information on employment policies and working conditions.

To this list, Ralph Nader adds two additional types: information on
political activity and tax information.[23]

Both the *specific* nature of the information and the degree of its
availability are major issues in the continuing controversy over
corporate secrecy. Although the slogan of a major oil company

public relations campaign in the mid-1970s was "Exxon Wants You To Know," the actual political thrust of this firm and nearly all major corporations has been in the direction of the restriction of information. Corporations have traditionally sought to limit the external flow of information by controlling the number of recipients of information, as well as the comprehensiveness of the data made available.

The specific kinds of information included in Senator Nelson's list can be classified into two broad categories, based on the degree to which information is restricted. First, there is information withheld from the public but shared with one or more government agencies. The second category, which is more restrictive, consists of information withheld from the government as well as from the public. Since it is beyond the scope of this chapter to examine in detail each particular manifestation of corporate secrecy, we will instead consider selected examples within both categories.

The Linkage Between Corporate and Government Secrecy

While this first category is less restrictive in terms of the overall availability of information, it also introduces significant problems of governmental accountability. In effect, such corporate secrecy increases the scope of governmental secrecy by making the government a partner in the withholding of information by private corporations. In Chapter 2, we examined problems of secrecy involved in business advisory committees in the federal government. It will be recalled that business interests represented in the committees vigorously sought to clothe their proceedings with a shroud of secrecy, thereby limiting the ability of other groups to have an input in policymaking. Furthermore, secrecy has served to magnify the power already inherent in the privileged access of corporations in the councils of government.

There are other important areas of secrecy shared by corporations and government agencies. Some regulatory and law-enforcement actions are either conducted or concluded behind closed doors. For example, as recounted in Chapter 5, the Automobile Manufacturers Association and the four major domestic automobile manufacturers were charged with conspiring to restrict competitive development of automobile pollution-control devices between 1954 and 1967. In 1969, as the result of a grand jury investigation, the Justice Department commenced a major civil antitrust suit against the automakers. The entire action is instructive for what it did not reveal. A Justice Department summary of the grand jury investigation stated that the evidence proved "the existence of an industrywide agreement and conspiracy among the auto manufacturers, through AMA, not to compete in the research, development, manufacture and installation of motor vehicle air pollution control devices."[24]

Before the Justice Department decided to proceed with a *civil* suit in January 1969, Antitrust Division attorneys had prepared a confidential memorandum presenting substantial evidence and recommending that a *criminal* charge be brought. This lengthy memorandum did not surface until 1971, when it was obtained and released in the *Congressional Record* by Representative Phillip Burton.[25] The first instance of nondisclosure was thus the recommendation for criminal action itself—a recommendation that was overruled in favor of civil action.

But the most striking manifestation of government-corporate secrecy was the settlement of the civil case by a consent decree in September 1969. In it, although the auto industry agreed not to conspire further to inhibit the development of antipollution devices, it did not admit that it had done so in the past. In the context of the problem of corporate secrecy, the provisions of the consent decree thus constitute a striking example of the convergence of government and corporate secrecy. The decree could not be used as *prima facie* evidence by later litigants (such as the State of California) who claimed injury from the conspiracy, and there was no provision for release of the grand jury transcript and other evidence to later litigants, although the court impounded the evidence gathered for possible later use. There was no safeguard against the destruction of past evidence, and, finally, there were no requirements for future reporting of relevant information such as records of subsequent auto industry meetings on pollution control.[26] Furthermore, the public was denied the full range of information that would have emerged at a public trial. While this and other similar antitrust consent decrees are manifestations of government secrecy, it is a form of secrecy that serves the needs of defendant corporations and is a response to their needs. Indeed, the suppression of information may itself be a major corporate goal in bargaining over the terms of a consent decree.

Regulatory agency actions are also sometimes clothed in secrecy, thus protecting manufacturers' financial and advertising positions. At one extreme, the Food and Drug Administration in 1973 decided to keep secret future recalls of particular defective and potentially hazardous medical devices and drugs. Normally, FDA-initiated recalls are publicized on a weekly list published by the agency. FDA spokesmen defended their actions by arguing that the policy was to prevent patients with devices such as heart pacemakers from being literally frightened to death by public announcements that might not even be relevant to their case. This policy was severely criticized by the Nader-sponsored Health Research Group, which stated that the secrecy was in the interests of the medical device and drug industries rather than the medical consumer.[27]

More frequently, regulatory information is partially shielded from disclosure in a way that makes it less useful than it should be. For example, the Food and Drug Administration issued a warning to consumers that certain "walker-jumpers" and "baby bouncers" were hazardous and could mangle an infant's hands. The FDA press release contained a description of the design elements to avoid, but it did not list the particular models or brands that were considered dangerous. The only apparent purpose of withholding this kind of information appears to be to avoid damage to particular brand names—a policy that shows far greater concern for the agency's business constituency than for its wider public constituency.

Another particular area of corporate secrecy in the regulatory field concerns manufacturing processes. Thus, Ralph Nader criticized the Department of Agriculture for refusing to disclose the Campbell Soup Company's quality control process to prevent botulism—a process USDA maintained was a trade secret. Citing the Bon Vivant case, Nader said: "No single company . . . should be permitted to claim a proprietary interest in lethality. Any regulatory scheme is bankrupt which permits producers to argue that they need economic incentives—such as those which flow from trade secrecy—to save their customers from injury and death."[28] This instance of secrecy, however, illustrates the complexity of the problem. It is not at all self-evident that the details of the quality control *process* must be in the public domain to assure effective protection as long as that process meets government standards. On the other hand, it might be argued that such processes should be made available to all, even though the company presumably has proprietary rights to other aspects of its quality control program that might be closely intertwined with health and safety. In any event, it is not clear that the public interest would be best served by eliminating all confidentiality in the relationship between regulators and regulated industries. The question must be whether or not disclosure, on balance, will benefit the public interest as defined by regulatory legislation.

Finally, there are areas in which government agencies regularly collect legally required information from corporations but keep it strictly confidential. The most common example of this type of information is Bureau of Census data on business firms and income-tax data. The Census Bureau collects extensive data on business firms broken down into "establishments" (individual plants, stores, and so on). This includes information such as new assets, number of employees, and manufacturing capacity and output. Only the aggregate data on each standard industrial category are released. Similarly, only aggregate corporate income-tax data is released by the Internal Revenue Service. The actual returns are kept confidential. It should be emphasized that both census and tax information on corporations are also unavailable to other government agencies that might find them relevant to their regulatory functions. Furthermore, the degree of secrecy has been increasing. For example, in 1965 the Federal Trade Commission, under pressure from the Senate appropriations subcommittee on the independent agencies, promised not to seek access to corporate tax returns, even though it was legally entitled to do so. A short time later, the Bureau of the Budget formulated rules to greatly restrict access to corporate tax returns by all government agencies.[29]

These exercises of confidentiality are the same as those that apply to individuals; and in the case of individuals there is great concern that the information be strictly controlled and closely held. This similar treatment is a manifestation of the policy assumption that corporations, in their legal standing, are equivalent to private individuals. This corporate right of privacy is actually sought not as a civil right, however, but as a competitive right. That is, it is argued that confidential information surrendered to the government would reveal too much valuable information to competitors if it were publicly disclosed, transforming proprietary information into a public good. In this instance, the control of information is thus utilized to prevent economic disadvantages for the corporation—not, in itself, an unworthy motive. Legitimate competing public claims on this information should not, however, be dismissed as though the issue were exclusively, or even primarily, one of civil liberty.

Unilateral Secrecy

There is a substantial area of policy-relevant information that is withheld not only from the public but from the government as well. There are vast quantities of information in a multitude of categories that are privately held by corporations. Only if greater central direction of the economy were sought would most of this information be expected to be released. Under the present system, to claim that corporations should have no secrets at all is to deny the legitimacy of private ownership and direction of economic activity. However, even in a private-enterprise economy, government intervention is considered desirable in some areas, and its effectiveness heavily depends upon information that only corporations can supply. In terms of the breadth of its impact, the most significant of these areas is information about the allocation of financial resources.

Although detailed information on the financial status of publicly held corporations is required to be reported to stockholders and to the Securities and Exchange Commission, the scope of this information can be likened to the old adage about statistics and bikini bathing suits: what they show is revealing, but what they conceal is vital. This criticism is particularly relevant to large multiproduct corporations, especially conglomerates. Financial information is conveyed to the public primarily through two forms: the annual corporate report to stockholders and Form 10-K, filed annually with the Securities and Exchange Commission. Although Form 10-K has considerably more detailed financial information than most annual reports, it is also limited as an instrument of disclosure for public-policy purposes. The major problem is that the business firms themselves are permitted to define their line of business, and information is provided and condensed into extremely broad categories. These are usually the same broad categories that are presented in annual reports; while the information about each category is more detailed in Form 10-K, within each category the information is not particularly useful.

Two examples of current financial reporting in 1972 Form 10-K reports vividly illustrate the limited utility of present procedures. R. J. Reynolds Industries has expanded its activities far beyond its original tobacco business. In addition to various tobacco products, Reynolds now has a variety of subsidiaries in processed food products (nine separate product lines), packaging, aluminum products, shipping, and oil. However, in the corporation's annual report, as well as in its Form 10-K for 1972, it breaks down its financial data into just three categories: tobacco, transportation, and "other." The category of "other"—which presumably includes foods, oils, and aluminium—reported earnings of $501 million for the year. With a category so broad, in effect no useful financial information is provided on the firm's performance in its various "other" activities.

An even more wide-ranging conglomerate, International Telephone and Telegraph, has a similarly broad aggregation of product categories. ITT breaks down its revenues into three categories: manufacturing, consumer, and business services; divestible operations; and Hartford Fire Insurance Company, which it owns. Thus, there is no public access to information on ITT earnings for hotels, publishing, bakeries, home building, or any of its many other specific lines of business.

Furthermore, the extent of corporate secrecy has been increasing over the past fifteen years as a consequence of the growth of conglomerates. Since 1960, ITT has acquired more than one hundred companies—many of them extremely large, such as Avis, Continental Baking, and Canteen. After these acquisitions, financial information on those companies, previously available, was buried in the broad consolidated categories used by ITT and thus became unavailable to the government, the public, and stockholders.

Although information for public consumption is provided in very limited form, other data provided to the government are far more specific and, as noted above, entirely confidential. Thus, the Standard Industrial Classification of the Bureau of the Census is broken down into ninety-seven major groups and totals hundreds of specific product and service categories. It is particularly revealing to compare the lump-sum categories used in the Standard Industrial Classification. Even tobacco products are divided into four categories in the SIC. Food products, which Reynolds Industries own report does not even list separately, itself contain eighty-seven categories such as canned fruits, sausage products, and other specific product lines.

It should be noted that the aggregated financial reporting practices of ITT, Reynolds Industries, and others are not universal. Transamerica, another major conglomerate, divides its lines of business into insurance and investments: financial, title, and relocation services; and mortgage and banking services. These are broken down further, and income statements of specific subsidiaries are also provided. Thus, there is nothing inherent in conglomerate organization that necessitates broadly aggregated income reporting. It is a question of choice. Transamerica chose to be detailed and forthright, and its example diminishes the various arguments conglomerates have presented for withholding information.

Regardless of how forthcoming a corporation may be, there remains a major problem of comparability. As long as corporations define their own lines of business, it is difficult, if not impossible, to compare the results from firms in the same product line. Defining lines of business in accord with the well-established Standard Industrial Classification categories would greatly facilitate comparison. In the preface to the Standard Industrial Classification Manual (1972) issued by the Office of Management and Budget, it is stated: "The Standard Industrial Classification Manual (SIC) is one of the most important tools that has been developed to promote the comparability of statistics describing various facets of the economy of the nation." Yet, the federal government does not require the comparability it touts.

One federal agency seeking to take advantage of the SIC system is the Federal Trade Commission. Since 1971, the FTC has sought product-line information for its *Quarterly Financial Reports*. At present these reports consist of only 31 lines of business broken down according to a single major category for each firm. Although the FTC had previously been blocked from requesting more detailed information from corporations by the Office of Management and Budget, legislation in 1973 freed the FTC and other regulatory agencies from the requirement that their data-collection activities be cleared by the Office of Management and Budget. Consequently, the FTC has sent detailed questionnaires to the 500 largest manufacturing corporations requesting sales, profits, advertising, and research and development figures for 219 product lines that closely follow the Standard Industrial Classification. The corporations that are the target of the inquiry are fighting it tooth and nail. They claim it is impossible in many instances to break down product information in the fashion that the FTC seeks, and a lengthy legal battle is in prospect. Furthermore, corporate interests are waging a rearguard action in attempting to get Congress to restrict the FTC's authority. Therefore, better and more complete information is still not being provided, and it is highly uncertain whether it will be provided in the future.

Once we acknowledge that presently provided financial information is inadequate, it remains for us to demonstrate why more information is necessary. Although our present concern is with corporate secrecy as a problem of public policy, we can start with the special stake of stockholders in the financial progress of their companies. The matter was succinctly stated by Donald F. Turner, former head of the Justice Department Antitrust Division:

. . . One of the principal tests of the efficiency of the management of a multiproduct firm is whether it is making a rational allocation of its capital and effort among its various lines of endeavor. One cannot begin to assess management performance in this respect if one knows only the overall rate of return on the company's entire operations.[30]

As Turner goes on to state, the stockholder's interest in this respect coincides with the public interest. As long as the private sector remains the primary allocator of economic values in society, there is a substantial societal interest in information relating to that allocation.

The control and withholding of information by multiproduct firms affects the basic premise of a capitalist economy. A competitive economy presupposes a supply of capital by many investors who are able to base decisions on information about *individual* industries. If profits in an industry are high, the theoretically expected investor reaction would be to invest capital. As a result, supply would increase, which, in turn, would result in lower prices and the elimination of monopoly profits. However, as John Blair points out:

. . . this sequence of events cannot even begin if investors are not able to determine the profitability of different industries. And such is the case where conglomerate corporations have come to account for a substantial share of an industry's output. In such circumstances investment becomes less a matter of rational decisionmaking by an informed investment community than one of simple trust in the business acumen of rival corporation managers.[31]

As a result of this loss of information on which to base rational economic decisions, there are two further political consequences. First, such withholding of information greatly disadvantages the small competititors of conglomerate subsidiaries. For example, a corporation that is only in the hotel business must disclose its own profits publicly but is unable to determine the profits of conglomerate-owned hotel chains such as Sheraton. To the extent that such information is a competitive resource, current SIC regulations and conglomerate practices undermine the position of small business. Second, since financial information is unavailable to the larger community of investors, decisions about capital flow are concentrated in the hands of those few conglomerate managers who do have detailed information on the profitability of each of their subsidiaries. Control over economic decisionmaking is thereby further concentrated.

The Impact of Corporate Secrecy

While corporate secrecy has important economic implications, as discussed in the previous section, for our purposes the most important issues posed by secrecy involve political accountability and political power. There is, first, the impact of corporate secrecy on the government. In policymaking in areas already subject to regulation—consumer protection, financial dealings, antitrust, and so on—corporate secrecy tends to reduce the ability of government agencies to carry out their regulatory mandate. There is therefore a compelling public necessity to decrease substantially the bounds of corporate secrecy in order to enforce previously enacted regulatory policy. Moreover, as noted above, corporate secrecy has led to the involvement of the government as a partner in secrecy. To the extent that the government is so involved, significant problems of political accountability are introduced. Thus, secrecy in the advisory system reduces the accessibility of government agencies to other business and consumer interests that are not represented. This lack of accessibility and lack of information undermines the very basis of political accountability.

Beyond the problems of accountability arising from the corporation-induced increase in government secrecy, corporate control of information relevant to the development of public policy introduces significant problems of accountability stemming from the unilateral power and social impact of major corporations themselves. As was extensively argued in Chapter 5, corporations are political as well as economic entities with the ability to make public policy. Thus, as with any other political entity, accountability requires a greater degree of information than has previously been available.

Moreover, the ability of the corporation to function as a political entity is increased by control of information, and thus the threat to political accountability from corporate secrecy is accentuated by the political and economic power inherent in secrecy. To the extent that information is an important political resource, the control and withholding of information yields political power. This power is illustrated by the advisory committee system. While participation in advisory committees is a source of political influence in any event, such participation in secret is an even more potent form of influence.

Secrecy is a source of power not only in relationships with the government but in terms of power in society. As Ralph Nader stated: "Without the ability to deny to the government, the small businessman, and the ordinary citizen literally every kind and form of information about their activities, large business enterprises simply could not dominate—as they often do—our economic and political life."[32] Indeed, secrecy has a "synergistic" effect—to use a term much favored by conglomerate producers—when combined with the existing power of corporations. Thus, the normal competitive advantages that would accrue to large business are accentuated by their ability to gain information about their smaller competitors without yielding the same kind of information in return. Similarly, the degree of control exercised by the eight major oil companies over America's energy supply is greatly enhanced by their unique knowledge of what makes up that supply. At least since Francis Bacon it has been observed that, in an uncertain world, information readily translates into influence, and large corporations are no exception to that rule.

In conclusion, secrecy not only acts as a barrier to the realization of corporate accountability, but excessive secrecy magnifies the power of corporations—making accountability that much more urgent. A reduction in corporate secrecy is not, by itself, a cure-all reform. At the very least, releasing information about corporate policies, profits, and products would provide the opportunity for greater public knowledge and intervention. As a political reform, simply providing that opportunity is the indispensable beginning toward greater corporate accountability—accountability that is every bit as essential for corporations as for government agencies.

In summary, we have examined three theories of corporate accountability—shareholder democracy, consumer sovereignty, and a variety of legal restraints—and found them inadequate to the task. Additionally, we have seen that the problem of corporate secrecy poses an overall barrier to any effective method of accountability. We now turn, in the final chapter, to various proposals that have been offered in response to vast corporate political power.

Notes

1. Morton Baratz, "Corporate Giants and the Power Structure," *Western Political Quarterly* 9 (June 1956), p. 415.
2. Peter Drucker, *The Concept of the Corporation* (New York: John Day, 1946), p. 72.
3. Michael S. Barum, "Social Control of Science and Technology," *Science* 172 (May 7, 1971), p. 535.
4. Jacques Ellul, *The Technological Society* (New York: Knopf, 1964), p. 5.
5. Adolf A. Berle and Gardiner C. Means, *The Modern Corporation and Private Property* (New York, 1932, 1968).
6. Ibid., p. 69.
7. Ibid.
8. Ibid., p. 88.
9. This section draws on Marvin A. Chirelstein, "Corporate Law Reform," in *Social Responsibility and the Business Predicament,* James W. McKie, ed. (Washington: Brookings Institution, 1975), pp. 42–46.
10. Ibid., p. 46.
11. Thomas Schelling, "Command and Control," in ibid., pp. 79–80.
12. Ibid., p. 95.
13. John Kenneth Galbraith, *Economics and the Public Purpose* (Boston: Houghton Mifflin, 1973), chapter 5.
14. *The Trustees of Dartmouth College* v. *Woodward,* 4 Wheaton 518, 636 (1819).
15. James W. Hurst, *The Legitimacy of the Business Corporation in the United States, 1780–1970* (Charlottesville: University of Virginia Press, 1970), pp. 8–11.
16. H. H. Gerth and C. Wright Mills, *From Max Weber: Essays in Sociology* (New York: Oxford University Press, 1946), p. 233.
17. Francis E. Rourke, *Secrecy and Publicity: Dilemmas of Democracy* (Baltimore: Johns Hopkins University Press, 1966), pp. 32–34.
18. *Bollard* v. *Volkswagen of America,* Civil Action No. 17845-3, U.S. District Court, W.D., Missouri. Decision reprinted in U.S. Congress,

Senate, Select Committee on Small Business, *Role of Giant Corporations*, hearings before the Subcommittee on Monopoly, 92nd Congress, 1st sess. (1971), pt. 2B, Appendixes, Corporate Secrecy: Overviews, p. 3018 (hereafter cited as *Role of Giant Corporations Hearings*).

19. John Kenneth Galbraith, *The New Industrial State* (Boston:Houghton Mifflin, 1967), pp. 23–34.
20. *Role of Giant Corporations Hearings,* 91st Congress, 1st sess. (1969), pt. 1—Automobile Industry, 1969, p. 98.
21. Kermit Vandivier, "Why Should My Conscience Bother Me?" in *In the Name of Profit,* Robert Heilbroner, ed. (New York: Doubleday, 1972), p. 30.
22. *Role of Giant Corporations Hearings,* pt. 2, p. 1203.
23. Ibid., statement of Ralph Nader, pt. 2, pp. 1064–73.
24. Mark J. Green, *The Closed Enterprise System* (New York: Grossman, 1972), p. 257.
25. *Role of Giant Corporations Hearings,* pt. 2A, pp. 1662–89.
26. Green, *Closed Enterprise System,* p. 260.
27. *Washington Post,* September 10, 1973, p. A2.
28. *Role of Giant Corporations Hearings,* statement of Ralph Nader, pt. 2, p. 1066.
29. Willard Mueller, "Corporate Secrecy vs. Corporate Disclosure," in *Corporate Power in America,* Ralph Nader and Mark J. Green, eds. (New York: Grossman, 1973), p. 125.
30. *Role of Giant Corporations Hearings,* pt. 2, p. 1136.
31. John Blair, *Economic Concentration: Structure, Behavior and Public Policy* (New York: Harcourt Brace Jovanovich, 1972), p. 604.
32. *Role of Giant Corporations Hearings,* statement of Ralph Nader, p. 1063.

9
Remedies and Reforms

The giant corporation is the dominant institution in our economic system. Led by a handful of men in a highly concentrated network of economic and political power, these institutions have greater influence over the lives of all of us than do most government agencies, congressmen, or judges. Nonetheless, there is no prevailing system of accountability, no theory of legitimacy relevant to the power being wielded. As Richard Barnett argued:

> We will have to stop thinking of global corporations as merely over-grown versions of the local drugstore or machine shop. When a corporation reaches the size and power sufficient to dominate the political life of whole communities, it is no longer just another piece of private property. It is a social institution and our laws must reflect that reality.[1]

Because of the barriers to corporate accountability and the failures of the traditional methods of control noted in the previous chapter, a variety of reform efforts have been proposed or initiated within the past few years. This chapter will review the major reform proposals and will conclude by advancing a theory of reform reaching toward political accountability.

The Remedial Approach

In terms of actual implementation, the most common approach to abuses of corporate power has been to formulate specific public policies (usually legislation) in response to specific problems. This approach is very much in keeping with the pragmatic, nonideological trend in American reform movements.[2] A major area typified by this kind of response to corporate power has been consumer-protection policy, which goes back at least as far as the late nineteenth century. For example, in response to rate discrimination and other abuses fueled by the monopoly power of the railroads, reformers enacted state laws and then the federal Interstate Commerce Act to regulate service and rates. The law was therefore addressed specifically to particular abuses in need of reform in a particular industry. Similarly, scandals involving the safety of food and drugs were met with the Pure Food and Drug Act of 1907 and the Food, Drug, and Cosmetic Act of 1938.

The more recent period of consumer-protection policy is even more typical of the remedial approach. Starting with the congressional hearings on the prescription drug industry chaired by the late Senator Estes Kefauver between 1959 and 1962 and reaching a crescendo by the end of the 1960s, there was a steady stream of consumer protection laws proposed and implemented in response to particular problems. These included the Ralph Nader-inspired automobile safety bill, as well as legislation on flammable fabric standards, meat and poultry inspection, radiation safety, product safety, truth-in-lending, truth-in-packaging, interstate land sales, and credit-card-holder protection—to cite the major enacted legislation. This legislation was characterized by replacing corporate decisionmaking in specified areas of public importance with partial or complete government decisionmaking.

Congressional interest and activity in consumer protection trailed off considerably following the peak years of 1966–1968. But beginning roughly in 1970 there was new concern in an issue intimately related to corporate power—the environment. Despite earlier warnings, such as Rachel Carson's alarming book *The Silent Spring* (1962), it finally reached public consciousness that the safety of the physical environment could not forever be taken for granted. Again, a large part of the problem could be traced to corporate power—decisions by corporate officials greatly contributed to air pollution, water pollution, and the depletion of natural resources. The remedial response to the newly discovered environmental crisis was somewhat more comprehensive than in the case with consumer-protection policy. Rather than being addressed narrowly to a particular type of business, environmental legislation covered virtually every industry that contributed to overall air- and water-pollution levels. The general aim of the legislation was to set up a system whereby absolute limits were established on the amount of pollutants that could be released into the atmosphere, streams, lakes, etc. (For a more detailed discussion, see Chapter 7). While covering more territory than consumer legislation, the major environmental laws still have been remedial in approach and have left a wide latitude of corporate decisionmaking in their actual implementation.

A variety of other areas of corporate abuse have also been met with specific remedies. Hazardous working conditions have been met with the Occupational Health and Safety Act, although only with limited success. Small businessmen operating under franchise from large corporations have been aided by occasional legislation and administrative regulation. Problems of campaign finance have been addressed by the Campaign Finance Reform Act.

We will make no attempt here to assess the adequacy of all the legislative remedies responding to corporate abuses and public pressure against those abuses. Some laws clearly have made major headway against particular problems; such as is the case with the Consumer Product Safety Commission. Others, however, have been only minor palliatives—remedies that may have been trivial (for example, truth in packaging) or completely underfunded (for example, occupational safety). However, the real problem with such remedial approaches is that, at best, they only alleviate symptoms of excessive corporate power without addressing the basic issues posed by the existence of that power. The fact that consumers have had to seek legislative remedies to problems with products and services itself suggests that consumers are relatively powerless in the marketplace. Rather than addressing that basic power imbalance, however, only its specific manifestations are touched.

Furthermore, legislation that promised to bring about more fundamental reform by attacking basic areas of corporate power has been repeatedly thwarted. The book that provided the final impetus toward the original Pure Food and Drug Act of 1906—Upton Sinclair's *The Jungle,* published in 1906—was actually written in the hope of attacking the more basic problem of horrible working conditions and virtual wage slavery prevalent at the time. As Sinclair himself observed, he aimed at the nation's heart and hit its stomach instead. More recently, Senator Estes Kefauver's original efforts in regard to the drug industry were aimed at the great market power of the drug firms. Instead, the reform effort was deflected to the issue of drug safety and efficacy. While the resulting legislation was an important step forward, it was only a remedy to specific problems caused by the great power of the industry; that great power, however, was not fundamentally diminished or made accountable.

In short, specific remedies to specific corporate problems may resolve those problems—but then again they may fail. The road toward corporate reform is littered with legislation that was inadequate to start with or was inadequately funded or administered by regulatory agencies. Indeed, it has been suggested that pressure from the public for reform has been deflated by the establishment of inadequate laws and agencies that provide only "symbolic reassurances" to citizens rather than meaningful reform.[3]

Finally, implicit in the case-by-case remedial approach is the assumption that corporate abuses such as illegal campaign contributions or the marketing of hazardous products are isolated episodes of evil behavior in an otherwise beneficent corporate system. While the argument of this book is not that corporate activities usually have evil consequences, it still must be recognized that the kinds of problems discussed in the preceding chapters call for more than a simple patchwork system. To the extent that we are committed to a basically "free enterprise" system, a remedial approach may be the best we can achieve. But before we settle for such an approach, we should first examine the possibility of more fundamental reform proposals that, in the long run, may be even more in keeping with our underlying democratic and capitalist values. It is to these broader reforms that we now turn.

Toward Reform

Corporate Responsibility

One broad theme for reform is generally termed *corporate responsibility*. In brief, this term encompasses a variety of proposals revolving around the concept that corporate power should be and can be used for benign purposes. As Neil Chamberlain notes:

> Many who believe in the potential goodness of our major corporations are convinced that only their present selfishness prevents them from making the desired social contribution. . . . If all major corporations would only recognize the consequence of their present social failures and the social benefits latent in more responsible uses of their power, we could experience a veritable revolution without bloodshed.[4]

While the demand for corporate responsibility comes largely from social critics outside of business, some executives within corporations also maintain that they could make a positive contribution to social welfare if they were given free rein to apply the technological expertise of their industries to social problem solving. Based on management science, especially techniques of systems analysis, Chamberlain terms this concept the *Social Engineering Thesis*.

Actually, vague notions of corporate responsibility extend at least as far back as Andrew Carnegie and the "social gospel" movement of the late nineteenth century, and they encompass present programs of urban renewal and job training for the disadvantaged. There are, however, at least two basic problems with the movement for corporate social responsibility. First, as Chamberlain argues, "neither of these approaches [corporate responsibility or the Social Engineering Thesis] has any prospect of implementation and . . . the only initiatives that can be expected even from our largest and financially strongest corporations will be necessarily limited in scope and substance, barely touching the most grievous social problems."[5]

Even if we tempered our expectations of corporate good works and relied on corporate responsibility to contain the negative consequences of corporate activity, a more basic, problem would remain. The concept of corporate responsibility accepts the reality of corporate power and focuses on its potential as a socially beneficent phenomenon—if only that power can be used for "good" ends. The problem with this solution is that it does not get at the problem of accountability. Instead of holding centers of power accountable to citizens, it simply stresses that such power can be used in ways that will benefit citizens. Instead of despotism, we are given benevolent despotism. Inherent in our own Constitution is the Madisonian concept that benevolence alone is not a sufficient standard of conduct in civil governments. It is no more sufficient when applied to private governments.

Antitrust

A foreign observer has called antitrust policy an American religion.[6] Given our high level of economic and industrial concentration, it is hard to go that far in characterizing American antitrust policy, but it is nonetheless true that American public policy has been far more opposed to cartels and monopolies than Europe and Japan. This theme in our economic policy has its roots in the late nineteenth century, when political pressure from the Populist and later the Progressive movements militated against the rapidly spreading trusts of the day, such as John D. Rockefeller's Standard Oil. The first major action against the trusts was the Sherman Act in 1890. The act prohibited "every contract combination . . . or conspiracy, in restraint of trade," and made it illegal to monopolize or attempt to monopolize trade. There is some controversy over whether or not it was merely a symbolic sop to public pressure. Regardless of the original intent of Congress, however, the act was limited by the Supreme Court, which, in 1911, invoked the so-called "rule of reason" that only unreasonable trusts were to be proscribed—for example, those that used their economic power in a predatory manner. Well-behaved trusts were to be considered legal.

As a result of court decisions and a pattern of lax enforcement, pressure from the Progressives mounted and the Clayton Act of

1914 was passed. Although intended to nip monopoly in the bud by prohibiting anticompetitive mergers effected by stock acquisitions, the Clayton Act was in fact easily circumvented by simply establishing mergers through acquisition of assets. Thus, the Clayton Act and the Federal Trade Commission Act, passed the same year, did nothing to prevent the formation through merger of giants such as Bethlehem Steel, Republic Steel, Allied Chemical, and General Foods, to cite just a few. It was not until passage of the Celler-Kefauver Act in 1950—backed by strict court interpretations—that mergers between competitors were effectively prohibited. By that time, as noted earlier (see Chapter 6), substantial economic concentration existed, and the merger movement turned to the conglomerate form in the 1960s. In short, regardless of their intentions, the antitrust policy of the United States did not prevent substantial industrial merger activity and concentration within industries such as steel and chemicals until 1950; even then there was no effective public policy to slow down the great conglomerate blitz that followed. Nonetheless, the attraction of antitrust as a reform continues to have a hold on many serious critics of corporate power.

The basis of antitrust philosophy is the belief that, through free and unfettered competition, the most efficient and equitable distribution of goods and services will take place. Antitrust policy is thus the public-policy counterpart of the demonstration of classical economics that monopoly results in the production of too few goods at too high a price. But there is more to antitrust policy than an economic dimension. As we have seen throughout this book, a high concentration of economic power readily leads to excessive political power. Thus, an attack on the former is simultaneously an attack on the latter. To the extent that the free-enterprise system is congruent with democratic values, the prevention of monopoly yields the political bonus of a wider distribution of power. Democratic values are also seen as inherent in antitrust policy in regard to the role of the government. In the absence of monopolistic conditions, the economic marketplace is believed to be largely self-regulating. Thus, in the antitrust credo, the role of government should be limited to maintaining the necessary conditions for free and vigorous competition. According to this belief, if such a healthy competitive situation can be made to prevail, more direct and severe government regulation becomes unnecessary. Thus, by maximizing freedom of action in the private sector and minimizing government's role, the democratic values in capitalism are maintained. All this is not to claim that all antitrust advocates are unreconstructed capitalists or that they all believe in minimum government. Rather, we have sought to emphasize that antitrust policies are completely consistent with traditional American economic and political beliefs.

There are, however, two basic objections to relying on antitrust policy as an instrument of reform. First, the application of antitrust laws has hardly been objective or nonpolitical. There has been as much partisanship and exercise of political influence in the design and implementation of antitrust policy as in any other sphere of economic policymaking. Antitrust cases have even been brought in order to win votes as they were in 1948 when suits against manufacturers of farm implements and against meat packing houses courted the farm vote. More commonly, solidly based antitrust actions have been dropped due to the intercession of high-level executive or congressional politicians.[7] In one of the most notorious of such cases, the government settled out of court its case that ITT divest itself of the Hartford Fire Insurance Company after ITT offered to help underwrite the 1972 Republican National Convention. Thus, it can be argued that antitrust has been so tinged with political enforcement that it has itself been a result of corporate political power; to depend on antitrust policy as a reform is inherently futile. The foxes cannot guard the chicken coop.

Another objection to antitrust policy is more basic. It has been argued that the financial and technological requirements of our modern economy require bigness. Only giant corporations possess the resources to afford the economies of scale of modern industrial life, the antitrust critics contend. Furthermore, even if such enterprises are larger than absolutely necessary, bigness is so endemic and so extensive in our economic system that the latter-day trust busters are only playing Don Quixote against the conglomerate and multinational windmills. As John Kenneth Galbraith, a resolute critic of antitrust, argues:

. . . Were only a handful of great corporations exercising power over prices, costs, the consumer and over public attitudes, perhaps their dissolution into smaller units and therewith the dissolution of their power might be possible. But a government cannot proclaim half of the economic system illegal; it certainly will not do so if its test of sound public policy is what, in general, serves the goals of this part of the economy.[8]

Beyond the argument that we cannot undo the past, there is also considerable sentiment in favor of giant corporations on other grounds as well. Particularly in regard to the need to meet industrial competition from Europe and Japan, corporate officials stress the need for an American response from corporations whose size and power are not diminished. It is further argued by Galbraith, as well as by corporate spokesmen, that only giant enterprise can afford the research and development expenses essential to develop new technologies in vital fields such as energy exploration.

Although the past history of antitrust should give us some reservations about relying on it as our fundamental reform, the real issue is not pure competition versus monopoly. It is essential to preserve competition within the economy, and the ultimate question is how to balance that need with the need for innovation and the ability to compete in the world market. Furthermore, if immense concentrations of capital are indeed needed in fields such as energy, there is also precious little evidence that giantism leads to innovation. For all its size, General Motors rapidly lost ground to foreign automakers that did a better job of filling the need for reliable cars with high gas mileage.

Given our underlying political and economic system, some policy of promoting competition is essential. The inadequacies of past antitrust policies only point to the need for more vigorous and even-handed enforcement and, perhaps, to new policies dealing with conglomerates and multinationals. The basic theme of antitrust is still valid: one way to check power is to prevent the vast accumulation of power in the first place.

Federal Chartering

A less widely proposed reform is federal chartering of large corporations. As was discussed previously, the original concept of the corporate charter was tied to the notion of the charter as a privilege. In moving away from that theory, however, we have reduced the regulatory features of the corporate charter to a ludicrous level. The individual states became the primary agencies for chartering, and a classic case of Gresham's law set in. As corporations grew in size, they no longer did business in only one state. Instead, although they were chartered in one state, they could do business in many different states. This led to a virtual contest among several states to see who could offer chartering terms that were most lax in exchange for the extra revenues that issuing a charter would bring. The early winner in the contest was New Jersey, which captured more than half of the nation's large corporations at the end of the nineteenth century. However, New Jersey's place was taken by Delaware in the early part of the twentieth century, and that little state has held the chartering championship ever since. At present, about one-third of all companies traded on the New York Stock Exchange and half of the one hundred largest corporations in the country are chartered in Delaware.

What are the inducements that brought this corporate bonanza to Delaware? Basically, Delaware charters are a bill of rights for corporate management and directors. The original 1899 business code permitted any classification of stock to be issued with or without voting powers; annual meetings could be held outside the state; and directors were permitted to issue new stock, change the terms of authorized stock, retire preferred stock, and change by-laws without the consent of stockholders. Later modifications gave directors, but not stockholders, power to propose charter amendments. Stock options and bonuses were expressly allowed without any safeguards or disclosure requirements. Also, in the event of criminal or civil cases, officers and directors could be indemnified by corporations for court costs without approval by the court or shareholders.

Advocates of a federal charter for corporations, foremost among whom is Ralph Nader, argue that the charter should protect the rights of stockholders and society rather than only management. The major arguments in favor of federal chartering revolve around the inadequacy of the states as controllers of large corporations. As Ralph Nader notes:

. . . Even *if* state business codes and authorities did not so overwhelmingly reflect management power interests, they would still be significantly incapable of following through to enforcement. . . . Our states are no match for the resources and size of our great corporations; General Motors could *buy* Delaware . . . if DuPont were willing to sell it.[9]

The federal rather than state government is urged as the chartering agency in order to reverse the results of the race among the states to be the lowest common denominator in charter requirements. At present, it would be folly for any one state to significantly tighten charter requirements because adversely affected corporations could simply be chartered in another state.

The key factor, of course, is not where a charter is issued but what it requires. The problem of jurisdiction only relates to the ability to enforce the requirements of a charter; what is required is another matter. Basically, the advocates of federal chartering urge a return to the earlier concept of the charter of incorporation as a privilege subject to a variety of restrictions for the purpose of promoting the public interest. The charter is conceived as a set of obligations that giant corporations would be required to meet as a condition of their very existence.

Although there are a variety of views of what such a charter would require, Ralph Nader's suggestions are both typical and comprehensive.[10] These include the following. First, real corporate democracy would be established, with substantial increase in the rights of shareholders and a consequent decrease in the unilateral prerogatives of management. For example, loans to corporate officers would be prohibited, and all compensation schemes for corporate officials would have to be submitted to stockholders for approval. Second, antitrust would be a condition of the charter; corporations beyond a certain size or having a certain proportion of a market would be prohibited from merging. Third, there would be corporate disclosure instead of corporate secrecy. Fourth, rules would be promulgated for protecting and indemnifying consumers for unsafe or shoddy products. Finally, the charter would "constitutionalize" the corporation. Thus, the charter would apply to the private government of the corporation many of the same guarantees available to citizens of public governments—for example, freedom of speech as one particular protection for employees.

As the above list indicates, the federal charter is actually an umbrella for a variety of specific reforms of corporations. The question is whether such an umbrella is the best strategy of reform in terms of either feasibility or efficacy. While there was a good deal of interest in Congress in federal chartering in the early part of this century and again in the 1930s, the efforts were derailed, and there has been little serious interest in the subject since that time. Furthermore, if it is now difficult to obtain enactment of laws against corporate secrecy, it would be far more difficult to combine every substantive reform currently being proposed into one comprehensive chartering act. While political feasibility isn't everything, it is still a factor to be weighed in any evaluation of a reform proposal.

More fundamental is the question of why any "umbrella" is needed over these various reforms. While the Nader proposals and other suggestions for inclusion into a federal charter requirements are related, they are not closely related. At least their interrelationships are not so apparent as to warrant the enormous political effort that would be necessary in the unlikely event that such a proposal is enacted. There is also left open the question of how much should be put into a charter. Clearly, not all problems of corporate accountability can be handled in this way, but how many should? What are the boundaries? There are no clear guides. Furthermore, having a federal charter does not eliminate the race among the states to offer the easiest terms to corporations. The states individually still can be played off against each other in matters such as taxation, zoning and land-use laws, labor standards, and so on. Since it takes only a few lax states to undermine tighter laws, it is difficult to see why everything should be crowded into a charter or why a comprehensive charter is a necessary instrument of reform.

There is, however, one basic aspect of the federal-charter proposal that stands out and perhaps outweighs any drawbacks—the concept of accountability. Inherent in the notion of the charter is the accountability of the giant corporation to the society of which it is a part. Corporate officials would be forcefully reminded that great public power cannot be used exclusively for private ends or in disregard of the public interest. This recognition would not weaken the character of the corporation as a business with a right to seek a profit, nor would it be even a further intrusion of government into business. Rather, a requirement of federal chartering for the largest corporations would be an assertion that, like all citizens, corporations not only have legal rights but obligations as well. In exchange for the very substantial privilege of corporate organization granted by society, corporations would comply with whatever policy requirements were determined to be in the public interest. At the very least this would be a major step toward accountability by asserting the public nature of giant corporations.

Governing the Corporation

The fourth major proposal for corporate reform consists of suggestions to change the internal governance of the corporation—to forcefully assert certain kinds of public-interest claims in the process of running the corporation. While greater corporate accountability is not the only purpose of such reform proposals, it is at least implicit in them. Without claiming that this is an exhaustive list, we shall mention three frequently heard proposals for reform in corporate governance.

First is the proposal for having public-interest members on the board of directors of a corporation—directors who would press the interests of the wider public in the corporate boardroom. One immediate objection to this plan can be surmised from the earlier discussion of the role of directors. While directors *theoretically* represent the shareholder interest, in fact they have little control (and frequently little interest) in running the company. To insert a public-interest representative in a group that traditionally has little power may be no more than an exercise in symbolism. To counter this weakness, the iconoclastic former president of Avis, Robert Townsend, has proposed that giant corporations should each have a full-time public director with a staff of various experts and a budget in the neighborhood of $1 million. Townsend argues for the necessity of public directors:

. . . It is no exaggeration to say that all the big-company managements I am familiar with are basically engaged (whether they are conscious of it or not) in screwing their stockholders, employees, customers, and the general public as well, while living off the fat of the land themselves. In my judgment, the government is not going to do anything about it; neither are the labor unions. Public directors could produce miracles of reform if they were selected properly and given an adequate bankroll.[11]

The public director would be able to attend all meetings within the company, have access to all records, and would be generally able to pursue an in-depth look at corporation policies. It is obvious that anything less than what Townsend proposes would fall far short of the mark. For example, to have a black person on the board as representative of black interests is not only tokenism, it also guarantees nothing about the giant corporation's compliance with equal-opportunity requirements.

Nonetheless, even the beefed-up public-director proposal has considerable difficulties. A public director would be only one member of the board, and it is far from certain that such a person could prevail in a conflict with management. To assume that the public director would somehow, by his very presence, prick the conscience of management or other directors is really to make a flying leap of faith. There is also a more fundamental problem. Who is to be the constituency of the public director? Who is the public that he or she represents? At the very least, the public director might more effectively protect the interests of stockholders than the present system of part-time directors with limited resources. There could be closer supervision of executive salaries, prerequisites, and the like. But this hardly constitutes a profound system of political accountability.

Moreover, it should be clear that the interests of the stockholders are no more coincidental with the public interest than the interests of management. And, if the public director can represent wider interests, even in opposition to management and stockholders, how does he or she become an instrument of political accountability? It is a little far-fetched to assume that anyone would be effective under those circumstances. Even if the director could be a representative of wider interests, the question would be which wider interest? After all, the interests of consumers are not the same as the interests of workers or those of people living in the community in which the giant corporation has its plants. All this is not to dismiss the concept of the public director out of hand. As an instrument of disclosure and even as a sort of early-warning system of corporate abuse, the public director could serve a valuable function—but only if adequately funded and staffed, as Townsend suggests. But even this element can be only one part of a total system of accountability.

Another mode of reform in governance is the move for "ethical investing."[12] The idea is to encourage large institutional investors such as pension funds and universities to take the social record of a corporation into account in making investment decisions. This move could take the form of avoiding investment in some companies altogether or, more commonly, marshaling large blocs of stock for or against various proposals put forth to the stockholders. The most notable attempt at ethical investing was Campaign GM, which succeeded (through the intercession of the Securities and Exchange Commission) in requiring General Motors to place various proposals on the annual stockholders proxy ballot. This attempt was notable not only in the publicity it received but also in the sad fact that the proposals received less than 5 per cent of the votes. Even if it had succeeded or had prospects of succeeding, a problem with ethical investing is that it tends to focus on a few highly publicized issues, which may not necessarily represent the most important areas of corporate social impact. Finally, it is hard enough for stockholders to assess the financial health of their corporation. To expect them to evaluate the far more ambiguous area of social responsibility is not realistic.

Finally, various models of worker control of the corporation have been proposed. Thus, it has been argued that workers should be involved in decisions relating to method and speed of production, hours, pay, and even product development and sales. Worker control is advanced in order both to reduce the alienation of the worker and to make the workplace more democratic; and there is a good deal of merit in these arguments. It is a cruel irony that, within industrial society, those who have the worst jobs—and often the most essential—are also paid the least. Giving the people who actually do the work in corporations some greater control over their working lives might in fact tend to remedy their inequitable position. But is worker management a means of obtaining corporate accountability? Probably not. Workers may be counted upon to deal with corporate impacts that directly affect themselves; but in all other respects, they would seek only to maximize the economic success of the corporation. Company success, after all, is the road to continued employment and higher pay for workers. It is simply romantic Marxist nonsense to expect worker-managers to react much differently from present corporate officials to problems of the environment and consumer protection. Labor unions have, at times, been active advocates of consumer protection legislation, except when it threatens jobs.

In looking at the larger picture of internal governance of the corporation, there is a more fundamental problem. It is not at all clear who *should* run the corporation. While as a society we take for granted the varied prerogatives of management, freedom of management is based on the unfounded notion that management is ultimately accountable to the stockholders. But we have seen that this is only a convenient fiction. Increasingly, the position of management may be seen as not legitimate—particularly to workers. As Peter Drucker notes:

. . . A legitimate government is a government that rules in the interest of its subjects. But that the enterprise cannot possibly do. The first concern of the enterprise must be for profitability and productivity, not for the welfare of its members.[13]

Drucker goes on to argue that the legitimacy of the corporation is established by using its power in the interest of the enterprise as a whole and of society. He notes, however, that workers do not accept such a rationale and only see that corporate authority is not discharged for their benefit and is hence not legitimate from their point of view.

Indeed, the question of who should rule or share in the ruling of giant corporations (and economic enterprise generally) is very much an open question. By what right does a self-perpetuating management exercise power in an enterprise it does not own? There is no satisfactory answer short of saying, in effect, "That's the way things are." But what about returning power to the actual owners, the shareholders? Not only is this easier said than done, but the shareholders are owners only in the most limited sense. In large corporations, individual stockholders (even institutional stockholders, such as banks and mutual funds) own only a fraction of the stock. It is not clear that they own anything tangible. Rather, they make an investment, a dignified gamble, in stocks whose market value they hope will increase. The concept of shareholder democracy has further difficulties as concisely noted by Robert Dahl:

. . . The first, and it seems to me lethal [objection], stems from the underlying and usually unexamined assumption that investors, whether individuals or firms, have some special right to govern the firms in which they invest. I can discover absolutely no moral or philosophical basis for such a right. Why investors and not consumers, workers, or for that matter the general public?[14]

Dahl notes that investors are not particularly interested in running corporations; nor are they competent to do so. Furthermore, it would be impossible to establish an equitable basis of voting. Our normal democratic theory calls for one man, one vote. But why should one share of stock entitle someone to more voice in the firm than an employee, who has a much greater stake in the firm? While Dahl tentatively edges toward the idea of worker control, based on their stake in the business, we have already seen that this in no way establishes the accountability of the corporation to the broader society over which it has power. In the interest of fairness, we might want to improve the position of workers or stockholders, but reform in the governance of giant corporations will not in itself establish the accountability that is essential from giant corporations.

The criticism of various reform proposals in the preceding pages should not be taken to mean that the quest for accountability is futile, nor that these proposals are without merit. Undoubtedly, if we had more vigorous antitrust actions (especially directed toward multinational conglomerates), public-interest directors, federal chartering, worker representation, and so on, we would be much better off than we are now. However, the problem of corporate accountability is more fundamental than is acknowledged in the various reforms that have been discussed, and a more fundamental theme of reform is needed.

Toward Accountability

The basic problem is that corporations exercise considerable power over people to whom they are not accountable—in neither theory nor practice—and that fact simply flies in the face of democratic theory. While there are different theories of the criteria of democracy, running from the minimum requirement of having a choice among competing elites all the way to the movement for participatory democracy, the *sine qua non* of most democratic theories is political accountability—some mechanism whereby citizens have formal means of control, either periodically or continuously, over those who make binding decisions affecting them. Corporations qualify as such decisionmakers, but there is no such means of control over them.

In discussing corporate accountability, the underlying point to be emphasized is that, in many respects, the quest for corporate accountability must be conceived of as part of a quest for greater overall political accountability. That is, to the extent that they are political entities with great discretionary power, the need for political accountability is as urgent for corporations as for the formal institutions of government. Furthermore, in order to obtain greater accountability from corporations, it is necessary to increase governmental accountability by reforming the government agencies that maintain and promote corporate power in a setting insulated from public control. Indeed, it will be argued that, by dealing with the problem of corporate accountability, we can also make some headway into resolving problems of governmental accountability. Thus, as Chapter 8 argues, some governmental secrecy is a consequence of corporate secrecy; lessening corporate secrecy would thus lessen government secrecy—secrecy that limits political accountability.

One potential objection to this emphasis on political accountability can be noted and dispensed with at the outset. It can be paraphrased as follows: Why emphasize political accountability from corporations when such accountability has proven to be difficult to obtain even from the formal institutions of government? We would offer two replies to such an objection. First, the difficulty of obtaining accountability is hardly a reason for abandoning the attempt. It only stresses the necessity for accountability. Secondly, and somewhat perversely, it may actually be possible to obtain greater political accountability from corporations than from governments. This likelihood stems from a proposal to rely more on the ultimate weapon of accountability—competition.

Another objection to corporate reform, whether it involves pollution control, consumer protection, or basic structural reform, is that the costs would be too high. One response to such an objection is simply, "So what? Democratic values are more important than economic values." While such a response may reflect the preferences of many people, it nonetheless accepts the corporate premise that reform is economically unsound. A more desirable response is that the costs to society need not be high and that, in fact, the economic costs are probably lower than the costs of the status quo. We can have our cake and eat it, too. As we have seen, excessive corporate power itself entails heavy costs on society. The power of corporations in government, as well as corporations acting as private governments, has led to costs such as pollution, administered prices higher than competitive prices, and artificial scarcities of energy resources. The basic cause of these corporate imposed costs is an unhealthy concentration of economic and political power. In terms of the economy, we have reviewed the problems of economic concentration. In political terms, we have seen an imbalance of political power in favor of corporations. The economic and political viability of reform therefore stems from the benefits that would accrue if these concentrations of power were dispersed. Indeed, political accountability requires no less than an assertion of greater political and economic pluralism by breaking down the present barriers to competition.

Rationality, Competition, and Accountability

As generations of students have learned from economists ranging from Adam Smith through George Stigler, and as we have seen in Chapter 6, monopolies distort the efficiency of the economy and result in higher prices than would otherwise accrue.[15] Oligopolies—industries controlled by only a few firms—have the same tendency but to a lesser degree. As John Blair noted in his major work on economic concentration: "Under today's conditions one of the effects of concentration, as compared to a more competitive or polyopolistic economy, would appear to be higher costs, particularly those arising from managerial diseconomies. A corollary effect would appear to be a slower rate of invention, and possibly also, a slower rate of innovation." Additionally, oligopolies result in higher prices and lower rates of production than would otherwise prevail.[16]

In short, giant corporations in concentrated industries tend to be economically irrational. Economic rationality refers to the most efficient relationship between inputs (labor, capital, and so on) and outputs (production, revenues, and the like). The essence of economic rationality—for both firms and consumers—is the goal of obtaining the maximum output per unit input. The actual behavior of firms usually departs from this ideal model as other goals, such as stable growth and share of the market, enter the calculations. Nonetheless, a rough version of "getting the biggest bang for the buck" is still a major goal, and the economic theory of the firm constitutes the basis of economic rationality.

For our purposes, it is important to note that, just as they are economically irrational, large corporations tend to be politically irrational in the same sense; that is, they distort the optimal distribution of political resources. A system of political rationality has inherent in it the same value assumption that applies to economic rationality—the goal of maximum political influence on policy (outputs) per unit of political input. In democratic systems, the votes of individual citizens are the basic inputs. Thus, the most rational system would be one in which citizens' votes in the aggregate have the maximum possible leverage on policy. In a purely rational system, the democratic creed of "one man, one vote" should also mean "one man, one unit of influence." To the extent that smaller aggregations of voters or nonvoting organizations exert political power that blocks or minimizes the policy outputs that should be obtained by larger groups of voters, political rationality suffers. Just as oligopolies result in higher economic prices to consumers, they may also result in higher political prices to obtain a given unit of influence.

The reform effort to obtain greater political rationality is the same as that needed to obtain greater economic rationality: the deconcentration of economic power and a novel reliance on competition. While this may appear, at first glance, like merely reverting to more antitrust policies, actually the reform theme being proposed here goes considerably beyond current antitrust policies and suggests instead a basic overhaul in the relationship between business and government. This approach seeks to redress the current imbalance between corporate power and other interests in society by aiming for political and economic structures and incentives that will lead to a more responsive, and hence accountable, economic and political order. Rather than detail every possible specific reform, we will outline broadly the direction we feel reform should take in order to achieve a more accountable economic and political system. There are several policies that would go a long way toward achieving this goal.

First, there must be substantial deconcentration of the economy. One useful measure along these lines is a bill introduced by Senator Philip A. Hart and cosponsored by several other senators in 1975. The bill, entitled the Industrial Reorganization Act (S. 1959) would make unlawful the possession of monopoly power by one or more corporations in any line of commerce. There would be a presumption of monopoly power if, over a specified number of years, either of the following conditions obtained: (1) there has been no substantial price competition among corporations in any line of commerce; or (2) if any four corporations account for at least 50 per cent of sales in a given line of commerce. When one of these criteria is met, the offending corporation would be required to reorganize and divest itself of some of its component parts, unless it could show that its monopoly power was due solely to the ownership of lawfully utilized patents or that such a divestiture would result in a substantial loss of economies. The act would also establish an Industrial Reorganization Commission to pursue other instances of monopoly power.

While bigness is not necessarily bad, giantism, with its distortion of economic and political resources, almost always is. There is a real threat to our political and economic institutions from corporations that have massive amounts of economic and technological resources. As the preamble to the Industrial Reorganization Act states: "The preservation of a private enterprise system, a free market economy, and a democratic society in the United States of America requires legislation to supplement the policy of the antitrust laws through new enforcement mechanisms designed to responsibly restructure industries dominated by oligopoly or monopoly power." Again, competition is seen as an antidote to concentrations of political and economic power.

It must be emphasized that such a proposal would not seek to revert to a bygone era of small shops and cottage industry. Nor does it even fulfill the romantic vision of self-sufficient communes and a society no longer dependent on the outpourings of heavy industry. Even if ITT were broken down into three or four divisions or if GM were broken down into its component product lines, we would still have several very large corporations. But that is precisely the point. With components the size of the Chevrolet or Buick auto divisions or the Frigidaire home appliance division, what possible rationale can there be for those components to be combined in one behemoth of a company? Given the enormous power harnessed in just a few hands, whatever marginal economic advantage there is to companies of this size pales in the face of the threat to democratic values and the public interest posed by such concentrations of power. By deconcentrating, the nation could easily enjoy the economies of scale necessary for efficient production and technological innovation. But we would have the additional benefit of having industry responsive to our needs rather than the other way around. Vigorous antitrust and deconcentration would therefore respond to one essential goal of reform—the control of power. Power to affect society unilaterally would be lessened by increasing the number of centers of power.

In addition to dispersing excess concentrations of power, a reform program would also have to address several problems that act as a catalyst for the irresponsible use of corporate power. That is, economic concentration is not the only source of the abuses of power. There are several other features of our political-economic system that almost guarantee that corporate interests will have a negative impact on society and that power will be abused. It will be recalled that the present economic system is such that government is the major element in the environment of most business corporations. Corporations thus have every incentive to influence the government; indeed, from the corporate perspective it is imperative that they do so. While it is clearly impossible and undesirable to remove the government from economic management, there are still a number of areas in which the incentives for the misuse of power and corruption could be significantly reduced.

One basic reform in this direction would be to reduce the number of things that government can do for corporations—particularly in regard to the creation of wealth. This would entail substantial deregulation of business activity. While it may appear strange to call for less government regulation while attempting to dismantle corporate power, it must be recalled that much of what passes for regulation is actually the utilization of government to create wealth or to protect existing corporations from competition. Such regulation is thus part of the problem rather than part of the solution. The solution would be to maximize economic freedom and decentralize economic decisionmaking by relying much more on the play of competition in the marketplace. The abolition of the Interstate Commerce Commission, for example, would allow consumers rather than a government agency (under pressure from regulated industry) to determine the ultimate shape of prices and service in the surface transportation industry. Similarly, airlines try to influence the Civil Aeronautics Board, through legal and illegal means, because the board controls their rates and routes. If this government power were removed, a great incentive to corruption would also be removed.

Even in those areas requiring some government intervention because of technological factors or the existence of a natural monopoly, greater competition could be introduced. The government clearly must allocate television and radio frequencies, but in doing so administratively it simultaneously creates wealth. Instead, the government could simply auction off broadcasting licenses. Corporations would then pay what they were worth, a bureaucratic threat to freedom would be eliminated, and an incentive for the exercise of massive political pressure would be reduced.

For the first time since the 1930s the whole issue of government regulation of business has become a major national issue. Conservatives and many businessmen are leading an assault on most facets of government regulation, particularly in the areas of consumer protection and the environment. While this would no doubt be convenient for many corporations, it would be less convenient for the rest of us. Therefore, it must be emphasized that deregulation must be selective. Since the purpose of the reforms proposed here is political accountability, the operative concept is *choice*. Deregulation makes sense only where consumer choice is a realistic option. Although conservative critics deny the distinction, there really is a basic and unambiguous line between regulation that protects monopoly and regulation for health and safety—a distinction based on the crucial concept of choice. Ralph Nader and Mark Green have cogently laid out the difference:

. . . A traveler can compare the prices of taking a plane or bus between Washington and New York City and arrive at a choice without the need of a CAB or an ICC. But can consumers smell carbon monoxide seeping into a car, detect that the drug they are giving their children is mutagenic, or taste cancerous pesticides that went into the production of their food?[17]

Another feature of reform would be to minimize the amount of discretion available to government administrators in implementing regulations. Congressionally passed legislation, of necessity, always allows a good deal of latitude to the agencies administering the law. But frequently the latitude is so great that agencies are left with the power to make decisions worth a fortune to affected business interests; and such decisions are made with little in the way of legislative guidance or limits. Thus, whenever possible, definite standards ought to be written in the law. For example, apart from its other goals, one valuable feature of Senator Hart's industrial-reorganization bill is that it simply sets size limits beyond which corporations cannot merge. This effectively prevents government agencies and the Department of Justice from having much discretion over the matter, and hence prevents the kind of corruption so evident in past antitrust proceedings.

Similarly, we saw earlier that the existing pollution laws present regulators with a real Hobson's choice of either flouting the law or closing down important plants that do not meet standards. Understandably, there is a lot of political pressure on the environmental agencies to choose the first course. However, rules assessing fixed taxes on pollution would not only charge companies for their externalities but also reduce the all-or-nothing power of government over corporations. That is, instead of having the power to decide whether or not particular deadlines would have to be met—a power inviting corruption—administrators would have only to assess predetermined tax rates based on the emission of pollutants. There are always going to be areas in which bureaucrats need to have discretion, in which they are going to be the ones making the real policy decisions—for example, in food and drug safety or income-tax audits. But the task for innovative policy- and lawmakers ought to be to reduce such discretion to the necessary minimum, not out of any abstract fear of "big government" but in order to reduce the incentives currently existing for giant corporations to run big government.

As we have seen in earlier chapters, economic concentration is not the only source of corporate political power and abuses. Regardless of the preceding reforms, business corporations will continue to wield a good deal of political power because of superior organization and other resources that will remain with business regardless of any conceivable (and feasible) reforms. The problem with such power is not that it exists but that it usually far outweighs the political power exercised by other social interests. Therefore, mechanisms must be established to redress the balance of forces—not to overpower legitimate corporate interests but to prevent the shutting out of other competing public interests.

One such reform is the proposal for an Agency for Consumer Advocacy. Such an agency would represent consumer interests before the regulatory agencies. This would tend to alleviate the enormous advantage now held by corporations that can readily muster more legal resources than any voluntary consumer group. Taking advantage of the adversary process inherent in our legal system, interests other than those of affected corporations would be forcefully pressed before the regulatory agencies.

Another possibility along these lines would be to make it easier for consumers to bring legal action known as class-action suits. These lawsuits would enable many individuals, each having relatively small claims against a corporation (for example, a defective television set), to band together and aggregate their claims into a single suit. Whereas it would not make any sense for any one of them to go to the trouble and expense of bringing suit individually, by being able to band together they could hire competent legal counsel and not be overwhelmed by the superior resources of the corporation. The principle of class action has suffered setbacks in the courts in the last few years, but this just means that we must look to Congress and the state legislatures to establish the means for facilitating this method of balancing corporate power.

In Chapters 2 and 3, we examined the exercise of corporate political power through campaign contributions and lobbying. In redressing the imbalance of power in these areas, we must take care not to abuse the constitutional guarantees of free speech and the right to petition government—rights that accrue to business interests just as they do to other social interests. However, as we discussed in the preceding chapter, *one useful remedy would be to break the bounds of secrecy within which campaign and lobbying abuses are more likely to flourish.* The provisions for more complete disclosure in the Federal Election Campaign Act Amendments of 1974 are a good start. Similarly, there should be more realistic and comprehensive requirements for the disclosure of the amounts spent by corporations for lobbying and the nature of their lobbying activities. There could also be more stringent prohibitions against the acceptance of gratuities from corporations by legislators in addition to the present rules that apply only to administrators.

Finally, in many areas we need new approaches to enforcement and better enforcement of laws to protect consumers and workers from abuses of corporate power. One of the virtues of removing the government from excessive regulation such as exists in the Interstate Commerce Commission is that more effort can be concentrated in the essential regulatory areas of health and safety. At a time when citizens are properly concerned with the growth of government bureaucracy, the solution is not simply to spend more time and money on regulating business. Rather, the effort must be made to identify those areas, such as occupational safety and pollution, in which more vigorous government regulation is needed and to remove the government from the business of creating wealth and protecting existing monopolies.

Competition and the Political System

The basic theme of the reforms suggested here is a revitalization of competition, achieved either through freeing the economic marketplace from regulatory restraints, decreasing concentrations of economic power, or aiding consumer, environmental, and other widely dispersed interests to match the inevitable political muscle of large corporations. Competition should be relied on to be the foundation of reform because there is a very direct and profound relationship between competition and political accountability.

In the economic sector, competition increases the aggregate influence of participants (as buyers or sellers) dealing with a particular market. In a competitive market, instead of prices being set unilaterally by one or a few sellers, they are set by the aggregate demand of many potential buyers in relation to supply. The sellers are thus automatically accountable to the buyers in terms of price and supply. Of course, by definition, individual buyers and sellers by themselves have no influence on the market. But neither—in a truly competitive market—are they faced with economic entities that are insulated and unaccountable to the vagaries of the market. Furthermore, consumer preferences in terms of product design, quality, and so on are more likely to be realized when there is real competition among sellers. For example, it was not until the advent of foreign competition that American car manufacturers began to offer truly compact cars. Therefore, competition increases the options available to consumers and forces firms to be accountable to the aggregate preferences of those with whom they do business.

Competition is also central to political accountability. The utilization of competition to obtain political accountability has both old and relatively new precedents. Inherent in most versions of democratic theory is the necessity of citizens having the opportunity to make choices between alternative elites and policies. There can only be choice if competing alternatives actually exist. Conversely, there is an incentive for government leaders to be responsive to the desires of citizens as long as those leaders are forced to compete for citizen votes.[18]

The reforms proposed above rest on two sets of assumptions central to the American political tradition. The first assumption is that Lord Acton was correct: Power corrupts, and absolute power corrupts absolutely. Highly concentrated power in corporations has led otherwise decent people to do indecent things. This leads to the second assumption that the way to control power is not to depend on self-control but to check power with competing power. This assumption is, of course, the very basis of our constitutional system of checks and balances. This proposition was concisely set forth by James Madison in *The Federalist Papers* No. 51:

. . . the great security against a gradual concentration of the several powers in the same department consists in giving to those who administer each department the necessary constitutional means and personal motives to resist encroachments of the others. . . . Ambition must be made to counteract ambition. The interest of the man must be connected with the constitutional rights of the place.

In short, competition not only increases consumer choice in the economic marketplace and citizen choice in the political marketplace, it also provides incentives to competing organizations to be more responsive to the desires of those whose support and patronage is needed.[19] Furthermore, we can reduce the discretionary power of each unit in a market (or in government) by increasing the number of units and seeing to it that no one unit has hegemony.

The Gains of Breaking Down Corporate Hegemony

In aiming toward greater political accountability from the corporate sector, moreover, we can go beyond the benefits of efficiency and accountability that would accrue in the corporate sector. In fact, the breaking down of corporate hegemony would lead both to corporate political accountability and to greater political accountability from the institutions of government—in short, to greater total political accountability. This is accomplished broadly in three ways.

- First, the ability to translate economic power into political power is greatly reduced simply by reducing concentrations of economic power. Public policymaking by corporations is also reduced by increasing the number of competing units, thus decreasing their ability and range of making binding decisions. Furthermore, the incentive for exerting political influence is reduced to the extent that government is unable to protect or extend corporate positions of hegemony.
- Second, the proposed reforms envision eliminating the price-setting function of agencies such as the Interstate Commerce Commission, thus lessening (or tending to eliminate) the control exerted by *insulated* centers of political power. Thus, we abandon the hopeless attempt to make agencies such as the ICC accountable to a broader public by simply abolishing the function for which they should have been accountable.
- Third, the overall policymaking power of citizens would be increased by decreasing the market power of the government and establishing agencies such as the Agency for Consumer Advocacy, through which citizens could wield power. The aggregate preferences of citizens could ultimately set prices and conditions of service in industries, such as transportation, that are presently regulated. Thus, once again, consumer sovereignty might be a revolutionary political as well as economic reform.

It should be noted that the second and third impacts of reform also respond to the need for greater economic rationality. The economic benefits respond to a problem increasingly noted by economists: government regulation has led to serious economic dislocations and has stifled the beneficial use of technological innovation.[20] Thus, there would be an intriguing set of spillover benefits stemming from reform. These can be graphically summarized in the chart on the following page.

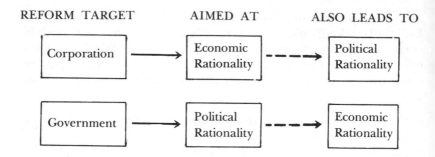

The model of corporate political accountability that emerges relies on a greater degree of overall political accountability by reducing the hegemony of corporations interacting, individually or in collusion, with similarly insulated centers of government power. It argues for a self-regulating system of political accountability by relying on consumer/citizen sovereignty in the economic/political marketplace.

In conclusion, just as the roots of corporate power derive from many sources, so too is there no single magic remedy. Nonetheless, there are several potentially fruitful reform possibilities based on the central concept of competition. A reliance on competition is not only an attainable and even moderate reform, it is also far more in keeping with our democratic heritage than the present insulation of corporate governmental power. In short, corporate accountability is political accountability. The Madisonian prescription of checks and balances is as valid today as it was 200 years ago.

Notes

1. Richard Barnett, "Not Just Your Corner Drugstore," *New York Times*, June 19, 1975, p. 35.
2. See Daniel Boorstin, *The Genius of American Politics* (Chicago: University of Chicago Press, 1953).
3. See Murray Edelman, *The Symbolic Uses of Politics* (Urbana: University of Illinois Press, 1967).
4. Neil Chamberlain, *The Limits of Corporate Responsibility* (New York: Basic Books, 1973), p. 3.

5. Ibid., p. 4.
6. Andrew Shonfield, *Modern Capitalism* (New York: Oxford University Press, 1969).
7. Mark J. Green, *The Closed Enterprise System* (New York: Bantam Books, 1972), pp. 30–62.
8. John Kenneth Galbraith, *Economics and the Public Purpose* (Boston: Houghton Mifflin, 1973), p. 216.
9. Ralph Nader, "The Case for Federal Chartering," in *Corporate Power in America*, Ralph Nader and Mark J. Green, eds. (New York: Grossman, 1972), p. 79.
10. Ibid., pp. 85–89.
11. Robert Townsend, "A Modest Proposal: The Public Director," ibid., p. 259.
12. *The Ethical Investor* (New Haven: Yale University Press, 1972).
13. Peter Drucker, *The New Society: The Anatomy of Industrial Order* (New York: Harper & Brothers, 1949), pp. 99–100.
14. Robert Dahl, "A Prelude to Corporate Reform," *Business and Society Review* 1 (Spring 1972), pp. 17–23.
15. George Stigler, *The Theory of Price* (New York: Macmillan, 1952), pp. 204–20.
16. *Economic Concentration: Structure, Behavior, and Public Policy* (New York: Harcourt Brace Jovanovich, 1972), pp. 199–254, 403–550 passim, 523.
17. Ralph Nader and Mark J. Green, "De-regulation is Another Consumer Fraud," *New York Times*, June 29, 1975, p. 14F.
18. See Anthony Downs, *An Economic Theory of Democracy* (New York: Harper & Row, 1957).
19. Scholars also urged increased competition within the bureaucratic sector of government in order to obtain greater accountability to citizens. It has been argued that competition among government agencies as well as between government agencies and private institutions would make public bureaucracies more efficient and responsive. See, for example, Matthew Holden, "Imperialism in Bureaucracy," *American Political Science Review* 60 (1966), pp. 943–51 and William Niskanen, *Bureaucracy and Representative Government* (Chicago: Aldine Atherton, 1971).
20. See, for example, William M. Capron, ed., *Technological Change in Regulated Industries* (Washington: Brookings Institution, 1971).

Index